Prepositional network models

A hermeneutical case study

Andrzej Pawelec

Prepositional network models

A hermeneutical case study

WUJ Jagiellonian University Press

This volume was supported by the Jagiellonian University – Institute of English Philology

COVER DESIGN
Anna Sadowska

REVIEWERS
Elżbieta Tabakowska
Henryk Kardela

ISBN 978-83-233-2868-1

WYDAWNICTWO
UNIWERSYTETU JAGIELLOŃSKIEGO

www.wuj.pl

Wydawnictwo Uniwersytetu Jagiellońskiego
Redakcja: ul. Michałowskiego 9/2, 31-126 Kraków
tel. 012-631-18-81, 012-631-18-82, tel./fax 012-631-18-83
Dystrybucja: ul. Wrocławska 53, 30-011 Kraków
tel. 012-631-01-97, tel./fax 012-631-01-98
tel. kom. 0506-006-674, e-mail: sprzedaz@wuj.pl
Konto: PEKAO SA O/Kraków, nr 62 1060 0076 0000 3200 0047 8769

CONTENTS

INTRODUCTION

This book has a two-level structure. Its central part is a case study of a cognitive approach to the representation of lexical "senses", which is sometimes called "prototype semantics" (cf. Kleiber 2003 [1990]). This initial delimitation of the "object" of investigation merits some comment.

The label "prototype semantics" serves well as a sign of opposition to previous, more openly structuralist[1] approaches to the representation of lexical senses. It is, however, potentially troublesome in respect of both its segments. While one may read the label's meaning as "an application of the prototype theory of categorization to semantic issues", it is not obvious that one can cogently talk about the prototype theory. What is beyond dispute is the existence of prototype effects, which may have relevance for psychological theories of concepts.[2] Moreover, the notion of "prototype" as used in cognitive psychology (see section 0.2. below) need not play the central role in the linguistic study labelled "prototype semantics". There are other features of "prototype phenomena" which may be as important in language study as the notion of "prototype" itself, i.e. graded and nondiscrete aspects of linguistic categories, or "family resemblances" between their members. In short, psychological "prototype effects" could be only a suggestive analogy to some linguistically relevant phenomena.[3]

The label can be also misleading as concerns the "semantics" segment. As understood traditionally, "semantics" is centrally opposed to syntax and pragmatics. However, in cognitive linguistics (CL, further used also as an adjective), which

---

[1] I am hinting here at complex relations between the descendants of Saussure's structuralism (neostructuralists, generativists and cognitive linguists). This historical issue will be formulated below and will constitute a significant element in my conclusions (see 5.2.).

[2] This is the position of Eleanor Rosch – the founder of the prototype approach in psychology. In Lehrer's summary, Rosch "argues that the notion of prototype does not in itself constitute a theory. She claims only that any theory of concepts must be consistent with what is known about prototypes" (Lehrer 1990: 381, note 1). Lakoff traces an evolution in Rosch's view on this matter – as pointed out by Vandeloise (1990: 409), reflecting rather his own changes of view than hers – but faithfully reports her position that prototype effects do not constitute a theory of categorization. Nevertheless, he claims simultaneously that Rosch "launched a general challenge to the classical theory" (Lakoff 1987: 42–45), thus giving substance to Vandeloise's charge.

[3] This general statement points to a complex of entangled issues central for "prototype semantics", concerning the relations between goals of psychologists and linguists (the role of linguistic evidence in ventures of different kind; the possibility of transferring – or "generalizing" – data from one research context to another; ultimately, the status of both disciplines or their mutual relationship). It is enough to point out here a peculiar role of words in psychological experiments: "prototype effects" studied by Rosch and others are elicited when words are treated as lists to be ordered according to some abstract criterion (e.g. what is a better example of a type?) rather than as used in communication.

developed the prototype approach, both syntactic and pragmatic phenomena tend to be explained in semantic terms (see 0.3.). Thus, the label "prototype semantics" can be used by a cognitive linguist to cover phenomena outside the range of traditionally conceived semantics.

This problem recurs in my description of the field under investigation, i.e. "a new approach to the representation of lexical 'senses'". In traditional terms, I will explore the domain of "lexical semantics", and more specifically, the category of "prepositions". Since cognitive analyses and models cross standard morphosyntactic boundaries, "prepositional" will actually refer not only to prepositions, but also to other categories, in which the lexical items chosen for discussion may be included.[4]

The crucial part of my agenda concerns the representation of lexical "senses" – a technical term for distinct meanings of words, ascribed to them out of the context of use. It is assumed both in the new cognitive paradigm, as well as in the more traditional schools (neostructuralist and generativist ones), to which it is usually opposed, that words have senses which can be analysed in isolation. Without this assumption, arguably central for the very existence of lexical semantics, "the rationale for distinguishing lexical from sentence/utterance semantics would evaporate" (Zlatev 2003: 454).[5] The distinction reveals a gap between word senses, as represented out of context, and their meanings in use. Since the latter seem to be almost infinitely flexible,[6] an analyst may feel an obligation to show how to get from postulated/attested senses to actual meanings. In lexical semantics, there are three general positions on this issue, which may be labelled with the terms: homonymy, polysemy, monosemy. The gap between senses and meanings of a word is least acute for the homonymy position, which allows, in principle, as many separate senses as one detects in use (or posits), but this is bought – ultimately – at the price of incoherence, if senses in use, or actual meanings of a word, are potentially infinite in number.[7] The gap is most acute for the monosemy position, assuming a theorist would like to derive actual meanings from a single postulated sense. The polysemy position occupies the middle ground. It may be viewed as more realistic than the other two and reflecting common-sense intuitions: words

[4] Terminological problems of this kind occur whenever a new approach offers its own theoretical grid to cover some "common ground" (terminology follows methodology). This issue primarily concerns future developments: whether a compromise is possible (an integration of perspectives or a "division of labour" of some kind) or not (which may mean that a particular perspective wins out as more encompassing or that both coexist as incommensurable).

[5] It is not obvious to what extent Zlatev's formulation covers some dynamic approaches to lexical meaning, which treat word meanings out of context as e.g. "pre-meanings" (Croft, Cruse 2004: 97ff.) or "parameterised lexical concepts" (Dunbar 1991: 112ff.), since such theoretical constructs require actualization to have some specific content. In such cases the postulated distinction between "senses" and "meanings in use" is problematic (see 0.4.).

[6] As pointed out by Croft and Cruse, the "possible readings of any word are nondenumerable" (2004: 111–112).

[7] Since the homonymy position – represented by generativists – is focused on abstract "competence", the issue of "performance" is not treated as problematic.

have a number of related senses (see 0.4.).[8] In a CL formulation, words constitute "natural categories of senses" (Lakoff 1987: 418).[9]

Thus, however, the polysemy position adds another dimension to the problem of representation. It is not only the number of senses of a single word form or lexeme[10] which is at stake (one, several, many), but also their relatedness. On the level of representation, the proffered solution is a format containing "chains" or "networks" of senses. The problem to be solved is how to find a principled way of distinguishing separate senses and how to locate the central sense(s), as models proposed by various theorists for a single lexeme turn out to be remarkably different in those respects. Those problems of representation reflect, in turn, the more substantial issue of meaning extension: on what grounds particular relations between senses are established? Specifically, what kind of reality is revealed by such networks of related senses: is it historical (social process), psychological (semantic representations in the mind underlying actualizations in a context) or logical (relatedness of ideas)? Or a combination of those possibilities? So much for the central questions of the case study (as they, *prima facie*, appear; cf. 4.3.).

Prepositional network models – as stated in the subtitle – will be the "object" of a hermeneutical exploration. This is the second layer, or the vantage point from which the case study is approached. There are several possible justifications for a "hermeneutical" approach to prepositional networks. At the historical level, one may argue that cognitive lexical models signal a return to the concerns of prestructuralist diachronic semantics, rooted in philological hermeneutics, within a new paradigm.[11] This claim has been forcefully put forward by Geeraerts in a series of publications (1988b, 1992b, 2002) and by Tabakowska in the context of Polish linguistics (2004). From this perspective, network models could be treated as a chapter in the history of linguistic ideas – "the return of hermeneutics to lexical semantics", as formulated by Geeraerts (the title of 1992b). At the methodological level, one could point out that linguistics is primarily a hermeneutical or interpretative science, opposed in its methods to natural sciences (as argued most persistently by Itkonen, e.g. 1977, 1981, 1997, 2008; cf. also Zlatev 2003: 459).

---

[8] Lewandowska-Tomaszczyk describes these positions and provides references. As she points out, the positions are related to the "granularity question": "Which level of detail is most appropriate for semantic description?" (2007: 152).

[9] See 1.3., note 28 for a discussion of Lakoff's phrase. It is invoked here in an intuitively appealing "evolutionary" meaning which seems to underlie network modelling: with the passage of time, words develop a number of related senses.

[10] "Word form" may be termed a "morpheme", "lexeme" (cf. Szymanek 1993: 14–18 for some definitional problems), or a "lemma", as in corpus linguistics (Glynn 2009). I will treat word forms as unproblematic for the purposes of this study; they will be marked with italics in the text (italics will also be used conventionally in quotations and to mark foreign words).

[11] On the prestructuralist linguistics, see Jankowsky (1972) and chapters from more comprehensive treatments, e.g. Jespersen (1922: book I), Harris and Taylor (1989: chapters 11–13), Seuren (1998: chapter 2). On the cognitive paradigm in general, see Gardner (1987); Varela, Thompson, Rosch (1993); Baumgartner and Payr (1995), Bechtel and Graham (1998). On CL, see e.g. Ungerer and Schmid (1996), Croft and Cruse (2004), Evans and Green (2006).

From this point of view, network models appear as intuitive reconstructions and interpretations of the structure of a given linguistic material rather than empirical models of actual processes and relations (whether historical, or psychological). Finally, at the level of foundational assumptions about the nature of meaning and language, one could try to show that insights developed in hermeneutical phenomenology by some of the great philosophers of the 20th century (Husserl, Heidegger, Merleau-Ponty, Gadamer, Patočka, Ricoeur) throw light on the whole domain of linguistics and on specific problems recurring in the work of cognitive linguists (some of whom claim that CL mounts a challenge to philosophy at that very level of foundational assumptions about meaning and language).[12]

The hermeneutical exploration offered below may be related to all three motivations. As concerns the historical development of the discipline, I believe – without putting into question specific parallels between cognitive and prestructuralist work pointed out by Geeraerts and Tabakowska – that network models remain importantly structuralist, and thus they cannot be properly opposed to this paradigm. Indeed, Geeraerts in the articles mentioned above places CL in the line of descent going down from structuralism, while Tabakowska opposes CL only to its immediate predecessor – Chomsky's transformational grammar (TG) – and presents it as a correction of "generativist excesses". As she says about Langacker: his "theory of language is based on solid structuralist foundations" (1995: 6). I will show, however, that CL – following Chomsky – has significantly weakened those foundations.[13] Thus, a "hermeneutical" exploration could be a voice in the discussion about the place of CL in the history of linguistics (see 5.2.).

That discussion is clearly linked to the methodological status of cognitive analyses. I have repeatedly argued against the "naturalistic" interpretation of CL, which was put forward most notoriously by Lakoff and Johnson in the whole series of their publications: Lakoff, Johnson 1980; Lakoff 1987; Johnson 1987; Johnson 1993a; Lakoff 1996; Lakoff, Johnson 1999 (to mention only book-length statements).[14] In a slogan formulated by Turner, they (used to) claim that "the central fact of the humanities [in our context: linguistics] is the central nervous system" (1991: 48).[15] Even though other towering figures within CL (notably, Langacker) assume a more cautious stance in relation to its place within cognitive

---

[12] E.g. "The problem [is] not one of extending or patching up some existing theory of meaning but of revising central assumptions in the Western philosophical tradition" (Lakoff, Johnson 1980: ix–x).

[13] This is not an original claim, as is evident in the debate between CL and its neostructuralist critics, see e.g. Coseriu's criticism of prototype semantics as reported by Rúa (2003: 19, 30–31) and Taylor (1999: 26ff.); see also Taylor's discussion of the "two-level model" (1995) and the relations between CL and structuralist semantics in general (1999). My position is opposed to Taylor's.

[14] I criticised that ideological project in detail in Pawelec (2005a, b, c, d; 2006a, b; 2007a, b).

[15] Turner belonged at one time to what may be characterized as "Lakoff's circle". I argued (see Pawelec 2005a: 11–12) that this group of researchers from various domains collaborating with Lakoff on a common agenda includes also Kövecses, Núñez and – via Turner – Fauconnier. See e.g. Kövecses 1986, 1988, 1990; Lakoff, Turner 1989; Fauconnier 1997; Fauconnier, Turner 2003; Lakoff, Núñez 2001. A possible formulation of this agenda may be found in note 17 below.

science,[16] there looms a fundamental question about the status of linguistics as practised within the cognitive paradigm: is it a branch of psychology of some kind (neuropsychology?; social psychology?) or is it (relatively) autonomous, with its own agenda? Following several authors – apart from Itkonen and Zlatev, also, importantly, Sinha (1993, 1999, 2009) – one may argue that CL should be reinterpreted: it is not primarily a branch of empirical (or even speculative) psychology but a hermeneutical or interpretative study of linguistic forms as developed, used and intuited within particular communities.

The last motivation (i.e. an assessment of CL from the perspective of hermeneutical phenomenology) is the most far-reaching one and at the same time most difficult to substantiate. On the one hand, CL is heterogeneous, while I focus on a small (and arguably noncentral) aspect of this venture. On the other hand, it would be out of place to present here in a sketchy (or rather skeletal) form the views on meaning and language as developed by hermeneutical philosophers.[17] Apart from the general reason that ideas of all great philosophers constitute takes on the whole of reality and, as such, require an all-out effort to be appropriated, hermeneutical philosophy is perhaps unique in its dedication to both external dialogue with other currents of thought (not only in philosophy, but also in science and art) as well as internal dialogue among its practitioners.[18] As such, it is less amenable to a summary presentation than most. Consequently, what I would like to offer is an introduction to the hermeneutical "view" (0.1.), occasional quotations and remarks bringing to light its divergence from the cognitive perspective, and, finally, a hermeneutical take on linguistic meaning and linguistics in general (see chapter 5.), to make this position more transparent to linguists without a background in philosophy in the context of more specific aims of this study.

However, the problem goes deeper, as manifested by my hypothetical statements about what the hermeneutical approach <u>may</u> involve in this case. No sane

---

[16] See Langacker's modest statements: "Some portions of the present work can be regarded as an exercise in speculative psychology. I speak unabashedly about cognitive events, and sometimes go into considerable detail about their architecture and their relationships. All of this must be accepted in the proper spirit. Since I claim no privileged access to the operation of the human mind, there is obviously a substantial (some might say intolerable) element of speculation in any such proposals concerning the specifics of cognitive activity [...]. I have adhered rather strictly, in developing my proposals, to the dictates of both psychological plausibility and linguistic necessity; I have relied almost exclusively on seemingly indisputable cognitive abilities (e.g. the ability to compare two events and register a discrepancy between them), and I invoke them for linguistic constructs that must somehow be accommodated in any comprehensive and explicit analysis" (Langacker 1987: 6). If we go further down the line, the label "cognitive science" may be used to package loosely connected ventures, which look for prestige and, ultimately, better funding (cf. Turner 2001: 154).

[17] I presented the gist of the positions taken on language by Merleau-Ponty, Gadamer and Ricoeur in Pawelec (2005a: ch. 7). My aim was to give substance to the claim that the ideological agenda of Lakoff's circle, when confronted with genuine philosophical work, does not carry any conviction. That agenda is advertised by Lakoff and Johnson as follows: "more than two millenia of a priori philosophical speculation about [mind, meaning and language] are over" due to empirical discoveries in cognitive science (1999: 3).

[18] As stated famously by Gadamer: "The ongoing dialogue permits no final conclusion. It would be a poor hermeneuticist who thought he could have, or had to have, the last word" (1993: 579).

person could believe that one can meaningfully prove anything on that scale (whether on the historical, methodological or philosophical level), particularly on the margins of a study focused on some problems of lexical representation in CL. My invocation of the hermeneutical perspective should be taken in the proper spirit: as an expression of my conviction that those problems of representation are rooted in the wider contexts invoked above, thus they can be made more transparent if one takes them into account. "Taking into account" means "showing that they are ultimately relevant" – that they should be invoked at some level of the discussion (see 0.5.).

I do believe that a step in this direction is justified and hopefully welcome, for several reasons. First of all, CL enters into a dialogue with other approaches to language and meaning. Even though in the initial phase of development its stance towards alternative positions was sometimes unnecessarily combative, as evidenced by "revolutionary" slogans and occasionally a patronising attitude to critics,[19] CL has now moved into a period of stabilisation and rapprochement with tradition, inviting open dialogue.[20] Such developments seem propitious for a renewed hermeneutical assessment, since previous ones – most notably by McLure (1990, 1993) – met with incomprehension, as is evident from Johnson's response (1993b) to the latter publication, which was in turn an answer to Johnson's call (1992) for treating CL's aspirations seriously.[21] Second, from the start CL is openly "interdisciplinary" and in search of foundations. One could hope that a hermeneutical (read: more encompassing) view on some vexing issues in lexical representation may contribute (on a modest scale) to efforts aiming at a clarification of CL's identity. That general justification, finally, is clearly linked with the hermeneutical aspects at the more specific historical and methodological levels, as mentioned before. Even though the questions raised in these contexts are different, they are all related to each other and also crucially to the basic issue of CL's self-identity. Thus, I would like to offer the present study as a small contribution to the self-interpretation of the discipline.

In more substantial terms, this book aims to reveal a deep divergence of perspectives between the cognitive and the hermeneutical approaches to the meaning

---

[19] In this respect, the debate around a well-documented psychological critique of Lakoff and Johnson's "philosophy of embodied realism" (Rakova 2002) is symptomatic. In their answer, Johnson and Lakoff tend not to notice substantive issues and prefer to ascribe to the author a "false mentality", e.g. "She is seeing our work through idealized cognitive models of the mind and language – including metaphors – derived from traditional forms of philosophy" (Johnson, Lakoff 2002: 258). In his commentary, Krzeszowski points out that their position "must result in communication breakdowns" (2002: 268). In a more general context, see J. Taylor's comments on "polemical aspects" of CL (2007: 567–569).

[20] As clearly evident thanks to the presence and content of several articles in Janssen, Redeker 1999 (e.g. Harder, Sinha), Geeraerts, Cuyckens 2007 (e.g. Harder, Nuyts, Sinha, Taylor) and Evans, Pourcel 2009 (e.g. Croft, Harder, Sinha).

[21] I have offered a hermeneutical assessment of the ideological aspirations of CL (under the banner of "second generation cognitive science") in Pawelec 2005a, as well as, more recently, of some linguistic aspects of CL's paradigm (2006c; 2008; to appear: a, b).

of words. My whole argument at this fundamental level could be summarised as follows: the issue of the representation of lexical senses (available out of context) presupposes the issue of distinct meanings of words in use, which in turn presupposes the question of the transformative power of words (in linguistics, articulated by Humboldt as *energeia*, cf. 5.0.). Anything I say below should be placed in the context of this sequence, which I hope to make more transparent. If a label could be helpful, I propose to complement an *a posteriori* static cognitive approach with a dynamic (or "genetic") "expressive" one. Again, a venture of this kind cannot be convincingly argued for, exhaustive etc. Whenever a fundamental change of perspective is urged, one can only appeal (as shown by Merleau-Ponty and Charles Taylor[22]), starting with some problems inherent in an interlocutor's position and trying to show that a more encompassing view may throw some light on them.

A possibly presumptuous undertaking of this kind will suffer from standard maladies afflicting such "fundamental" and "centrifugal" ventures (as my presentation so far has perhaps already made abundantly clear). While pointing to more embracing perspectives on matters at hand (a "synoptic" view), I will invoke data and arguments from various quarters, whenever I find them illuminating.[23] Thus, I will often cross domain boundaries (I will try to signal, though, where I tread). Nor will I try to offer exhaustive expositions of available material, once I feel that enough to exemplify a position is presented (copious references may be viewed as a partial atonement – or further evidence of damnation). As a result (since particulars are there, waiting in the wings), I may also fight at places a losing battle with my parenthetical remarks and footnotes.[24] Nevertheless (as a possible defence), what I am doing is intrinsically related to the character of the field under investigation, which is openly interdisciplinary. Thus, I take seriously the call for an integration of perspectives on mind and language adopted in different ventures and disciplines placed under the umbrella term "cognitive science". To be sure, I am not equally competent in all domains of inquiry: this study is primarily a review of a particular method of lexical representation in CL, while all additional matter serves as the background to make this assessment more meaningful. The

[22] For Merleau-Ponty, see note 8 in 5.1.; for C. Taylor, see e.g. (1989: 87) in the moral context.

[23] Even though this strategy may superficially resemble a search for "converging evidence", treated by Lakoff and Johnson as a sign of success in interdisciplinary ventures (e.g. Johnson 1992: 345), I believe it is almost directly opposed to it. Lakoff and Johnson apparently assume that "data" exist independently of theories and may be picked at will, whenever they seem to confirm one's point. They do not pay much attention to the problem of integration of knowledge coming from different research domains (as opposed to e.g. Donald 2004). As Lakoff admits in his only "methodological" statement I know: "I generally prefer not to engage in methodological discussions and would rather just get on with my work" (1990: 39). The hermeneutical approach, however, does not aim at the integration of data at the "objective" level but rather treats problems arising at that level as symptomatic of assumptions and limitations of particular research methods. Cf. remarks in the next paragraphs on my aims in the present study.

[24] I paraphrase here (and exemplify) Beardsmore's remark on Kripke's book on Wittgenstein, as quoted by Pateman (1987: 113). My apology may sound flippant but the peculiarities mentioned above may be also taken as evidence that I have striven at clarity as far as my approach allows (and within my limitations). I would be glad if I had found a more direct way to say what I meant.

present work – as noted in the subtitle – is a "case study" of a cognitive style of theorizing about lexical representation.

To limit the centrifugal tendencies inherent in my approach, I chose to focus on a highly specific "objective" domain, i.e. network models of two prepositions (particles, adverbs, prefixes etc.): English *over* and Polish *za(-)*. I present this material in, perhaps, tedious detail (even though the actual material covered is by far richer) to document the way in which researchers grapple with problems posed by the phenomena, when inspected from their vantage point. It is important to underline that I do not propose any solutions to particular problems, nor do I look for a more successful way of dealing with the phenomena in question. Rather, what appears as problematic at the "objective" level is treated as a symptom of the vantage point adopted by researchers. I aim to make better visible some of their deeper assumptions (rooted in the paradigm they work within), which may go beyond (and sometimes even against) their self-declared positions. This is one cause of the presumptuousness mentioned above and also of the possibly irritating habit to place "object" and "objective" in inverted commas (see 0.1.).

Such an approach may seem reminiscent of the patronising attitude I charged Lakoff and Johnson with (as exemplified in note 19 above). However, I am far from mounting the charge of false consciousness against the authors of the models analysed below, nor do I think that hermeneutics (as opposed to "scientism") has an emancipatory mission, because it "knows better". As for the former point, scientists develop a given position – they try to capture as many recalcitrant phenomena as they can within a chosen paradigm. Their work is normally viewed as hypothetical,[25] i.e. not as something to believe in, but rather as a possible explanation of a range of phenomena (when one takes for granted a set of assumptions), to be compared with alternative approaches, which apply other methods to an overlapping, or a complementary, range of phenomena. The charge of false consciousness makes no sense in this context. One may only point out limitations of a particular position but this is true in all such cases: science is perspectival. While science (or a given discipline) as a whole aims at a more comprehensive perspective, embracing all relevant phenomena (a "synoptic" view), fragmentation and a competition of paradigms is the norm. A wider perspective may be achieved only thanks to a laborious integration of more partial approaches (transforming the significance of their respective "data" in the process). As for the latter point, since hermeneutics is not situated at the "objective" level (it is not a method), it cannot directly participate in the task of integration. Hence, it has no right (or intention) to admonish or emancipate scientists. Hermeneutics rather reveals the conditions of "objectiveness" in general, as well as in particular "objective" domains, thus

---

[25] In theory rather than in practice, though, as shown by sociology of science. Cf. the pioneering study by Fleck (1986 [1935]) – an insider's account of how Wasserman's test shapes biological "data" – and the classic work by Mannheim (1955). The standard work on "paradigms" in science is Kuhn (1996). On "paradigms" in society at large, see Foucault (1994).

aiming at a better self-understanding.[26] I will try to make the relation between science and hermeneutics – central for the second layer of this work – somewhat clearer in 0.1. Naturally, this is a broad subject, debated on both sides, and one cannot go into details. The present study as a whole may be taken as an exemplification of that dialogue.[27]

As for the method, primarily I report research found relevant in CL to throw light on the notion of "linguistic categorization", as it has been theoretically discussed and developed in particular examples of network modelling of prepositional polysemy. My contribution is to place that research in the wider perspective on language offered by hermeneutics, in order to reveal some of its inherent limitations. Importantly, this should not be viewed as a negative task, but in the context of Ricoeur's remark: "An awareness of the validity of a given method is essentially linked to an awareness of its limits" (1985: 150).[28]

As for the order of presentation, the first layer of the book – the "case study" – consists of four chapters. In Chapter 1, I present and discuss the "foundational" accounts of network modelling by Langacker and Lakoff. Chapter 2 contains several attempts to improve Lakoff's model of *over*. In Chapter 3, I present and discuss (mostly from the diachronic perspective) a Langackerian model of the Polish lexeme *za(-)*. Chapter 4 investigates the issue of the cognitive "diachrony within synchrony". The second "hermeneutical" layer of the book, which provides the framework for the case study, consists of two parts. In the preliminary Chapter 0, I try to characterize "the hermeneutical situation", or the, *prima facie*, nontransparent background of the issues taken up in the case study. In Chapter 5, I oppose the hermeneutical view of language to the position adopted by CL (and linguistics in general).

---

[26] Let me add that I view myself as a member of the CL community in a rather uncomfortable role of a doubting Thomas, who questions on the hermeneutical grounds the "objectiveness" of constructs often taken for granted, e.g. the cognitive unconscious, conceptual metaphors or image schemas. The role is uncomfortable because it is one thing to claim in general that some constructs do not make sense as explanatory devices of a specified kind – e.g. the unconscious as conceived by Lakoff and Johnson was criticised long before by Ricoeur in reference to "naive interpretations" of Freud (1985: 212–213) – while it is quite a different thing to be able to show it in the terms accepted within the CL community. The latter task was undertaken e.g. by Zlatev (2007b) in his criticism of the cognitive unconscious, and (2007c) in his criticism of image schemas. Some problems with the conceptual metaphors paradigm are pointed out by Croft, Cruse (2004: 198–204); see also Ortony (1988).

[27] Which took place mostly in the natural and social sciences, e.g. C. Taylor (1985, 1995). As for cognitive science, the hermeneutical position was presented by e.g. Dreyfus (1992) and Dreyfus, Dreyfus (1986). First generation CL (Chomsky's TG) was defended against a hermeneutical (Wittgensteinian) challenge by Pateman (1987).

[28] Ricoeur's comment concerns structuralism and the issue of its "initial truth", often hardly visible in later phases of its development and in some far-reaching applications. Thus, the task of finding defensible limits of a method is linked to this initial stage of divergence and the process of growth, when a particular perspective establishes itself against available positions and is found more generally attractive. As is normal in history, it may be found attractive for various (also wrong) reasons.

To some extent, this book is a hybrid. It is a continuation of a study written in Polish (Pawelec 2005a), covering (with a substantially different focus) a similar range of material, i.e. CL research available primarily in English. Writing the present book in English was thus easier in some respects, but the Polish background remains present (several of my references and some examples are in Polish, one case study concerns a Polish lexeme and, when writing, I often had my Polish interlocutors in mind and sometimes employed Polish stylistic conventions). Still, I hope that the book will not prove impenetrable to the English-speaking audience. All translations from other languages (if not noted otherwise) are mine. Sometimes, I had to rely on Polish translations of classics from various domains or Polish editions of books in English, when I had no access to the original. In such cases I tried to add in the bibliography references to an English edition. Several items in the bibliography – along a standard identification, usually in a full version, but sometimes without pagination or all conventional details when those were not available – are marked as internet sources in one way or another. This may mean that I consulted a given work on the Internet as a reprint of an actual edition or in an author's format or as pre-publication material or (as a last resort) in the chopped versions offered for free by "Google Books". It may also be the case that I had access to a printed edition (at some stage of writing) but I wanted to make the reader aware that a text is available on the Internet. In all such cases I did not provide long and largely meaningless web addresses with dates of access, as is usually done, since the texts are also provided with standard references and may be more easily googled. In this context, I feel obliged to express my deep gratitude to several authors who place their current (and in some cases, past) work on the Internet. Without this aid, the present study could not even be conceived. This does not in any way diminish my indebtedness to the Library of my Institute of English Philology (and the late Brygida Rudzka-Ostyn, who bequeathed her unique CL book collection to the Jagiellonian University) as well as to the Library of the UNESCO Chair for Translation Studies and Intercultural Communication in Kraków.

This study would have never been completed without a generous support offered by Elżbieta Tabakowska, who has been an invaluable mentor and partner in an ongoing dialogue about language (and life), spanning now more than a quarter of a century. Henryk Kardela expressed faith in this project at a critical juncture. While both of them have read and commented on the manuscript, full responsibility for all remaining quirks and errors is mine. The book has been financed by the Institute of English Philology at the Jagiellonian University. I owe deep gratitude to its director, Elżbieta Chrzanowska-Kluczewska, who has been invariably supportive of this venture.

CHAPTER 0. THE HERMENEUTICAL SITUATION

0.0. Introductory remarks

In this preliminary part of the book, I will discuss several topics which are relevant as the background for an assessment of the material presented in chapters 1–4. Only the first section is truly introductory, i.e. it is intended to make tangible for a novice the hermeneutical viewpoint, which I adopt in my approach to network modelling and CL in general. The subsequent sections are intended for readers who are well-acquainted with relevant CL literature. Their goal is to "problematize" issues usually taken for granted or passed over in standard presentations of the domains in question. In other words, I attempt to show that some of the assumptions underlying particular treatments are arbitrary or of limited adequacy or beside the point, when one focuses on the issues from a wider perspective. Consequently, I do not offer "introductions" to particular fields of inquiry, but rather critical comments on some of the basic claims put forward in those fields. By its nature, an approach focusing on gaps and questionable assumptions cannot be systematic. I will try to retrace my steps and introduce some order in the final section (0.5.). Let me point out that the possibly irritating approach adopted here is my way to deal with the "hermeneutical situation", i.e. one which is not transparent at first sight, in terms offered by CL theorists.

0.1. The hermeneutical perspective

In this section, I will try to present "the hermeneutical perspective". I will focus on two issues: the "manifestation" of things and the scientific approach to phenomena (both in the natural and human sciences). In section 0.5. and chapter 5, I will return to some questions mentioned below.

In a well-known Oriental parable, a group of blind men, asked to identify an object, touched various parts of an elephant ("it's like a rope!", "it's like a pillar!" and so on). Consequently, they could not agree on what they dealt with. Originally, the story justified a call for harmony and co-operation. Rhetorically, the call was probably effective, since the elephant was a common sight and such grave (but entirely predictable) "misrepresentations" of it must have seemed ludicrous. Nowadays, the story is sometimes used to illustrate the "perspectivism" of science: particular "takes" on reality are limited, we can only see what is revealed from our partial perspective.

Even though it seems true that our cognitive predicament is best described as groping in the dark – a good reason for the lasting attraction of the elephant story – the parable does not go to the heart of the matter. Namely, how can we reveal the true shape of reality (or cut nature at its joints)? That is so, first, because the elephant is an example of "middle-size dry goods" (John Austin's expression). As such, it can be directly apprehended (unless one is blind – then it turns out to be oversized for an apprehension at one go). More importantly, second, the story presents an unsuccessful identification of something already known. It does not get in focus the more fundamental problems: how can we reveal anything at all?; how can we identify something we do not know? Both questions are on the hermeneutical agenda.

I will return to the latter one in the next section (0.2.), when presenting the issue of categorization. As for the former one, it is clearly related to the functioning of the senses. The elephant story is not very helpful in this respect, since it merely plays the limitations of one sense (touch) against a greater recognitory potential (in the context of the activity) of another one (sight). A different example (provided by psychologists) could be more relevant. Let us imagine a blind person using a stick for the first time to find her way around. Such an activity will be initially experienced as tapping. But after a while, the stick will become "part of the body", an extension of the hand "meeting" things within reach. As such, the stick is integrated into the "body schema"[1] and increases the power of one sensory channel (touch) to such an extent that it can serve as a replacement of the sense we chiefly rely on when moving around (sight). This example shows at least two conditions of the process of "revealing" things. First, it is possible only as active exploration: primarily, as a movement directed at a goal. Tapping could be integrated into any number of activities. It is transformed into "sight" of a kind only when employed in this role. This transformation involves a miracle of sorts: one gets access to reality in a new way,[2] something "appears" as a result of one's special involvement (this miracle is at the centre not only of perception, but also linguistic expression). Second, the miracle is possible because the stick (and the very activity of tapping) "conceals itself", leading "directly" to phenomena. We can become aware of things because we normally stop being aware of our revelatory engagements with reality. As a result, all perception (and symbolic expression) leads to a kind of "self-forgetting": one's role in the process of revelation is

[1] Merleau-Ponty's notion. See the discussion in Morris 2004.

[2] Of course, not entirely new: in this case the stick extends the potential of touch. The more foundational question concerns the genesis of a new sense (a new channel of revealing reality).

backgrounded and the reality revealed seems available "as it is" (rather than "as it is for us" due to our involvements[3]).

In this context, we can try to see the difference between Husserl's original project of phenomenology and Heidegger's hermeneutical transformation of it. Phenomenology raises the question I posed above: "How things make themselves manifest?". It is important to appreciate what it achieves at the point of departure, when this basic question is asked. The question is an attempt to tackle the problem of the "bridge" between "consciousness" and "objects" (or mind – body dualism): when we start from consciousness, we get only "correlates" of consciousness (as in philosophical "idealism"); when we start from objects, consciousness must appear as an object of sorts (as in philosophical "materialism").[4] Phenomenology tries to overcome the "subject" – "object" dualism by thinking them together – by making "appearance" ("that something appears") basic, and the "subject" – "object" dichotomy as a subsequent step. It is enough to make two points here about Husserl's project of doing philosophy. First, his is the last attempt to provide a necessary account (i.e. without any arbitrary assumptions) of phenomena. Second, his account takes the form: "the subject (consciousness) meets an object", which is not true to the original intent of phenomenology as an inquiry without arbitrary assumptions (cf. Michalski 1998: 26ff.). As we have seen above, it is not necessary that things appear as objects of consciousness, because primarily[5] they are correlates of our engagements with reality.

That point was made by Heidegger in *Sein und Zeit* (1994 [1927]). He showed the essential primacy of practice as the source of phenomena. Husserl's attempt to achieve certainty was thus doomed to failure, because it was not originary – it was based on seeing ("the subject perceives an object"), while the primary way of manifestation is through movement, action. As Patočka puts it: "At the very protofoundation of consciousness, of thought, of the subject, there is acting, not mere seeing. That explains why so much is opaque, obscure, in our clarity" (Patočka 1998: 96–97).

We can see now how Heidegger's position ties in with the example of tapping. If, at the very source (originarily), things appear as correlates of involvement, of a primordial interestedness, then their appearance is opaque: they manifest themselves not as they are,[6] but primarily as useful, as *pragmata* – not objects we see but "something handy" (the tapping serves the aim of finding one's way, i.e. de-

---

[3] Individual processes of "revelation" in the animal realm are taken over by biological populations, while in human communities they "sediment" into a culture, see Merleau-Ponty (2002) for the notion of "sedimentation". Importantly, individual revelations are transformed by "sedimentation" into social "horizons", see Gadamer (1993) for the notion of "horizon".

[4] Cf. Kołakowski (1975: 66ff.) for a critical account of Husserl's attempt.

[5] Phenomenologists look for the "originary" access to phenomena, i.e. necessary conditions of encountering them.

[6] The expression "things as they are" looks dubious to our relativistic mindset, since we know they appear differently to different people (the lesson of the elephant story). Philosophy, however, seeks certainty. Philosophers, as opposed to scientists, try to make sense of phenomena in such a way that they make no arbitrary assumptions. Husserl (in Kołakowski's account) was the last philosopher

tecting potential obstacles rather than revealing things as they are). Additionally, their appearance involves self-concealment (whatever infrastructure is necessary for a manifestation of phenomena, it is necessarily backgrounded). Heidegger shows that this is true not only of perception, as in the example, but generally. Thus, the world as a correlate of our involvement cannot be made transparent directly through "seeing" (as in Husserl's phenomenology), for it is based on self-concealment.[7]

We should try to keep in mind this hermeneutical point of departure: "the world" is not the universe of things (out there without anyone watching), but "the meaningful whole" as revealed in the history of engagements, which are normally lost from view (there is no intention to deny reality here, and no subjectivism). We can see now that the problem of interpretation, of making things more transparent – in our context, the issue of theorizing – is rooted in the foundational process of manifestation, of revealing "the world" in "the natural attitude", with its accompanying forms of self-concealment. The world of common sense – the world "as we live it",[8] with its own ways of understanding: prejudices, stereotypes, myths, folk etymologies etc. – is the actual point of departure for all theoretical efforts to understand reality (and it is, to a large extent, shaped by those "objectifications"[9]).

Let us now ask about the distinction between natural and human sciences, which is relevant in our context, since CL is often treated as belonging to natural sciences (as opposed to linguistics *sans phrase*, which is normally classified as belonging to human studies). Natural science goes beyond the natural attitude and assumes the "hypothetical" stance. It provides an interpretation, a clearer vision of some parts of the commonsensical world (than e.g. myths), employing empirical, objectifying methods. The hypothetical attitude is based on the assumption that phenomena reflect various functional wholes of causally linked entities – "objects" of study – which we may (ultimately) capture. One may adopt that assumption for "manipulative" reasons (thus, it becomes a driving force of technology) or for "contemplative" reasons (one wants to understand reality as such a whole). As a result, we live (mostly) in a "disenchanted universe".[10] However, the natural science vision is "trumps" not mainly because it removes some self-illusions (something that remains unclear and bothers us in our practical dealings with things), but primarily because it offers more powerful tools for our com-

to believe that a direct non-arbitrary path to "things as they are" is available. Since Heidegger, "foundationalism" is rejected and more roundabout ways are explored.

[7] See a commentary to Heidegger's *Being and Time* (Dreyfus 1991).

[8] Husserl's *Lebenswelt*, cf. Patočka (1986).

[9] This leads to a paradox from the objectivist point of view: in social studies, as Plamenatz noticed, the "object" of theory may change under its influence; specifically, false theories of democracy sometimes shape democratic practices (Plamenatz 1973: 27–33). The paradox dissolves when we see man as a "self-interpreting animal", falling prey to illusions while seeking clarity. The term is explained by Charles Taylor (1985, II: 26).

[10] The term is Weber's. The process (with serious reservations concerning Weber's diagnosis) has been described in a ground-breaking way by C. Taylor (1989, 1991, 2004, 2007).

merce with the natural world.[11] Only when that objectifying stance toward reality is perceived as distorting, as it was perceived by Heidegger – cf. C. Taylor (1995: 100–126) – or harmful, as in the ecological movement, can we begin to seek a clearer vision of our relations with the material world.

The problem of self-illusion and self-interpretation is much starker for the sciences of man, for they try to explain <u>what people do</u>. Thus, they should offer accounts which are clearer than self-interpretations in the natural attitude. To be sure, the objectifying stance can produce a lot of empirical data and reveal new phenomena in the human sciences, but it constantly runs the risk of "changing the subject"[12] – of providing accounts which to a smaller or greater extent disregard the way people experience and articulate phenomena. That seems an inevitable result of reducing (or rather hoping to reduce) the phenomenon under study to the theoretical grid one adopts. As Plamenatz noticed, deriving definitions of phenomena from one's theoretical assumptions is the most widespread sin in political philosophy, leading to theories divorced from reality (1950: 81–82). A related error was called by William James the "psychologist's fallacy": "the mistaking of a doctrine, which may be good as far as it goes, for the very processes it is about".[13] More generally, one could talk in this context not only of hypostatizing, but of *hysteron proteron* methodology: what is a result of the process of revealing reality or expression (concepts) is invoked to explain this very process (as in linguistic mentalism[14]). These are all signs of "self-concealment", which may be remedied by a hermeneutical investigation.

The hermeneutical approach, true to its phenomenological roots, tries to be faithful to phenomena, rather than to one's theoretical assumptions (to repeat, it is not a method). It is practised in various ways. Of particular relevance in our context is Ricouer's "detour" – a "long route" to a more originary view of phenomena, through a dialogue with various objectifying methods. In other words, since one cannot fathom reality from a chosen perspective, a hermeneuticist should choose a "detour" through encounters with all available sources of evidence and types of investigation to reveal what is valid in them, how they help us "uncover" phenom-

---

[11] To be sure, many scientists (*qua* ideologists) attempt to shatter some self-interpretations, e.g. about the exalted status of humanity. In that role, they have no advantage over other participants in the debate: they must provide better self-interpretations (reducing self-obscurity). As such, scientific facts – e.g. that we are "naked apes" in evolutionary terms – are no "trumps". To accept that we are <u>just</u> naked apes (rather than, e.g., God's children), we must find that description a better one than available alternatives as our self-interpretation.

[12] Donald Davidson's expression, quoted in C. Taylor (1989: 56).

[13] Richards (1965: 116). Another version is called the "linguist's fallacy": attributing theoretical knowledge of language to ordinary speakers (McLure 1993: 42).

[14] "Linguistic mentalism" treats language primarily as a mental entity. In Chomsky's TG, language is identified with syntactic "deep structures"; in Langacker's CL, with semantic conceptualizations. I will oppose CL's mentalism to hermeneutical "expressivism" (the primacy of expressive behaviour in relation to conceptual structures) in 5.1.

ena.[15] And as already pointed out, we cannot know what is valid in a given method unless we specify the limits of its application (Ricoeur 1985: 150).[16] The analysis undertaken below may be viewed as an attempt to specify some limits of application of network representations of lexical senses, or their claims to validity.

Finally, as is perhaps clear by now, I place "object" and "objective" in inverted commas to emphasize (when it seems relevant) the necessary involvement of observers in the process of revealing reality (my aim is to counter the assumption that reality is directly accessible). That convention is not meant to deny that objectifying methods – both in the natural sciences and in human studies – are fully legitimate (within their limits).

0.2. Prototype effects and categorization

In this section I want to raise three issues, which are interrelated: what are prototype effects?; how are they related to the question of categorization?; what is linguistic categorization in relation to both previous issues? The hermeneutical question posed above: "how can we identify something we do not know?" is central for the issue of categorization. I will mostly follow the standard CL account, adding comments and trying to widen the perspective.

The notion of "linguistic categorization" is of primary importance in this study. John Taylor, who used the phrase as the title of his book – the first monograph presenting prototype approach in CL – pointed out its ambiguity. Whenever we use the same word to refer to various specimens of something, we categorize, or name "sameness in difference" (Taylor 1989: vii). Since words can refer to linguistic entities, "linguistic categorization" may not only involve categories pointed out verbally in the world, like DOG,[17] but also linguistic categories, like WORD or LEXEME.

In this way one may enter the long-standing philosophical debate about the relations between language, thought and reality (cf. 5.1. for some empirical evidence). Taylor mentions traditional philosophical positions concerning "sameness in difference". Nominalism claims that "sameness is merely a matter of linguistic convention; the range of entities which may be called dogs [...] have in reality nothing in common but their name". Realism asserts, on the other hand, that

---

[15] Thus, there is no hermeneutical perspective, properly speaking. I use this word to refer to the hermeneutical approach, based on the insights presented above. On the hermeneutical "detour", see Ricoeur (1985, 1986, 1989).

[16] Ricoeur's own attempts of this kind (e.g. 1977, 2003, 2004) and Gadamer's opinion quoted in the Introduction (note 18) show clearly that this is an unending task.

[17] Categories, like concepts, will be typed in capitals.

"categories like DOG [...] exist independently of language and its users", while the words "merely name these pre-existing categories". The third position, called conceptualism, proposes that "a word and the range of entities to which it may refer are mediated by a mental entity, i.e. a concept". Conceptualism may be given a nominalist or a realist interpretation: according to the former, concepts are taken to be formed by convention; according to the latter, they are supposed to mirror existing categories (i.e. cut nature at its joints). In Taylor's view, CL adopts the conceptualist position which is intermediate between its nominalist and realist interpretations. As he puts it: "To the extent that a language is a conventionalized symbolic system, it is indeed the case that a language imposes a set of categories on its users. Conventionalized, however, does not necessarily imply arbitrary. The categories encoded in a language are motivated to varying degrees, by a number of factors – by actually existing discontinuities in the world, by the manner in which human beings interact, in a given culture, with the world, and by general cognitive processes of concept formation" (Taylor 1989: vii–viii).

Taylor's resume plunges us in deep philosophical waters concerning the relations between language, mind and reality. However, the position of CL against that background is hardly transparent. At this early stage, let us try to see better what is involved in Taylor's final claim that linguistic categories (in either sense) are non-arbitrary or motivated. Let us notice that "motivation" conceived in this way (as the opposite of arbitrariness) is very unspecific: it may cover any factors which influence categorization.

As an example, let us consider the categorization of colour (the point of departure in Taylor's account). In their pioneering study, Berlin and Kay (1969) put forward the following claims. First, all human beings (with the exception of individuals with vision defects, e.g. daltonists) possess the ability to recognize eleven basic colour categories mentioned below, even though not all linguistic communities verbalize each category. Significantly, there is an order of verbalization summarised as follows:

1) All languages contain terms for white and black.
2) If a language contains three terms, then it contains a term for red.
3) If a language contains four terms, then it contains a term for either green or yellow (but not both).
4) If a language contains five terms, then it contains terms for both green and yellow.
5) If a language contains six terms, then it contains a term for blue.
6) If a language contains seven terms, it contains a term for brown.
7) If a language contains eight or more terms, then it contains a term for purple, pink, orange, grey, or some combination of these. (Berlin, Kay 1969: 2–3)

These findings leave much room for speculation, e.g. why is the order of verbalization partly fixed and why does it take this particular form?[18] Provisionally,

[18] Berlin and Kay note: "Our essentially linguistic investigations have led, seemingly inescapably, to the conclusion that the eleven basic color categories are pan-human perceptual universals.

we can conclude that there is a non-trivial correlation between perceptual and linguistic categories. It is important to note in this context that Berlin and Kay chose to study colour categorization because colour perception can be investigated independently of linguistic expression, thus allowing a more objective correlation of data.[19] By using colour samples, they were able to show that even though the colour spectrum may be divided in incommensurate ways by different languages, there is a cross-linguistic agreement concerning what constitutes a good example of a particular colour ("focal" colours).

Taylor[20] (1989: 10–12) reports several experiments conducted by Rosch which confirmed and extended that finding of Berlin and Kay. When speakers of eleven different languages were asked to choose good examples of colour terms in their vocabulary, they picked out focal colours. When speakers of twenty three languages were asked to name samples of focal and non-focal colours, the names for focal colours were produced faster and they were shorter. In another experiment on short-term memory, speakers of English were compared with speakers of Dani, who have only two colour terms at their disposal. In the test, which concerned the recognition of focal and non-focal colours, the English subjects performed better overall (this may suggest that having relevant terms aids memory). Still, the Dani were as good as the English speakers in choosing the focal samples over the non-focal ones. In a long-term memory task, Dani speakers learned names for focal colours faster than for non-focal ones. Finally, English three- and four-year-olds paid more attention to focal colours and could match them better than non-focal ones.

According to Taylor, Rosch's experiments show that colour categories have a centre and a periphery. A colour term will denote "first and foremost" a focal colour, even if its range is subsequently extended to cover a large portion of the colour space (in languages with few such terms). When a neighbouring term appears in a language, the periphery will contract, while the centre will remain intact. Consequently, not all members of a colour category have equal status. As concerns motivation, Taylor does not fully endorse Rosch's view that the formation and reference of linguistic colour categories is shaped by perceptual-cognitive factors. Following Wierzbicka (for instance: 1990a), he adds that also "environmental" factors – the stability of colour features of important entities in the world, e.g. blood, vegetation or the sky – should be taken into account (Taylor 1989: 14–15).

But we can offer no physical or physiological explanation for the apparently greater perceptual salience of these particular eleven color stimuli, nor can we explain in any satisfying way the relative ordering among them. Existing theories of color perception, both classical and recent, offer several plausible suggestions for parts of the observed pattern, but none will serve as the basis of an adequate explanation" (1969: 109).

[19] Lucy (2000: xi–xii) comments on the problem of circularity when only linguistic data are used for the study of relations between thought and language.

[20] More or less the same experimental material is covered in other books on this subject, e.g. Lakoff (1987: 24–57); Ungerer, Schmid (1996: 1–20); Rúa (2003: 104–121).

To recapitulate, focal colours are apparently grounded in human physiology: we perceive and recall better some segments of the colour spectrum, which serve as natural perceptual reference points. Linguistic labels are supposed to refer primarily to such points. Since not all eleven focal colours have labels in languages under study – and there seems to be a structural regularity in the development of such terms – additional factors must be invoked, e.g. environmental salience of some colours.

Subsequent studies concerned other categories (it is clear that the categorization of colour is untypical, being so closely tied with sensory mechanisms). As reported by Taylor (1989: 40–42), Labov asked subjects to name the drawings of household objects (cups, mugs, bowls, vases) which "morphed" into one another. Apart from variable shapes, he also included functional elements. For instance, he asked subjects to imagine that the receptacles are filled with contents of different kind, e.g. coffee or mashed potatoes. Labov's experiments show that labelling does not reflect primarily inherent properties of such objects, but their functional roles, to some extent shaped by particular cultures.

Rosch investigated several "natural" categories, that is "concepts designatable by words in natural languages" (quoted by Taylor 1989: 43), e.g. FURNITURE, FRUIT, VEHICLE, BIRD.[21] She focused on their "goodness of rating". For instance, American college students were asked to rate sixty household items on the scale from 1 to 7 as "good examples" of the category FURNITURE. In the experiment, CHAIR, SOFA, COUNCH and TABLE were ranked the highest, while VASE, ASHTRAY, FAN and TELEPHONE – the lowest. Such "prototype effects" (interpreted by Taylor as "degrees of membership" in a category) were confirmed in other experimental paradigms (e.g. reaction time, frequency and order of naming).

Rosch found out not only that some items are "better members" of a category, but also that one level of categorization is more cognitively and linguistically salient that others.[22] The so-called "basic level", as exemplified by the middle term in the sequence: KITCHEN CHAIR (subordinate level), CHAIR, FURNITURE (superordinate level), contains perceptual and functional gestalts (entities we perceive as functional wholes, which can be represented by schematic drawings) and is expressed by terms which are generally short, structurally simple and used more frequently. Thus, "it is the basic level categories that most fully exploit

[21] As explained by Taylor, in psychology natural categories are opposed to artificial ones, e.g. sequences of letters or numbers, which are used in studies of concept formation (1989: 43, footnote). He also points out that natural kind terms may be opposed to nominal kind terms: the former refer to entities with "natural" boundaries (e.g. BIRD), while the latter to categories of artefacts (like TOY or VEHICLE), whose boundaries are a matter of definition (1989: 43–44) We may notice that "natural language" categories are also opposed to categories in artificial languages of logic. As concerns typing conventions, let me repeat that both categories and concepts are marked by capitals – these notions will be distinguished in 0.3.

[22] In Geeraerts's description (1992a: 221), "horizontal" prototypicality within one category as opposed to "vertical" prototypicality between hierarchically related categories.

the real-world correlation of attributes [and] cut up reality into maximally informative attributes". More specifically, they: "maximize the number of attributes shared by members of the category and minimize the number of attributes shared with members of other categories" (Taylor 1989: 50–51).

What kind of motivation is revealed by the existence of "prototype effects" and "basic level" categories? Taylor (1989: 52–53) presents several possibilities mentioned by Rosch and other authors: frequency of occurrence, order of learning, average properties of better members or (alternatively) their salient properties. Most satisfactory in his view is a "more general explanation" offered by Geeraerts, who argues that prototype categories are more efficient than "Aristotelian" ones (based on necessary and sufficient properties), since they are able to accommodate new data without necessitating a restructuring of the category system. Let us notice, however, that overall higher efficiency of a system is a result of some factors at play which still need to be explained. Moreover, if one wants to compare the performance of X and Y, they should compete at the same task (*tertium comparationis*). Aristotelian categories – as noticed by many participants in the debate – are more efficient in some areas, e.g. mathematics.

Harnad shows that Rosch's findings concerning "prototype effects" and "basic level" entities do not explain categorization – they have nothing to do with the generation of this capacity. As a cognitive scientist (dealing with "sensorimotor robotics"), he aims at describing mechanisms, asking "how" things work. From this point of view, Taylor's initial characterization of the phenomenon in question – "the seeing of sameness in difference" (1989: vii) – is a description of the result. We need to widen our horizon to see the process which underlies it.

Harnad defines categorization as "any systematic differential interaction between an autonomous, adaptive, sensorimotor system and its world" (2005: 3). Thus, we talk about organisms and not objects, which also "systematically and differentially interact" with their environment in some sense, like the sand in the desert building up dunes under the influence of the wind. The difference is this: while the sand produces the same output (a configuration) when there is the same input (wind conditions), an organism reacts in the same way when there is the same kind of input. A description of systematic and differential interaction of the sand and the wind is a description of "brute facts",[23] while a description of an organism's reactions – a description of "meanings".

Categorization is a sensorimotor skill which must be learned (like all skills). This is so even if a particular differential capacity (like colour perception) is inborn, since such abilities must have developed through evolution.[24] The "seeing of sameness in difference" is thus an inborn or acquired ability to recognize some sensory input as a kind of thing, requiring the capacity to abstract. In the context of linguistic categorization, it is important to gauge the extent of abstraction in-

[23] "Brute facts" as captured by physics (to repeat, all "facts" are revealed in involvement).

[24] The process of individual sensorimotor learning involves real-time trial-and-error, while the process of evolutionary adaptation involves genetic trial-and-error. See Harnad (2005: 10).

volved. Our sensorimotor systems with their skills acquired through evolution detect only some physical stimuli (e.g. the "visible" part of the light spectrum) and they do not give equal weight to them. For instance, a (relative) continuum of shades in black-and-white vision is transformed in colour vision into eleven clearly differentiated ranges of "focal" colours (in Berlin and Kay's account). Abstraction – understood in negative terms: as eliminating some features from a given whole – is thus only a superficial description of the process of categorization, which is intimately tied with differential weighting of input. When focal colours are extracted as invariants, the frequencies belonging to their range become "compressed" (we see them as shades of "the same" colour – as more "similar" than they would be in black-and-white vision), while there is "expansion" at the boundaries (equal-sized frequency differences look much smaller within a category than over the boundary).

This process of "articulation" of phenomena in perception was described by Ernst Cassirer in the twenties of the last century in the following terms:

> The building of the world of perception requires an articulation of the sensory phenomena – that is to say, certain centers must be created, to which these phenomena as a whole are referred and toward which they are oriented and directed. [This requires that] the even flow of appearances be interrupted in some way and that certain favored points be singled out. What was previously an unremitting flow of events now coalesces, as it were, about these favored points: in the very midst of the stream there form separate vortices, whose parts seem to be linked in a common movement. It is the creation of such dynamic rather than static totalities, this formation of functional rather than substantial unities, that gives rise to the inner relationships between phenomena. For now there is no longer any absolutely isolated thing; every element that is engaged with others in such a common movement bears in itself the general law and form of that movement and is able to represent it for consciousness. And now, wherever we penetrate the stream of consciousness, we find definite living centers, toward which the individual movements strive. Every single perception is a *directed* perception; aside from its mere content, it possesses a vector which makes it significant for a definite direction or meaning.[25] (Cassirer 1957: 221–222; emphasis in the original)

We can see from this quote that the term "abstraction" is a static, after the fact description of a deep reconfiguration of experience. Categories, or vortices around favoured points in the stream of experience, are formed as functional unities. Thus, they must be viewed in the context of activities which give them their meaning (*le sens*).

Let us consider, as an example, Harnad's distinction between relative and absolute discrimination (2005: 20). The former takes place in the context of successive pairwise presentation of two very similar shapes. Subjects, who are asked whether the shapes are the same or different, can normally spot tiny differences.

---

[25] Merleau-Ponty (2002: 223) quotes Cassirer as an important forerunner of hermeneutic phenomenology. Let me add in this context that the "directional" character, or the meaning of an act of perception is best expressed by the ambiguous French word *sens*: see the translators' notes to the English (2002: 499) and Polish (2001: 431) editions.

But when they are shown one of the shapes in isolation, and asked which of the two it is, they are unable to do so. The latter task requires identification or absolute discrimination. In order to identify something, one must know what to look for. If we extrapolate Harnad's example, we can begin to see better the difference between experiential categorization of animals and linguistic categorization of human beings. Animal categorization takes place in the context of their biological needs. The categories have more or less direct survival value: is "this" food or non-food?; friend or foe?; home or foreign territory? In other words, animals have no need to recognize "objects" (which have some identity in isolation) but only correlates of their drives, as activated in a particular environment.[26] Linguistic categorization, on the other hand, is more like identification in isolation: what is an X in absolute terms, i.e. in reference to other related entities (linguistic categories) at one's disposal?[27]

Against that background, we can appreciate better, perhaps, Harnad's claim (2005: Appendix 1) that "the Roschian legacy" of prototypes, family resemblances[28] and the basic level of categorization is a "non-starter" as an explanation for our ability to categorize. Specifically, if prototypes are "templates" for categories, then "*everything* is a member of *every* category, to different degrees" (this *reductio ad absurdum* follows directly from the observation that one can compare X and Y along any number of dimensions[29]). Moreover, many things we categorize have no templates (or "gestalts" – cf. Rosch's presentation of the basic level above). And finally, template-matching does not work in machine-learning models. Harnad concludes: prototype effects concern typicality judgements, which presuppose the ability to categorize, and not the other way round.

Models based on family resemblances – or polycentric categories – are clusters of either / or features: this is an X, if it corresponds to the description A, B or C. As based on "disjunctive invariants", such models are "perfectly classical".[30] What is more, we are not told how the ability to categorize in this way may de-

---

[26] This point is well illustrated by Köhler's often discussed experiments with chimpanzees: they used a stick to reach a banana only if the stick was placed in sight – when it formed part of the situation; otherwise, they did not look actively for it, which indicates it was not an independent "object" in their memory store, see e.g. Vygotsky (1962: 36).

[27] Linguistic identification is also driven by some needs but of a different kind than in the animal world. The point of the example was to highlight the difference.

[28] The notion is based on Wittgenstein's discussion of the meaning of the word "game" [*Spiel*], see Wittgenstein (1978: 31–33). It is used to distinguish "monocentric" categories (which refer to one kind of thing) from "polycentric" ones (which include several kinds of things, or subcategories).

[29] This idea is well captured in Watanabe's "Ugly Duckling Theorem" (see Harnad 2005: 19): the "ugly duckling" is no less similar to any of the white swans than they are to one another, as long as one does not treat whiteness as a privileged feature.

[30] Basically the same point is made by Geeraerts, in a more understated manner: "while the revolutionary nature of prototype theory is often said to reside in the fact that it rejects the classical view that lexical categories can be defined by means of a sufficient set of necessary conditions for category membership, the possibility that some lexical items cannot receive a definition in terms of necessary-and-sufficient attributes is not exactly absent from the classical tradition. Rather, it is traditionally taken as an indication of the polysemy of the item in question" (1993: 223–224).

velop. Let me add at this point that "linguistic categories" analysed in the present case study are such polycentric categories based on family resemblances.

The "basic object level" – as opposed to the superordinate and subordinate level – merely corresponds to "the default context" of everyday communication. To quote Harnad:

> If you point to an object, say, a table, and ask me what it is, chances are that I will say it's a table, rather than a Biedermeyer, or furniture, or "Charlie". So what? As mentioned earlier, there are many ways to categorize the same objects, depending on context. A context is simply a set of alternatives among which the object's name is meant to resolve the uncertainty (in perfectly classical information-theoretic terms). So when you point to a table and ask me what it is, I pick "table" as the uncertainty-resolver in the default context. [...] If [the room] contains four tables, I might have to identify this one as the Biedermeyer; and if there are four Biedermeyers, I may have to hope you know I've dubbed this one "Charlie". (Harnad 2005: Appendix 1)

To conclude: prototype effects are real enough. It is true that in "monocentric" categories some elements are perceived as more central, that in "polycentric categories" some subcategories stand out as more easily recognizable, and that labels for "basic level" entities are used more readily in the default context. The significance of such effects for the theory of categorization is much less clear.

In the context of linguistics, some light on the significance of prototype effects is shed by a discussion between Bolinger and Wierzbicka. Bolinger reacted to Wierzbicka's attack (1990b) on the abuse of prototype analyses: they are offered unnecessarily in the cases when a more rigorous feature-type analysis is possible. As an example, she points out the difference between the concepts BIRD and FURNITURE. In the former case (a natural kind term), one is never in doubt whether a particular creature belongs to the category, while the latter concept (a nominal kind term) is indeed vague: "one cannot draw a line between kinds of things which are included in this supercategory and things which are not – because by virtue of its meaning, the word *furniture* doesn't aim at identifying any particular kind of thing" (Wierzbicka 1990b: 355; emphasis in the original). In Wierzbicka's terminology, this is the difference between a "taxonomic" concept and a "collective" concept (or, in my paraphrase, a superordinate concept, comprising heterogeneous "basic level" objects).

In Bolinger's view there is no essential difference between taxonomic and collective concepts (and consequently, between natural kind terms and nominal kind terms). The discreteness of taxonomy is largely an illusion. For one thing, we see only the results of a long process of natural selection, which eliminated intermediate stages of evolution (e.g. birds with teeth); moreover, we are taught to perceive the natural order through the traditional classificatory lenses provided by Linnaeus and Darwin (1992: 114).[31] Thus, both the concept FURNITURE and the

[31] Bolinger does not mention this but there is a lively discussion in biology between proponents of partly inconsistent taxonomic criteria: morphological vs. genetic ones (the latter are proposed by "cladists"; see Gould (1983); cf. Lakoff (1987: 119–121)). In philosophy of biology, there is a debate

concept BIRD have fuzzy boundaries. If they differ, it is not because the latter is rooted in the natural order of entities or the former cannot be represented by one schematic object. The difference lies in the definitional criteria. FURNITURE, as an artifactual category, is identified relative to its function (things used to furnish rooms). Functional features – as opposed to morphological or genetic ones, as in the case of BIRD – are much more fuzzy. For instance, the feature "a piece of furniture is thought of as movable" on the one hand does not exclude "rugs" (1992: 115), while, on the other hand, seems to exclude kitchen furniture, which is fixed to the walls.

In her rejoinder, Wierzbicka points out that there is an important difference for definitional purposes between "a kind of thing", which has a stable position in some taxonomy, and "things of different kinds kept in one place, for the same purpose". Only in the former case should the taxonomic position be included in the definition, e.g. it is right to define PARROT as "a kind of bird" and it would be wrong to define BED as "a kind of furniture". This is based on the assumption that "there are no higher levels of taxonomy in the realm of artifacts" (1992: 120–122).[32]

In the present context, it is important to underline that Bolinger and Wierzbicka agree that both prototypes and features have a place in semantic description (their debate concerns a relatively minor issue: when should the information about the place of an item in a taxonomy be included?). This common assumption is in agreement with the results of a *prima facie* paradoxical result of an experiment by Armstrong et al., as reported e.g. by Lakoff (1987: 148–151) or Taylor (1989: 68–69). The study revealed that classically defined categories – ODD NUMBER and EVEN NUMBER – also exhibit prototype effects, that is subjects assign higher values to some members. Taylor places this result in the context of the distinction between "folk" and "expert" categories: even though some (or most) categories can be defined in a (relatively) discrete way by experts, in everyday communication people need only "cognitive reference points" for successful orientation. Thus, there is a "division of linguistic labour" within a speech community. As described by Putnam (1975), experts look for necessary and sufficient criteria of categorization, while ordinary speakers rely on "stereotypes" (Taylor 1989: 68–74). We may conclude that "prototype effects" reflect the ordinary cognitive strategy of relating new specimens to established "templates" or "gestalts" in a continuous effort to "domesticate" reality, as opposed to the expert task of "categorizing the world" as a taxonomic system of units defined in a discrete way.

---

whether to treat the species as a "natural kind" (a class of entities) or as an "individual"; see Bird, Tobin (2008) on "natural kinds" and Ereshefsky (2007) on "species" .

[32] Consequently, Wierzbicka would probably reject my characterization of FURNITURE as a "superordinate concept, comprising heterogeneous 'basic level' objects".

* * *

Let us return to the questions guiding this presentation. How can we identify (categorize) something we do not know? Within CL (and psychology) this question is normally understood as the problem of applying schemas (concepts) to objects which do not obviously fit them. This issue (is something still a cup or a mug?) is clearly secondary – it is the question of referential application. Genetically, the problem concerns the constitution of categories: how is it possible that reality appears as <u>types</u> of entities? What is the source of this "typicality" (proto-ideality)? As Harnad shows, types arise in sorting actions, when an organism looks actively for entities which could satisfy its needs. Primarily, types result from distinctions introduced by the goal of a given activity. In a more hermeneutical formulation, activities are "projective" stances: an animal treats its environment as if it were good for something. When it looks for food, shelter or a sexual partner, its reality polarizes into entities which apparently satisfy the need or not.

This "projective" – hypothetical – style of exploration is revealed by studies in biological deprivation. When entities normally chosen to satisfy an animal's needs are missing in the environment, almost anything can "trigger"[33] a relevant reaction.[34] In this way, time (and time-scale) enters the picture as a crucial factor. An animal exemplifies a set of generic distinguishing behaviour patterns, which must have evolved in the history of the species. The objective correlates of these patterns may be viewed as "protocategories". Thus, the categorizing history of individual exploration in successive generations sediments (we need not be diverted here by evolutionary mechanisms) into a generic "habit/at": an indissoluble whole of distinguishing behavioural patterns in an environment. This is why some entities are default options (or prototypes), while others may be included in a category as the need dictates. When the habitat changes (as a result of deprivation or unusual abundance, or an introduction of a new predator, or – most radically perhaps – due to a transfer to a different environment or a transforming genetic mutation), behavioural patterns must keep pace with the changes. On the one hand, then, there is a drive to fix categories (as this guarantees greater efficiency in standard conditions), while on the other hand, rigidity of categories would spell extinction (in times of change). To sum up the biological background sketched above: reality

[33] This behaviourist term reverses the genetic order (similarly to the "stimulus-response" sequence): it is only because an animal "projects" its environment as something (or takes up appropriate stances) that things appear as good for some purposes.

[34] "In a series of experiments with blond ring doves Craig removed the female from the male in a succession of gradually increasing periods. After one such period of deprivation, he experimented to see which objects were now sufficient to elicit the courtship dance of the male. [After a few days] the male was ready to court a white dove which he had previously ignored. A few days later he was bowing and cooing to a stuffed pigeon, later still to a rolled-up cloth, and finally, after weeks of solitary confinement, he directed the courtship toward the empty corner of his box cage where the convergence of the straight sides offered at least an optical fixation point" (Lorenz 1963: 48–49). Or as shown by Weiner (1994), in periods of drought a particular species of finch chooses types of grain it would not normally consider as food.

manifests itself according to what an organism searches for; biological needs are a kind of protoquestioning, while types of entities (categories) appear as yes – no answers (e.g. will or will not X do as food); a history of questioning underlies a particular exploratory infrastructure (the sensory apparatus and behavioural habits), while a history of answers constitutes a given habitat.

We may now approach the issue of "ideality", which surfaced in Taylor's characterization of CL in the context of the debate concerning "universals": CL is taken to be "conceptualist", with partly "realist" and partly "nominalist" leanings. This description has no philosophical significance, i.e. CL takes no position in the ontological/epistemological debate about the status of concepts. CL merely assumes that some concepts are non-arbitrary, i.e. that they reflect perceptual universals, e.g. focal colours.[35] When one inspects this example at close range, it may be used to dispel several misconceptions. As is evident from Taylor's presentation, focal colours – taken as centres of fuzzy natural categories, whose peripheries merge – are invoked to counter the structuralist view that concepts are sharp ("classical"), while it is only their referential application which may be problematic. Taylor's (more generally, CL's) position is based on the doubtful assumption that "colour categories" are natural concepts. If we accept it for the sake of the argument, we can see that the structuralist position is right: focal colours are sharp, i.e. clearly defined as opposed to their neighbours. Our sight responds differentially to those "concepts". The fact that some colour samples are judged as better examples does not mean that the "concepts" are fuzzy and that there are "degrees of membership". The "concepts" are there in the perceptual system – clearly opposed to one another. Their "definition" presupposes a boundary which – *eo ipso* – has no categorial status. Thus, by the very fact that we have "points of reference", there must be some "middle ground" with uncertain status.

Moreover, Taylor's argument does not take into account the fundamental fact that categories – basically, differential reactions – are not fixed like Platonic "ideas". Focal "red" may be recognized as such when confronted with "pink" or "yellow", but it could be also classified as a "light" colour or a "dark" colour, depending on its saturation. "Pink" could be opposed to "red" or treated as a kind of "red", depending on the oppositions in question. In other words, the system of "concepts" is one thing, while its application to reality for some tasks – another one.

We can appreciate now that the role of oppositions is absolutely central, when one invokes concepts or categories. Of course, once a category is constituted, we can think that e.g. "red" or "yellow" is directly accessible, no matter what other colour categories are available. But this is an illusion based on self-forgetting (to recall the hermeneutical diagnosis). As we have seen, colour vision requires a re-shaping of the black and white spectrum, constituted by shades of grey. In this

---

[35] The existence of perceptual universals does not solve the philosophical problem of validity: such universals are still contingent, i.e. reflect our generic way of viewing reality (as different e.g. from the way a daltonist, a bonobo or a bat views reality).

mysterious process (why do we see colours at all?), vortices are formed, which exert their pull on all data provided by sight.[36] As a result, there are no isolated colour perceptions: everything is drawn by one vortex or another. To be sure, this "conceptual" system does not run automatically: depending on the situation, i.e. the task at hand, the vortices may expand, contract, subdivide, merge along one dimension or another, revealing the same fragment of reality as X or Y or Z (cf. Eiser 1994 in a related context).

When one adopts some objective criteria of differentiation, e.g. "red" as defined by light wavelength, it may seem that oppositions are not necessary. However, an objective definition takes for granted the process of constitution.[37] We may translate "red" into a certain range of frequencies, because our vision has differentially cut up the visible light spectrum in a particular way. This shows that Rosch's argument about the development of colour categories, as quoted by Taylor, is wrong. It is not true that a "colour term denotes, first and foremost, a focal colour, and it is only through 'generalization from focal exemplars' [...] that colour terms acquire their full denotational range" (1989: 15). A colour term denotes first and foremost the range within the boundaries staked out by oppositions to neighbouring terms. If the Dani use two colour terms, then focal colours (which they can clearly recognize) are not treated as centres of their categories (they could rely, perhaps, on saturation, if they oppose "light" to "dark"). In general, "objective" perceptual data (e.g. focal colours, saturation etc.) provide only a motive, which may be taken up in conceptual expression, i.e. in a linguistic *reprise du sens* of perceptual articulation (see 5.1.).

As for the "basic level" categorization, it is at least recognized by Rosch and CL that gestalts are "maximally distinct". However, this is true in general: also at a given superordinate or subordinate level, because concepts tend to be maximally distinct within their standard context of use to remain functional (they are there to mark oppositions). One can claim that "trees" and "bushes" are distinct perceptual gestalts, i.e. natural categories. However, their opposition is symbolic: we learn to draw them differently in the kindergarten to mark "maximally distinct" types. In reality, particular specimens may very well look the same, while the gross perceptual differences represented schematically in drawings need not be primary in the conceptual constitution of these categories; cf. 1.2.2. on Langacker's "developmental story". As pointed out by Harnad, the "basic level" is special only because it provides the defaults in everyday communication (but the defaults may be very different in specialist or special contexts).

The definitional problems discussed by Bolinger and Wierzbicka concern the status of category boundaries and the opposition between "natural" and "nominal" categories. As for the former issue, Bolinger points out (rightly, in my view)

---

[36] As long as some threshold of light intensity is attained – at dusk we return to black and white vision.

[37] And distorts uncomfortable data or pushes them into the background, cf. 4.2. on the objective definition of *length* and *width*.

that all boundaries are fuzzy – whether those drawn by nature (between species) or those drawn by man.[38] As for the latter one, Wierzbicka is clearly motivated by her theoretical assumptions (concerning "natural" semantic primitives), when she says that *bed* should not be defined as "a kind of furniture", because FURNITURE is not a natural category and thus does not belong to a natural taxonomy. The real problem at issue here may be the difference between "folk" and "expert" categories, invoked by Taylor. In everyday communication we rely on "stereotypes", e.g. a "fish" lives in water and looks like a fish (thus, a whale is a "big fish"). Stereotypes serve as our "points of reference" (or "vortices") in everyday life, thus they may be as flexible as it is functionally relevant (beaver's meat may be a kind of "fish" on Friday in a Catholic country). Since experts aim at "carving nature at its joints", they look for natural relations between entities and "objective" differences. As opposed to "people in the street", they try to construct taxonomies not for some clearly pragmatic reasons, but to order the available material in a perspicuous way, revealing natural relations between entities. However, alternative definitions of entities are still the norm and alternate functional wholes may be postulated.

I hope to have shown that "prototype effects" cannot lead directly to any conclusions about the structure of concepts or categories (whether perceptual or linguistic). As we have seen, that position was actually adopted by Rosch (in reference to "mental categories"). Since the issues involved in the discussion raise several fundamental problems which cannot be satisfactorily investigated here, I hope to have given an idea of their complexity.

0.3. Cognitive linguistics as prototype semantics

The first question to be raised – in view of doubts about the significance of prototype effects for the theory of categorization – concerns a phenomenal success of prototype modelling within CL. It is perhaps easy to understand why Rosch's work was taken up with great enthusiasm by Lakoff. Since in his interpretation Rosch "provided a full-scale challenge to the classical theory [of categorization]", Lakoff used her work to bolster up his own project to revolutionize not only linguistics, but also several other disciplines, in which "the classical theory was taken for granted" (1987: 39). However, prototype models were also constructed and/or defended at that early stage by linguists who had no ideological axes to grind, e.g. Langacker (1987, 1988a, 1988b), Geeraerts (1988a, 1990, 1992a) or

[38] To repeat, this does not mean that we cannot have sharply defined concepts (Wierzbicka's concern).

Taylor (1988, 1989), and they were subsequently applied in a variety of fields by a legion of researchers.

One may suggest several reasons for this transfer of ideas. First (and most generally), cognitive linguists naturally looked for inspiration in other cognitive sciences as members of the same interdisciplinary research paradigm. Second, the focus on categorization – and more generally, on conceptual structuring of experience – meshed well with CL's aims, as characterized, for instance, by Fauconnier: "CL has emerged in the last twenty-five years as a powerful approach to the study of language, conceptual systems, human cognition, and general meaning construction" (2003: 1). Finally (and most specifically), the prototype approach seemed to be a promising alternative to the structuralist paradigm in linguistics,[39] as a way to a more realistic characterization of linguistic categories.

The last motive is clearly visible in the debate concerning the structuralist distinction between "linguistic" and "encyclopedic" meaning.[40] The rejection of such oppositions underlies the cognitivist position in lexical semantics, as expressed e.g. by Langacker: "The distinction between semantics and pragmatics (or between linguistic and extralinguistic knowledge) is largely artifactual, and the only viable conception of linguistic semantics is one that avoids such false dichotomies and is consequently encyclopedic in nature" (1987: 154).

In his discussion, Taylor ties the structuralist or "autonomous" position on this issue with the analytic-synthetic distinction, which he exemplifies (1989: 81) as follows:

(1) *Dogs are animals.*
(2) *Dogs have four legs / have a tail / bark / do not miaow / do not have horns, etc.*

Sentence (1) is analytic, that is true by definition – it is a statement about relations in the classical system of categories, defined in terms of necessary and sufficient conditions. Sentence (2), on the other hand, is empirically true, as it contains facts about dogs. Following Taylor, a structuralist linguist would argue that the definitional feature in (1) is purely linguistic (thus, belongs to the "dictionary"), while empirical facts about dogs expressed in (2) are of concern to zoologists and other specialists (the "encyclopedia"). Taylor admits that if a dog, for whatever reasons, lacks the features mentioned in (2), it will still remain a dog. Thus, they are not necessary for defining "dogness". He claims however, following philosophers criticising the analytic-synthetic distinction (Quine, Kripke, Putnam), that

[39] Whether in its neostructuralist or neogenerativist version, see Geeraerts (2002: 7); cf. Geeraerts 1988b: 673 and Geeraerts 1992b: 265. I believe, in accordance with Geeraert's historical classification, that it is a quarrel in the family: CL is also a structuralist school of thought. However, I will argue in 5.2. – as already mentioned – that CL shares important assumptions with its generativist predecessor, as opposed to Saussure's structuralism; cf. Pawelec (2005a: 156–157, 160).

[40] Or the opposition between "dictionary" and "encyclopedia" – the title of Haiman's seminal article; cf. Langacker (1987: 155).

the same conclusion must be drawn in the case of (1), for such relations reflect our present-day knowledge about the world, which may turn out to be false: "In the highly unlikely, but not totally inconceivable, event of dogs being discovered to be self-reproducing automata controlled by extraterrestrial minds" (Taylor 1989: 82).

Taylor refers above to Putnam's example (actually, about cats[41]), which cannot be discussed without analytic terminology. So far, I have talked interchangeably about "words", "terms", "categories" and "concepts". Now it is time to introduce some relevant distinctions.

Intension vs. extension of a term

To make the question of word meaning more manageable, let us focus on simplified (idealized) situations. The basic one is "naming": a personal name (X) provides a unique identification of a person (Y). X is a term (or a label), and Y is its "extension" – its range of application (in this case: a single person). X has no definitional meaning, no "intension", since it does not relate to other terms – it just points to an object or designates it (as in an "ostensive" definition). A more complex situation was discussed by Frege in his classic article[42] on sense and reference: the planet Venus is known both as Evening star and Morning star. These terms have different "intensions" or conceptual meanings (Frege's "sense"): "the star which appears in the evening" and "the star which appears in the morning". Their extension (Frege's "reference") is the same: they designate the planet Venus.

Concept vs. category

More often, terms designate classes of things – categories. For instance, the intension of the term "human being" is a properly defined concept (a set of features), while its extension comprises all individuals to whom the term legitimately applies, or the relevant category.

To quote Rúa: "It could be said that a category is a class of objects which is apprehended by means of the corresponding concept" (Rúa 2003: 20). As she points out, due to this inextricable link the terms "concept" and "category" are often used interchangeably. Their identification, however, can be justified only in the ideal case of a class term with a fixed intension (concept) and a fixed reference (category). The paradigmatic example concerns analytic terms: the definition of a concept determines the relevant category, e.g. the term "triangle" designates entities defined as "a flat figure with three straight sides and three angles". As Frege's

---

[41] Analytic philosophers often contrive outlandish thought experiments. A similar one by Putnam concerns "water" with a different chemical formula (not H_20 but XYZ) on "Twin Earth" (1975: 223), cf. McLure's account (1990: 510ff.).

[42] *Über Sinn und Bedeutung* published in 1892. English translation *On Sense and Reference* (1993).

example shows, however, the relation between "intension" and "extension" is a complex one already on the level of individuals. It is only to be expected that it gets even less tractable on the level of classes.

We talked about "terms" designating individuals or classes as an ideal case. In normal communication, we use "words" which are vague and/or ambiguous:[43] neither their extension nor intension is fully specified out of context. Only in some domains, e.g. trade or law, we stipulate ideally unambiguous intensions (but the problem of extension – i.e. which actual items or cases are covered by the concept – will still remain in force, necessitating further intensional specifications). Generally speaking, categories are "sets" of entities, while concepts are "delimitations" of relevant entities. It may be quite a different task to delimit a concept – to define it in relation to other concepts – and to devise a procedure for recognizing members of a category.

If we return to Putnam's example, we will see that he wants to define the meaning of *cat* or *dog* "extensionally", i.e. on the basis of some recognitory procedures devised by experts (which would fail, if it turned out that the classes are automata, merely imitating animals). In intensional terms, however, the meaning of *cat* or *dog* need not change – people could simply start to call the creatures "false cats" or "automatic dogs", to mark the additional distinction (their defective status).

We can see now that there is a gap between philosophical and linguistic aims. There may be no analytic terms (intensions) which necessarily determine their referents (extensions). Even the definition of the triangle quoted above may turn out to be too constraining, if we would like to call by this name (as would be natural) a three-sided figure drawn on the surface of a sphere (as in Riemannian geometry), which would <u>not</u> have straight sides and would <u>not</u> be flat. That does not mean, however, that a linguist cannot define concepts according to the present state of knowledge, or as actually used (how else?). Consequently, Taylor is wrong to suggest that philosophical problems with the "analytic – synthetic" distinction count as an argument against discrete definitions. Extensionally, it is enough to identify a set of differentiating features (from related categories) as possessed by standard specimens. Intensionally, the description of dogs in (2) above is not useful because it does not consistently oppose DOGS to CATS (or some other concept).

Langacker argues that the account of the meanings of linguistic expressions offered by autonomous semantics cannot capture their full richness, as it leaves out "recalcitrant data for an ill-defined 'pragmatic component'". He suggests that autonomous semantics is grounded in methodological and aprioristic considerations. Since it aims to describe language as a formal system, it focuses on a limited

---

[43] To define these terms (in their most widespread interpretation): "vague" is extensional (or referential) – it is appropriate when we do not know if a given word legitimately applies to a referent (all words referring to things are potentially vague); "ambiguous" is intensional – it is appropriate when a given word applies to different concepts, e.g. *school*: 1. with pupils; 2. of dolphins (most words which denote something are ambiguous).

set of semantic properties. That goal, says Langacker, is gratuitous: "The fact that autonomy of language would be highly convenient for linguists does not amount to valid evidence for its reality". Additionally, autonomous linguists do not think it is feasible to describe linguistic meaning as a matter of conceptualization. Langacker takes that stance to be pointless, "since meaning is, in the last analysis, a matter of conceptualization", and adds rhetorically: "what else could it possibly be?" (1987: 156).

Generally speaking, Langacker argues in the name of realism, advocating greater faithfulness towards the phenomena or a fuller characterization of the object of study. In itself, it is an admirable attitude – an expression of a truly scientific spirit. Still, the objections reported above, and some of their presuppositions, are questionable. The claim that autonomous semantics does not deal properly with awkward data may be justified as far as it goes, but it points to the legitimate problem of a demarcation between semantics and pragmatics (specifically, the issue of potentially infinite flexibility of word meanings in use). The same goes for the distinction between "dictionary" and "encyclopedia". As pointed out by Taylor: "an encyclopaedist approach also brings with it a demarcation problem. We do not, presumably, want to say that everything an individual happens to know about dogs will be relevant for a characterization of his concept DOG" (Taylor 1989: 83). Additionally, Langacker's claim that "autonomous linguistics" is based on the assumption of "autonomy of language" goes too far. It may be justified in reference to Chomsky's position concerning the autonomy of syntax, but it misrepresents the original impulse behind structuralism, i.e. how should one delimit a properly linguistic "object" of study?; cf. 4.1. Thus, the original problem remains: is linguistics to be conceived as a subdiscipline of psychology (or some other science), or rather as a separate field of inquiry? If the latter, what is its "object"? The final, apparently rhetorical, question posed by Langacker lies at the centre of the present investigation. Is meaning – specifically, linguistic meaning – to be equated with conceptualization? Are there any alternatives?; cf. 5.3.

At this stage, let us see how the cognitive "encyclopedic" approach differs from the structuralist "dictionary" approach. In Taylor's account, both positions are similar at the point of departure. They accept that linguistic meanings do not exist as separate entities – they are context dependent. For the structuralist, however, the context is conceived as "the syntagmatic and paradigmatic relations between signs within the linguistic system". Thus, meaning is a language internal issue. For the cognitivist, on the other hand, meanings are defined in the context of language external "cognitive structures, embedded in patterns of knowledge and belief" (Taylor 1989: 83).[44]

---

[44] The Chomskyan school, as represented by Jackendoff, accepts that semantic structures are "simply a subset of conceptual structures – just those conceptual structures that happen to be verbally expressible". Thus, "when we are studying semantics of natural language, we are by necessity studying the structure of thought" – quoted in Taylor (1996: 21). However, this position is still based on the "dictionary" view of semantics: the proper subject of semantic inquiry is limited to those aspects of

In what respect, then, does linguistic conceptualization differ for the cognitivist from conceptualization *sans phrase*? An answer is given in the title of a book by Langacker: *Concept, Image, and Symbol*. Out of all possible conceptualizations (the first segment of the title), a language sanctions a subset of construals, which may be creatively extended, imposing a particular image on a given conceptual material (the second segment), thanks to its symbolic nature, that is conventional pairings of the conceptual and phonological pole on any level of linguistic structure: "all valid grammatical elements and constructs are held to be symbolic" (the third segment). Consequently, "viable semantic analysis ultimately reduces to conceptual analysis", while grammar is symbolic: it forms "a continuum with lexicon" (1991: ix).

To understand the meaning of a linguistic form, we must place it in the context of relevant cognitive structures – its "domains". For instance, the word *hypotenuse* can be understood given the concept of the right triangle; *elbow* – within the configuration of the human arm; *April* – as part of the calendar. A given word gets its meaning by "profiling", or highlighting, a particular region in the relevant domains. Most semantic structures require several domains (or a "complex matrix") for their full description. For instance, the complex matrix for *knife* includes a shape specification (space domain), its canonical function (cutting domain), its relation to other pieces of cutlery and any other piece of information relevant for its characterization (for instance, knife-throwing acts in circuses). As we already know, Langacker opts for a fully encyclopedic view: "Any facet of our knowledge of an entity is capable in principle of playing a role in determining the linguistic behavior of an expression that designates it (e.g. in semantic extension, or in its combination with other expressions)" (1991: 3–5).

A given semantic structure – for instance, one designated by *hypotenuse* – emerges when a bounding schema profiles the relevant region (the side opposite to the right angle) in the domain (a right triangle), which is called in this context its "base". This is an example of "imagery", that is "our manifest capacity to structure or construe the content of a domain in alternate ways". In his theory of grammar, Langacker presents "conventional imagery", that is construals sanctioned by convention. There are several dimensions of conventional imagery: the "level of specificity" at which a situation is construed, the "scale" and "scope of predication", the "relative salience", the construal of a situation relative to different background assumptions and expectations, as well as perspective (1991: 5–12).

There is ample room in Langacker's theory for prototype effects, i.e. an unequal status of category members or a nondiscrete characterization of category structure. Since most lexical items designate an array of interrelated senses sanctioned by convention, Langacker represents them as a network. Some of the senses are "schematic" relative to others, which are their "elaborations" (at

---

a word's meaning that are perceived to be related to the syntactic behaviour of the word; see Taylor (1996) for a critique.

a lower level of specificity). Some senses are "extensions", when they conflict in some ways with their sanctioning schemas (low-level prototypes). The most entrenched, or cognitively salient, node is the category prototype. However, it is not always the case that there is only one node of this kind, nor can one always expect the existence of the highest-level schema (compatible with the specifications of every node). Consequently, the conventional meaning of a word is to be equated with the entire network (Langacker 1991: 2–3). From a complementary perspective, since a given word may belong to several morphosyntactic categories and its senses may be defined in alternate ways,[45] "a single network [can] be divided into lexical items in multiple and mutually inconsistent ways" (Langacker 1987: 388). Moreover, since grammar is symbolic, prototype effects may be found in all linguistic categories and constructions, e.g. in morphology, syntax, phonology (see Taylor (1989) for an overview).

* * *

There are several problems raised in this account which seem tangential to the issue at hand (the significance of prototype research in CL) but which are fundamental and central for my investigation (concerning the identity of CL in relation to its predecessors and the nature of its project).

The philosophical attempt to distinguish "analytic" from "synthetic" concepts, mentioned by Taylor, fails because concepts are grounded in reality: they offer a "perspective" on some referential domain. Even a geometrical concept like TRIANGLE is "perspectival" and *eo ipso* provisional: it makes sense as a way of questioning reality which is open and may always surprise us (i.e. necessitate a broader definition, integrating previous ones[46]).

Putnam also aims to demonstrate that "analytic" concepts do not determine their extensions – that reality may surprise us. However, his "thought experiments" do not adequately represent the relations between intension and extension. They suggest that the meaning of a term is purely extensional, to be determined by experts. In reality, however, we have a two-way process: intensions are provisional ways of capturing relevant distinctions, which may prove inadequate, when

[45] E.g. *mother* may be either a noun or a verb. Cf. Lakoff's comment on the noun: "even among [dictionary-makers] there is no single, generally accepted cognitive model for such a common concept as 'mother'" (1987: 76). While Lakoff's analysis of *mother* is contestable – cf. Wierzbicka (1990: 353–354) – and his objection is based on his own theoretical constructs, the general point stands: a lexical item's senses may be defined in alternative, criss-crossing ways; see for instance Geeraerts's analyses of *vers* (1990) and *fresh* (2007: 1166–1169).

[46] Thus, the analogy with the "elephant story" is limited: there is nothing to generalize in the partial "takes" provided by the groping blind men, since the story is about recognizing a known entity. Science is about discovering meaningful wholes, which one does not see clearly, in all of their manifestations.

unexpected data are brought to light; this normally necessitates a restructuring not of a single concept, but of the whole semantic field in question.[47]

We can see now that the relations between "intensions" and "extensions" are complex and cannot be reduced to a single formula. It may seem, then, that the structuralist approach foregrounding intensions – as formulated on the basis of paradigmatic and syntagmatic relationships of words – is questionable, since it backgrounds the issue of their application or actualization in context (as well as genesis). There is, however, an important difference between philosophical or scientific concerns ("what is the nature of concepts?", "how concepts arise?") and the concerns of a linguist ("how to represent linguistic knowledge?"). One may argue (as we shall see in 4.1.) that the structuralist position captures the intuitions of language users concerning the present senses of words (as opposed to the pragmatic issue of their application in language use).

How should one view Langacker's theoretical choices in this light? He apparently takes the opposition "dictionary"/"encyclopedia" to be interchangeable with the opposition between "semantics" and "pragmatics". In the former case, he rejects the dictionary approach to linguistic meaning, since any information (however idiosyncratic) could prove relevant in meaning extension or compositionality. In the latter case, he rejects pragmatics as "ill-defined", and on the grounds that linguistic meaning is a matter of conceptualization ("what else could it be?", he asks rhetorically).

I submit, first, that the distinctions are not interchangeable and, second, that they cannot be abolished. The first one is about types of knowledge, the second one (in the interpretation relevant for us) – about the application of linguistic knowledge in discourse. Specifically, "dictionary" contains answers to the question: "what do words mean?", while "encyclopedia" contains answers to questions about factual matters. To be sure, in order to know what e.g. *transcendental* or *dative* means one should master some relevant facts. However, it is one thing to know how words are used and another thing to know factual distinctions of one kind or another. At some point, such distinctions may prove important enough to be lexicalized and enter general circulation (whether in a community of specialists, or in the community at large). Langacker is right that potentially any piece of information may find its way to the lexicon but the question is about the status of lexicon (or linguistic knowledge, in general). Without the opposition with "encyclopedia" that issue is fudged.

When Langacker extends semantics to cover "an ill-defined 'pragmatic component'", he fudges another important distinction: that between intersubjective, socially available senses of words and their specific construals in use. In other words, he injects contextual interpretations into the semantic system. Once he

---

[47] Thus, a purely extensional approach to concepts makes no sense. Putnam's example of "water" with a different chemical formula shows clearly that such a "freak of nature" – if it could not be accommodated in the available conceptual framework – would require a wholesale reformulation of chemistry (not just of our concept of WATER).

takes this step, linguistic meaning is identified with conceptualization (hence the rhetorical question). However, since any utterance is open to a potentially infinite number of construals (based on more and more idiosyncratic information and scenarios), we require a distinction – in principle – between what is available socially, i.e. to standard language users in normal circumstances, and what is a matter of contextualized interpretations. In short, we need a distinction between semantics and pragmatics.

Linguistic "categorization by prototype", i.e. in reference to the most representative member or the template of a category, is not an issue in CL (as it is not a real issue).[48] Some nodes in the network are important because of their "cognitive salience". As cognitive "reference points" they provide sanction to elaborations and/or extensions. In the latter case, Langacker talks of prototypes. But they do not exert influence on the status of categories. Categories are taken for granted as networks of senses. Whether they are monocentric, or polycentric, their category status is assumed on some external grounds, rather than derived from the notion of "prototype". Consequently, it is more adequate to say that CL proposes "representation by prototype" or, better still, "according to prototype effects".

What is their role in the network representations of lexical senses? Since some nodes are "more central", the categories are "graded" – their members have unequal status. Specifically, as we shall see, they consist of "clusters". Since a network may comprise several clusters, possibly criss-crossing, it is "nondiscrete" – it need not allow of a consistent characterization. Finally, separate clusters could be conceptually so distant, that they may be connected only by "family resemblances".

0.4. The intractability of polysemy[49]

The notion of polysemy, understood as "the existence of a diversity of related meanings expressed by the same word form" (Lewandowska-Tomaszczyk 2007: 139), may seem straightforward. Under closer inspection, however, it turns out to be elusive. A principal aim of my analysis of network models at the "objective" level is to show some of the reasons for its elusiveness.

The term was introduced in the nineteenth century by Bréal in his study of meaning change.[50] He saw that polysemy results from the diachronic fact that

---

48 In Langacker's account. Prototypes play a more significant role in Lakoff's approach which is, however, much less tenable (see 1.1.). As I argued in 0.2., following Harnad, "categorization by prototype" is impossible, since category boundaries can be demarcated only in opposition to related categories.

49 The phrase is Geeraerts's (e.g. 2007: 1161).

50 The account in this paragraph is based on Nerlich, Clarke (2007: 593–594).

while words (word forms) acquire new senses, the old ones normally remain available. However, at any particular moment of language use polysemy does not really make itself manifest. With the exception of some special uses of language (jokes, puns), a word in an utterance is not normally felt to be ambiguous. Since in the context of discourse one is not aware of choosing from the multiplicity of senses listed in dictionary entries, polysemy appears to be "an artifact of lexicographers".[51] Consequently, Bréal distinguished a social classification of word senses (abstract and decontextualized) contained in dictionaries from "isosynchronic competence" of language users, that is "a half-conscious type of user knowledge which only works inside concrete situations".[52] Thus, the question arises about the relationships between individual situated semantic knowledge and social polysemy. It is clear that language users must somehow acquire the set of conventional senses linked with a word form; and that such conventional, or lexicalized, senses must somehow arise (assuming they exist). One can see that there are several possible levels of analysis involved here, e.g. the original individual extension (not sanctioned by the social norm and which may involve linguistic creativity of a kind); the social acceptance or propagation of a new sense: lexicalization (both these levels are important for linguistic diachrony); a specification of available senses of a word (a lexicographer's or a linguist's synchronic task); a developmental appropriation of available social senses (language acquisition); the use of lexicalized senses in discourse (with infinitely flexible meanings).

Both notions mentioned last – social "lexicalization" and individual flexible use in discourse – point at another relevant aspect of polysemy from the theoretical perspective. It is not enough that meanings conveyed by a lexeme are different; they must be sufficiently different to count as "distinct senses" (this is a conjunction of conditions: socially sanctioned difference of construals). Alm-Arvius tried to capture this point in her distinction between "lexicalised polysemy" and "incidental polysemy" (2007: 44). For her distinction to make sense, one must understand "polysemy" broadly,[53] following Croft and Cruse: not just as the existence of "distinct, established senses", but as "variation in the construal of a word on different occasions of use" (2004: 109).[54] The label "incidental" is not, however, quite adequate. It may cover "nonce uses", when a word is used idiosyncratically – as in creative extensions (Alm-Arvius does not cite examples). It

---

[51] Cf. a similar statement by Dunbar (following Barsalou) in his cognitive account of lexical senses (or concepts): they are "fictions created by theorists out of convenience". He adds: "the position of a lexicographer [is] a perfectly respectable stance but one tangential to the investigation of the comprehension of language" (1991: 54).

[52] Bréal was Saussure's mentor, cf. Joseph (2004: 61).

[53] If the former label is not to be pleonastic, and the latter – a case of *contradictio in adiecto*. The definition of polysemy by Lewandowska-Tomaszczyk, quoted above, is ambiguous in this respect ("meanings" may be interpreted as "senses" or as "construals").

[54] This definition still allows to retain the opposition between semantics and pragmatics, since lexical senses are treated as "pre-meanings", pragmatically actualized in discourse. Cf. note 5 in the Introduction.

is not felicitous, though, as a description of regular senses of an item, which are not felt to be sufficiently distinct.

An extensive discussion of such "sub-senses", which do not have the level of autonomy of full sense units, is provided by Croft and Cruse (2004: 116–140). By "autonomy" they mean "the ability of a unit to behave independently of other units that might be construed in the same context", i.e. to be antagonistic to them (p. 112). They distinguish two categories of sub-units which do not display such antagonism and, consequently, can be unified: "facets" and "microsenses". The former can be unified to form a global gestalt, while the latter can be unified into a superordinate category, or a hyperonym (p. 116).

The notion of "facets" may be illustrated by the following example:

(1) a. *Britain today lies under one meter of snow.* [LAND]
b. *Britain is today mourning the death of the Royal corgi.* [PEOPLE]
c. *Britain declares war on North Korea.* [STATE] (p. 117)

This global gestalt – which can be glossed as the "country" – comprises at least three[55] ontologically different entities. Since a difference of ontological type normally signals a substantial semantic distance, the question arises why facets are not felt to be distinct senses. Croft and Cruse speculate that they "operate in a kind of functional symbiosis". This is more than a regular co-occurrence of entities: the state is a political manifestation of a people settled on its territory. In Langackerian terms, these concepts "are *jointly* profiled against a single domain matrix" (p. 122).

The notion of "microsenses" may be exemplified as follows:

(2) a. *I got a card the other day from Ralph, who's on holiday in Tenerife.*
b. *Let me give you my card; let me know as soon as you have any news.*
c. *The box was full of cards of various sorts.*

Even though the senses (2a) and (2b) are covered by the more general sense in (2c) – and thus could be viewed as contextual specifications – they are partly autonomous. As Croft and Cruse put it: *card* has "a hyperonymic reading and a cluster of hyponymous readings, whose default construals are sister incompatibles". In other words, in the default context one expects not the hyperonimic reading but one of the hyponymous variants – a phenomenon which the authors term "default specificity". This is different from standard cases, in which the default reading is unspecific, or neutral with respect to some potentially applicable features, as exemplified below:

(3) *My best friend married my brother / sister.*

[55] Croft and Cruse note that in principle the set of facets of a sense need not be determinate (2004: 117).

In the absence of contextual pressure ("brother/sister"), the neutral reading of *friend* (without gender specification) will be construed, while the specific variants in (3) are "contextual modulations" (pp. 26–28).

As compared with facets, microsenses illustrate a converse problem: since they belong to one ontological type (the reason why a hyperonymic reading is possible), one would expect a neutral default sense, while in fact specified ones are the case. Thus, the question now is about the unexpected boundaries. As with facets, the answer concerns the domains in which microsenses operate: while joint relevance of domains counterbalances semantic distance in the cases of facets, distinct habitual contexts counterbalance semantic closeness in the case of microsenses (p. 131).

Even lesser autonomy is displayed by "ways-of-seeing" (WOS), that is different ways of looking at the same thing.[56] Croft and Cruse mention four types:

a. the part-whole WOS: an entity is viewed as a whole with parts (e.g. a horse as viewed by a vet);
b. the kind WOS: an entity is viewed as a kind among other kinds (e.g. a horse as viewed by a zoologist);
c. the functional WOS: an entity is viewed in terms of its interactions (e.g. a horse as viewed by a jockey);
d. the life-history WOS: an entity is viewed in terms of its life-history (e.g. a books as viewed by an author or publisher).

Even though they do not correspond to distinct concepts and they are not referentially distinct, ways-of-seeing display some autonomy. Take *hotel*: when viewed as a building, it will contrast with houses or factories; when viewed as a type of accommodation, it will contrast with hostels or motels (p. 137).

The lowest degree of autonomy is displayed by "active zones", i.e. extensional in nature "parts of something which are isolated for compositional purposes", and "semantic components", i.e. intensional in nature "parts of a more inclusive sense which are compositionally active". Specifically, a relevant segment of an entity or a sense is selected by the context, while some choices may be the default construals. Consider, for instance, the ambiguous phrase *an old friend*: under negation, the default reading of "old" would apply to the relationship, and not the person (pp. 138–139).

With "contextual modulations", as in (3) above, we reach the zero point of the scale: specifications are contributed by the context, rather than selected or triggered (p. 140). Before we return to the highest point of that scale in Croft and Cruse's account – i.e. "full sense boundaries" – let me first present some traditional distinctions and issues discussed in this context.

The most basic distinction is one between "homonymy" and "polysemy" not in the synchronic sense introduced at the beginning (i.e., in reference to one of the three levels of granularity in semantic representation) but in the diachronic sense:

---

[56] As the authors note, the term corresponds to what Pustejovsky calls "qualia roles"; see Croft, Cruse (2004: 137) for a comparison.

whether some identical word forms with distinct senses are derived from a common source (polysemy) or from different lexical sources (homonymy), and their formal identity[57] is due to various historical contingencies. As noted by Croft and Cruse, this etymological distinction "is a yes/no matter, [...] a question of historical fact, resolvable in principle, if not always in practice" (2004: 111). The situation gets complicated, however, as soon as one postulates that "related" senses in the definition of polysemy should be felt to be related. From this perspective, some senses of a polysemic item would not be normally related (e.g. *pupil* in the senses: "a pupil at school" and "the pupil of the eye"), while homonyms could be felt to be related, as pointed out by Langacker: "Many speakers treat the meaning of *ear* implied by *ear of corn* as an extension from the prototypical value of *ear* as a body-part term" (1987: 387).[58] Since CL accepts the standard of "psychological reality", a possibly uncomfortable situation arises when respondents begin to relate conceptually any homonyms (e.g. to treat *light* as antonym of *heavy* and *dark*), when asked to find "a similarity". As noted in 0.2., one can associate any two items along a potentially infinite number of dimensions. However, Langacker does not talk about a laboratory situation: the existence of "folk etymologies" shows that language users tend to assimilate in some manner what they do not understand, and the same word form – or merely a similarity of forms – may be a *prima facie* reason to relate its different senses; cf. Vandeloise's jocular treatment of Fr. *large*: 4.2., note 21. On the other hand, language "experts" (as in Putnam's position concerning the division of linguistic labour) may keep in check such tendencies. Clearly, to have a conception of polysemy based on "felt relations", one must take into account the interplay between individual and social level.[59]

In the previous paragraph, the presence of intuitively distinct senses was assumed. Linguists (and philosophers), however, look for diagnostic criteria of polysemy. There are three kinds of polysemy test available: logical, linguistic and definitional. According to the logical test proposed by Quine, "a word is polysemic if an assertion involving that word can be both true and false of the same referent", e.g. a feather is "light" (not heavy) but "not light" (dark)" – Quine's original example quoted by Lewandowska-Tomaszczyk (2007: 141). Thus, the test does not distinguish homonymy from polysemy in the etymological sense. As pointed out by Geeraerts, the test also neglects the influence of context. For instance, hedges like "technically speaking" make it easy to assert "X is p and not p", since they change the range of extension of a lexical item (1993: 247). Tuggy shows

[57] Some (complex) issues concerning the identification of Polish lexical homonyms by the lexicographer are discussed by Buttler (1988: 5–12).

[58] These examples are taken from Lewandowska-Tomaszczyk (2007: 142).

[59] Croft and Cruse also raise the issue of "plausibility" of a particular interpretation. And they point out: "There is a difference between (i) 'I can sense a connection between the two meanings', (ii) 'I understand your explanation of how one meaning gave rise to the other', (iii) 'If I had never met meaning B before, only meaning A, I would understand the word in sense B if I encountered it in a suitable context" (2004: 111). The question of the social status of an interpretation seems to be at least implied here.

in greater detail (using various scenarios concerning "painting") that the logical test does not really remove uncertainty whether particular meanings in context can be both predicated of someone or not (1993: 275–278). In general, the logical test is based on referential differences, while in many contexts this aspect may be irrelevant (e.g. are two types of the same activity referentially equivalent?) or negotiated (e.g. for definitional purposes).

The linguistic tests (there are several variants) are based on the observation that in some contexts the use of one word with two distinct meanings is felt to be awkward (a phenomenon called variously: punning, zeugma or syllepsis[60]). For instance:

(4) ?*George and his driving license* <u>*expired*</u> *last Tuesday.*

In another test, the anaphora signalled by *so* indicates the expectation of a single sense. As a result, the following sentence with two senses of *port* is zeugmatic:

(5) ?*At midnight the ship passed the* <u>*port,*</u> *and so did the bartender.*[61]

Still, it is possible to devise contexts (of the definitional type, as above) in which a sentence with anaphoric clause is acceptable:

(6) *Daddy, what is a race: a group of people or a competition? Well, son, a group of people is a race, and so is a competition.*

The definitional test is traced back to Aristotle: a word is polysemic if more than one definition is required to cover its range of meaning. In more detail, a definition of a word should be maximally general (to cover as much of its extension as possible), while at the same time minimally specific (to distinguish it from other words). Thus, a maximally general definiton of *port* ("harbour", "fortified wine") to cover both extensions – e.g. "an entity" – is excluded because it does not capture the specificity of *port* (in either of its senses) as distinct from other words. As a result, in Geeraerts' "popular paraphrase": "If you cannot achieve maximal generality, settle for the next degree of generality that you can attain". He points out that while previous tests are merely diagnostic, the definitional test is also explanatory: it "embodies a hypothesis about the principles of categorization that human beings employ", i.e. that they aim at generality or maximal abstraction (1993: 236–237). Let us notice, however, that the test gives no procedure for defining, thus it is hardly diagnostic as long as one does not come up with a

---

[60] The terms are distinct but all are applicable in this context, cf. Croft, Cruse (2004: 113).

[61] Geeraerts' example (1993: 229). The discussions of polysemy tests by Geeraerts (1993), Tuggy (1993), Croft, Cruse (2004: 109–115), Lewandowska-Tomaszczyk (2007: 141–144) mostly rely on the same set of examples invoked in the literature.

definition, while a definition may be contested or seem intuitively unconvincing and so on.

Geeraerts' discussion is an extended attempt to undermine the credibility of polysemy tests. He points out that they are not reliable (when one fixes the context properly) and that they may yield mutually inconsistent result. One such case concerns "autohyponymous words" such as *dog*, whose more general sense ("the species") includes extensionally the more specific sense ("the male of the species"). As a result of this unusual relationship, the word will pass the logical test ("Lady is a dog alright, but she is not a dog"). It cannot pass, however, the definitional test, since "male dog" properly belongs to "the species dog" (it is not an independent sense in the definitional context), while in the linguistic test only one of the senses will impose itself, e.g. "Fido is a dog, and so is Lady" (hence, the double meaning will not be detected). Without going into further details, let us notice that the cases of inconsistency put forward by Geeraerts are not standard examples of polysemy (e.g. *dog*, *newspaper*, *fruit*).

Geeraerts also mentions the "contextual" criterion considered above by Croft and Cruse, i.e. whether an interpretation is contributed or selected by the context. In the former case, cognitive linguists talk of "vagueness" rather than polysemy (the latter case). Traditionally, however, as pointed out by Geeraerts (1993: 228) and Zlatev (2003: 482), "vague" is opposed to "ambiguous" to differentiate "referential indeterminacy" from multiplicity of senses; cf. note 43 above. Consequently, Zlatev proposes to replace "vagueness" in the present sense[62] with the term "generality" (I have already followed this suggestion). Geeraerts argues against the contextual criterion, pointing out that not only the cases of generality, but also of polysemy are resolved (specified) in the context. One needs proper context to resolve the generality of *student*: to know whether it refers to a male or a female. Similarly, one needs context to resolve the ambiguity of *position*: whether it refers to a "mental attitude" or an "occupied place". Thus, if the contribution of context is necessary in both cases, it cannot serve as a criterion to distinguish generality from polysemy (1993: 267–268, note 16).

As we have seen, however, this objection does not take into account the difference between conventional "pre-meanings" (at the level of "full sense units") and actual meanings, or the difference between intersubjective senses and their referential specifications in use. In other words, Geeraerts questions the existence of full sense boundaries (or senses of words) before an actualization in context. Such, indeed, seems to be the conclusion of his article: "lexical meanings are not to be thought of as prepackaged chunks of information, but as moving searchlights that may variously highlight subdomains of the range of application of the lexical item in question" (1993: 263). We may return now to Croft and Cruse's

[62] Vague meanings could be defined as meanings "unmarked for a certain category distinction", e.g. *student* is vague with regard to the distinction between "male/female" (Lewandowska-Tomaszczyk 2007: 141).

exposition and ask about the grounds they give for the (pre-)existence of such boundaries.

They believe that the linguistic tests are basically correct and that they reveal "antagonism" between distinct senses of a lexeme. In other words, such senses are competitive: if one is at the focus of attention, the other one is backgrounded. This is what happens in standard use, as opposed to zeugmatic contexts, which evoke both senses. The (intuitively obvious) difference between polysemy and generality is clear from this perspective: in the latter case the function of the context is not to exclude some pre-existing senses (or to select a given full sense), but to add information which need not be specified. Geeraerts fudges this issue – like Langacker, discussed in 0.3. – which basically concerns the distinction between semantic information and pragmatic construal, when he offers the following hypothetical statement: "There seems to be no reason to restrict [contextual information] to purely linguistic contextual information, if only because any relevant piece of extralinguistic, encyclopedic or situational information could be turned into a piece of linguistic context by expressing it in words" (Geeraerts 1993: 267––268). The question, however, concerns not "adding" encyclopedic information (i.e. formulating it verbally), but "lexicalizing" it (i.e. making it conventionally available).

In Croft and Cruse's account, "pre-meanings" place various constraints on actualizations in context. Full sense boundaries place the strongest constraints on an actualization of distinct senses in a single context, but the boundaries are not absolute, as shown by definitional contexts pointed out by Geeraerts (hedges, crossword puzzles etc.). Since, however, such contexts are exceptional – and they may serve to "unify" any two meanings, or temporarily suspend their boundaries – the linguistic test is valid (Croft, Cruse 2004: 112–113).

What makes full sense units antagonistic? The most obvious reason is semantic distance: the senses (tend to) have few elements in common, belong to different domains, their referents have a different ontological status etc. However, as exemplified by the two senses of *month*: "calendar month", "period of four weeks",[63] some senses may be very close and still antagonistic. A deeper explanation ("but which is still in some ways mysterious") refers to the notion of "unification" presented in the context of "sub-senses": antagonistic readings resist any kind of unification mentioned there (Croft, Cruse 2004: 115).

* * *

The notion of "polysemy" raises several issues, which one should try to keep separate. The issue of polysemy tests is perhaps least troublesome. All of them take the intuitive presence of polysemy – i.e. antagonistic senses linked to <u>one</u>

[63] "It would hardly be possible to find an ambiguous word whose component units were closer" – Croft, Cruse (2004: 115).

word form[64] – for granted. Thus, they do not really "diagnose" it, since the antagonism is felt (to verify the antagonism, one could ask respondents rather than try to apply the tests). The tests are not reliable primarily because the role of context and contextual interpretation is no less elusive than the notion of polysemy. Additionally, there are unusual sense relations (autohyponymous words) and sub-senses, which are not straightforwardly antagonistic or unexpectedly antagonistic in some contexts (we will return to sub-senses below).

Traditionally, polysemy denotes a historical relatedness of senses linked to one word form, as opposed to homonymy, when two words – due to historical contingencies – acquire the same form. This case is not as simple, in principle, as Croft and Cruse make it, since the historical contingencies in question may actually involve the perception of similarity of etymologically different words. Thus, Langacker's example concerning the "*ear* of corn" could have – hypothetically – a diachronic significance, if both word forms converged because people felt their senses were related. As a result, the distinction between polysemy and homonymy would be much less secure.

In CL, "polysemy" is redefined as a "variation in the construal of a word on different occasions of use" (Croft, Cruse 2004: 109). Since such construals are "nondenumerable", "polysemy" in this formulation would lose all meaning (it could not be opposed to something) and, *a fortiori*, could not be modelled. As argued, we need a distinction between pragmatic construal in use and semantic availability of distinct senses out of the context of use. In Croft and Cruse's conception, semantic information takes the form of "pre-meanings", actualized in discourse. Distinct senses are most antagonistic in the whole range of such "pre-meanings": they place the strongest constraints on actualization in one context.

What are the sources of antagonism? We would have an answer, if we knew why full senses resist unification. Croft and Cruse's discussion of sub-senses is very instructive in this respect. Basically, they show that full senses do not have a common referential context, nor a close superordinate term, which could unify them. Antagonism is born when a word is applied to referentially distinct situations. A *key* in the lock is antagonistic to a *key* in the keypad because they articulate slots in different "frames" (to use Fillmore's term). It does not matter whether the former entity is a piece of metal or an electronic card or any other device invented for the purpose, since they all articulate the same slot in an intuitively distinct situation. Thus, senses form a complex with referential situations which they have helped to articulate. Apparently, it is those default "situations" which are antagonistic. Facets can be unified because in some contexts of use such ontologically different entities can fill the same "situational" slot (due to their "functional symbiosis"). With microsenses, we actually witness the origin of sense antagonism when distinct situational uses (e.g. *card* sent from holidays or used in banking) are splitting the more general meaning apart. Apparently, once a particular usage is felt to co-articulate a separate referential situation, it acquires

[64] As noted, they do not distinguish diachronic polysemy from homonymy.

the status of a distinct sense. For instance, the verb *tease* is felt to merit four sub-entries in *Longman Dictionary*:

1. To laugh at someone and make jokes in order to have fun by embarrassing them;
2. To deliberately annoy an animal;
3. To deliberately make someone sexually excited without intending to have sex with them;
4. (AmE) To comb your hair in the opposite direction to which it grows, so that it looks thicker.

It seems that once we can distinguish a separate (existentially different) context of use, however close the general meaning (as with the first three entries), we feel justified to postulate a distinct sense. On the other hand, *eating* "with a spoon, fork or chopsticks" may be referentially varied,[65] but such uses do not merit the status of polysemy, since they fill a single slot in the same situation type.

This interpretation of polysemy, I believe, accords well with Zlatev's critique of CL's "mentalism" and his suggestion that the "semantic pole" of linguistic symbols should be conceived not as a "conceptualization", but as a "situation (type)" (2003: 455). It is not easy to fathom the consequences of Zlatev's proposal for linguistics. I will return to it in my plea for "expressive linguistics" submitted in 5.3.

0.5. A recapitulation

One may rightly complain that the complex of issues discussed above is hardly penetrable, while my preliminary results are nothing more but one way of looking at this material. It should be remembered, however, that the issues, which I have tried to follow and elucidate, are raised in standard accounts of "prototype semantics". CL kindled such great hopes and evoked such an overwhelming response[66] precisely because it aimed at an integration of wide-ranging perspectives, encompassing philosophical inquiries into the nature of meaning, psychological studies of categorization and conceptual processing, anthropological explorations

[65] As pointed out by Weinrich – who in the sixties criticised accounts leading to an "infinite proliferation of senses" – one could ascribe a plethora of meanings to *eat*, since "eating with a spoon", "eating with a fork" etc. is performed differently; cf. Ravin, Leacock (2000: 10).

[66] Cf. Langacker's repeated expressions of gratitude to his graduate students: "Without the security of tenure, they have been willing to pursue a non-establishment vision they believe in, with full cognizance of the likely professional consequences. Regardless of theoretical orientation, I think we can all agree that such courage deserves to be admired, if not tangibly rewarded " (1991: ix). This statement, reminiscent of "first Christians mentality", is an indication how far CL has progressed in the last twenty years.

of culture systems and so on. As a countervailing force against the "generativist excesses" and the structuralist "prison-house of language",[67] CL attempted to build new interdisciplinary foundations for linguistics "with a human face". That impulse was liberating and beneficial, while it clearly entailed the risk of inflated ambitions and eclecticism. As a result, CL was in some ways misguided[68] both in its opposition to the predecessors and in its access to the cognitivist paradigm. I will return to the historical context in 5.2.

At this stage, with hindsight, let us try to see the issues discussed above in their (more) correct proportions. "Prototype effects" – treated by Rosch as data to be integrated into a psychological theory of categorization – were hailed by Lakoff as "a general challenge to the classical theory [of categorization]" (1987: 42). For Langacker, they were consonant with his conviction that "autonomous semantics" is unable to faithfully represent linguistic data, thus a more flexible approach is needed to achieve descriptive adequacy. I have argued that prototype effects studied by Rosch reveal an important difference between folk "categorization" based on cognitive reference points and expert categorization aiming at full taxonomies, i.e. comprising all relevant entities within a discrete conceptual system. The former stance is openly pragmatic – reflecting our everyday need to "domesticate" reality. In other words, folk "differential treatment"[69] is rooted in various existential motivations rather than in the theoretical stance. If one wants to have varied meat dishes on Friday in a Catholic country with fasting rules, a beaver provides better "motives" than chicken or deer to be identified with fish. Theoreticians, on the other hand, are supposed not to be swayed by such mundane considerations.[70] Their goal is a complete, hierarchical system of categories – a rational view of things as they are.

Consequently, Lakoff's interpretation of Rosch's data makes no sense. In everyday communication, people rely on local stereotypes of various kinds and are not normally bothered by delimitation problems or the overall consistency of their "conceptual system". Such a system is a theoretical construct proposed by some cognitivists (notably, those belonging to Lakoff's circle) to explain in a *hysteron proteron*, rationalist manner what people do in their situated, pragmatic, historical, contingent (and often thoughtless or unreflective) ways. Only if one proposes such a cognitive system in the cognitive unconscious (psychologist's fallacy), can one see any analogy between contextual use of language and theoretical categorization. As we shall see below – 1.1., note 11 – Langacker's arguments against the "classical model" of linguistic categorization are based on this misconception.

Prototype effects, as pointed out by Harnad, are relatively superficial phenomena. They cannot be relevantly invoked in a discussion concerning the constitu-

---

[67] The title of Jameson's monograph of structuralism and Russian formalism (1972).

[68] I refer to some formulations of CL's agenda. As we shall see more clearly in 1.1., CL has never been unitary in its assumptions.

[69] Harnad's definition of categorization in its basic or primitive form: "at bottom, all of our categories consist in ways we behave differently toward different kinds of things" (2005: 30).

[70] But see note 25 in the Introduction on sociology of science and "paradigms".

tion of categories. The genetic issue is foundational, as shown by roboticists, who attempt to elucidate it in a practical manner (by teaching machines to "create" categories), or by hermeneuticists, who try to uncover layers of constitution in their search for the most "originary" view. The latter venture is embedded in the philosophical inquiry concerning the status of "ideality", as reflected in the debate about "universals", cited by Taylor. Since CL aims to capture the linguistic results of unexplored processes of categorization, it cannot take a principled stand in that foundational debate.[71]

What, specifically, is CL's agenda? In Langacker's view, language is (symbolically anchored and mostly conventional) conceptualization. Linguistic units at all levels of analysis – morphemes, lexemes, collocations, idioms, syntactic structures, sentences, utterances – are packages of phonological form and semantic content. It is clear by now, I hope, that this identification of language with conceptual structure is *post hoc*. One can treat linguistic units in this way because they have been constituted in a history of expression (and actualized in acts of expression). One may ascribe a set of meanings to, for instance, the dative case in Polish or *over* in English because both forms have evolved in some historical (and unexplored) processes of linguistic articulation. Similarly (but at an individual, rather than social level), words and sentences in a context may be treated as conceptualizations because they have been interpreted, or used to articulate a given existential situation.

CL's approach – after (for many) stifling formalisms of TG – was a waft of fresh air; it opened exciting vistas before linguists who felt that language is primarily about meaning and only secondarily about formal structure. As a result – and this is my main claim in this book – CL has merely changed the focus from one factor in the equation to another, while sharing an important set of assumptions with TG ("linguistic mentalism"). The real challenge, however, is to genetically link both form and meaning: to show their mutual development as a way of domesticating reality. This statement should be taken in the proper spirit. My intention is not to belittle CL's tremendous achievements. As a correction of its predecessors, it has (re)introduced themes of primary importance into the research agenda. Specifically, since it takes language to be a mental faculty, it has not only returned in its own way to Humboldt – the father of modern linguistics, cf. 5.2. – but it has been able to show in a transparent manner how linguistic forms are correlated with semantic content. This is a task of vast proportions which involves an integration of linguistic and cross-linguistic material from all areas of research. Such conceptual representations reveal important analogies and continuities at various levels of schematicity. My point concerns the limits of CL's method or its proper "object" of study: this approach captures the results of social processes of linguistic articulation rather than hypothetical mental structures and processes in individual minds.

---

[71] To repeat, prototype research and CL assume the existence of categories and explore problems with their extensional applications or intensional definitions.

From this vantage point, the distinctions blurred by Langacker (and partly Geeraerts) – between lexical and encyclopedic knowledge on the one hand, and semantics and pragmatics on the other one – are pivotal because they express the basic opposition between what is social and what is individual: between intersubjectively available senses and individual (or special) knowledge, between generic (cultural) interpretations and individual readings in the context. Both distinctions bear directly on the issue of polysemy. As concerns the former one, some uses of a word (its senses) are felt to be available prior to acts of expression. To be sure, one can recognize the possibility of a novel use in an unusual context but such extensions are merely understandable – not socially available. As concerns the latter one, an "actualization" of a word is a situated application of its "semantic potential" to articulate some pragmatically relevant distinctions. Without a context, one takes for granted the most typical social scenarios ("default contexts"). In situated use, a pragmatic interpretation may involve very unusual scenarios. To conclude: we need to keep separate the social and the individual perspective to make sense of polysemy.

CHAPTER 1. NETWORK MODELS: FOUNDATIONAL ACCOUNTS

1.0. Introductory remarks

Network models[1] constitute a family of formats for representing lexical polysemy. Thus, they provide a particular type of answer to the question concerning the appropriate level of granularity of semantic definitions, i.e. "the level at which the relatedness of senses can be best observed and captured".[2] As pointed out by Lewandowska-Tomaszczyk, the monosemy position (espoused by neostructuralists) strives for the most parsimonious or schematic representation (a single sense), while the homonymy position (associated with generativists) is primarily concerned with deriving (any number of[3]) senses from sets of matrices of linguistic properties (2007: 152). Both approaches are obviously motivated by different theoretical assumptions. I have little to say about the generativist approach (see J. Taylor 2007; and more generally Seuren 1998), which in CL plays mostly the part of the polemical "bogeyman" (as will be exemplified in the next paragraph). That approach seems to be motivated by the idea that linguistics should be chiefly concerned with "the underlying reality of language" (cf. Katz 1971), thus (in semantics) it neglects many of its surface manifestations. The level of granularity considered appropriate in particular cases is achieved by combinations of atomic properties.

The motivation for the monosemy position is much more complex and important in our context in view of the claims that CL is solidly based on Saussurian foundations. For instance, in his discussion of cognitive models Taylor mentions the structuralist doctrine of "the unity of the sign" and in this context puts forward two claims. First, that "the 'indissoluble dualism' of the sign predicts the ultimate sterility of any approach to language which focuses only on form" (a snipe at TG[4]). Second, that in view of a widespread "formal and semantic polyvalence",

[1] As developed in CL. Network representations of semantic knowledge (in computational approaches) constitute a wider (and related) field, cf. Evens (1988).

[2] As already noted in the Introduction: note 8.

[3] This approach is focused on formalizing types of relations, thus it manifests "a practical disregard for the polysemy-homonymy distinction" (Lewandowska-Tomaszczyk 2007: 152).

[4] Examples of this kind in CL are legion. They are commented on by Taylor (2007), who urges a more conciliatory attitude. As I will argue below, and more extensively in chapter 4., CL shows a complementary disregard for the "indissoluble unity" of the sign, focusing on conceptual relations (rather than on the interplay between formal and conceptual structure).

which *prima facie* breaks the unity of the sign, the Saussurian heritage "imposes the need to search for unitary representations of the [...] one-to-one relationship between signans and signatum". And he concludes: "Respect for the unity of the sign, in both senses of the expression, lies behind a number of important developments in cognitive linguistics, as expounded, for example [by] Ronald Langacker [...] and George Lakoff" (Taylor 1990: 522–523). Such claims, however, are clearly exaggerated[5] and they misrepresent the structuralist position.

The notion of the unity of the sign may be understood in the light of the famous passage from Saussure: "The characteristic role of language with respect to thought is not to create a material phonic means for expressing ideas but to serve as a link between thought and sound, under conditions that of necessity bring the reciprocal delimitation of units" (1959: 112). For Saussure, the essence of language lies in the <u>combination</u> of sound and thought – not "pairing" (which produces "nomenclature", or a list of words) but "reciprocal delimitation".[6] Consequently, the sign can be a vehicle of meaning – in the system of oppositions – only if it preserves this unity (one-to-relationship between signans and signatum). This fundamental idea is missing in the CL paradigm.

To be sure, the Saussurian notion of the unity of the sign is difficult to apply: it seems hardly credible when confronted with the facts, i.e. the "formal and semantic polyvalence" noted by Taylor.[7] For instance, a monosemic representation of *climb*, which is used to denote both upward and downward movement (cf. Taylor 1989: 105–109), may seem clearly impossible and hardly desirable. Still, I will argue for the original Saussurian insight, as opposed to its skeletal version underlying CL in Taylor's account. I believe that, <u>at some level</u>, the unity of the sign is a necessary assumption, if one wants to understand language, while obviously it must be interpreted in a way which makes space for the facts. As a result, the polysemy position is *prima facie* the most "realistic" option and – consequently – it faces an additional problem of representation: it is not enough to define a set of distinct senses (as in the homonymy position), but one should also try to show how they are related.

In this chapter, I will present two "foundational" accounts of such modelling by Langacker and Lakoff, who approach (or sidestep) both basic problems mentioned so far (1. How to define distinct senses?; 2. How are the senses related?) in a different manner. Usually, only the differences in the format of their

---

[5] The only evidence of the "Saussurian debt" is Lakoff's definition of *there* constructions as "pairings of form and meaning" and Langacker's definition of "symbolic units" (Taylor 1990: 523; repeated 1999: 19, 41 note 1). As for the "search of the unity of the sign" (advertised in the title of Taylor's first article and taken below in his own meaning), that claim makes almost no sense in the context of network models: as we shall see, in Langacker's version, the unitary schema of a network is not necessary (and uninformative, if possible), while a lexical item is defined in an arbitrary fashion. In Lakoff's version, unitary representations are openly rejected as a realistic goal.

[6] In other words, a linguistic symbol is "a form, not a substance" (Saussure 1959: 113) – it is a way of giving shape to the material (sound and thought simultaneously).

[7] As he says: "instead of the one-to-one relationship of signans to signatum, we have a one-to-many, a many-to-one, or, more typically, a many-to-many relationship" (1990: 522).

approaches are pointed out and discussed (Lakoff's "radial" model is built around the prototype, while Langacker's "schematic network" involves both prototypes and schemas). I will try to show that these differences are secondary: they result from assumptions about the nature of linguistic categories as conceived by Lakoff ("natural categories of senses") and Langacker ("complex categories"). I will give a detailed resume of both positions, followed by a presentation of a critique (from the monosemic perspective) of Lakoff's model of *over* (Vandeloise 1990). Some of the points made by Vandeloise apply to network modelling in general.

In Chapter 2, I will present four subsequent attempts to improve Lakoff's model of *over*. In Chapter 3, I will present a Langackerian model of Polish *za(-)* – primarily a preposition, which in a range of its senses is an equivalent of *over*, and a verbal prefix. The model of the latter will be discussed in the diachronic context. In Chapter 4, I will raise the question whether network models represent "diachrony within synchrony".

1.1. Motivations behind the Langackerian and Lakoffian models

I want to ask first about the rationale for adopting the new approach to the representation of linguistic categories. In this respect, the accounts provided by the "founding fathers" of prototype semantics – Lakoff and Langacker – are significantly different. I will try to charter some of the differences below.

Lakoff's declared aim is incredibly ambitious and extends far beyond the domain of linguistics (as documented in note 12 and 17 in the Introduction). He wants to provide an alternative to "the traditional view" about the nature of language, mind and reality (he calls "objectivism"), "which is tied to the classical theory [of categorization, according to which] categories are defined in terms of common properties of their members" (Lakoff 1987: xii). The alternative proposed by him – a theory based on prototypes – is to serve as a lynchpin of a new view, bringing forth a revolution in philosophy and science. The wider implications of Lakoff's proposal go far beyond the present context.[8] As concerns language, Lakoff says:

> One of the principal claims of this book is that language makes use of our general cognitive apparatus. If this claim is correct, two things follow:
> – Linguistic categories should be of the same type as other categories in our conceptual system. In particular, they should show prototype and basic-level effects;

[8] As already mentioned, I analysed that ideological project of "Lakoff's circle" primarily in Pawelec (2005a).

> – Evidence about the nature of linguistic categories should contribute to a general understanding of cognitive categories in general. Because language has such a rich category structure and because linguistic evidence is so abundant, the study of linguistic categorization should be one of the prime sources of evidence for the nature of category structure in general (Lakoff 1987: 58).

It seems, *prima facie*, that Lakoff merely assumes that linguistic categories are like "other categories in our conceptual system" and are structured around prototypes, or "radially structured". I will look at his argument in greater detail below. Here, it is enough to point out that Lakoff treats prototype models in semantics as evidence for the existence of prototype-based categorization ("psychologist's fallacy"). As he puts it: "polysemy appears to be a special case of prototype-based categorization, where the senses of the word are the members of a category. The application of prototype theory to the study of word meaning brings order into an area where before there was only chaos. [...] Each of these case studies[9] demonstrates the reality of radially structured categories" (Lakoff 1987: 378–379).

Langacker, on the other hand, notices in a matter-of-fact fashion that: "Much in language is a matter of degree. [...] Nondiscrete aspects of language structure must be accommodated organically in the basic design of an adequate linguistic theory". He subsequently raises the issue which concerns us here: "whether the criterial-attribute model or the prototype model offers a better account of linguistic categorization". As he explains: "The criterial-attribute model characterizes a class by means of a list of defining features;[10] in its strict form, it requires that every member of the class fully possess every property on this list, and that no nonmember possess all of the listed properties. Class membership is thus an all-or-nothing affair; a sharp distinction is presumed between those entities that are in the class and those that are not". Langacker points out three "well-known problems" with this model. First, some indubitable members of a category may lack attributes intuitively judged criterial for it (e.g. flightless birds). Second, a set of features sufficient to delimit a category, i.e. "to pick out all and only the members" of a class, "might still be incomplete and inadequate as a characterization of that class" (e.g. "[featherless] [biped]" as defining humans). And third, in actual use the criterial attributes are not judged necessary to ascribe class membership. For instance, a baseball which is the wrong colour is still called a baseball.[11] Ac-

[9] There are three extended case studies in Lakoff's *opus magnum*. As he says (exemplifying again the "psychologist's fallacy"): "Since radially structured categories differ most radically from classical categories, it is important to have detailed case studies that document their existence" (1987: 379). In the first study (produced in cooperation with Kövecses), Lakoff discusses "idealized cognitive models" underlying in his theory linguistic expressions referring to ANGER. The second one is a radial "image-schematic" model of *over* (developed on the basis of Brugman's thesis), which will be presented in 1.3. below. The last one is a study of "symbolic" *there* constructions.

[10] Conventionally placed in square brackets.

[11] None of these arguments is a serious problem for the "classical" model. The first one ignores the distinction between "folk" and "expert" categories ("intuitively criterial" refers to the former, while necessary and sufficient features are searched by "experts"). The second one merely states that the search for essential features is difficult (it misrepresents the nature of this search: its point is not

cording to Langacker, the prototype model avoids these problems. First, "it does not require that every member of a category possess a given feature (or even that there be any salient property shared by all members)". Second, "the characterization problem is avoided because the prototype model is not inherently minimalist in spirit; instead it encourages the fullest possible characterization of prototypical instances, if only to specify the basis for assimilating the full range of non-prototypical instances to a category". And third, "the prototype model allows an entity to be assimilated to a category if a person finds any plausible rationale for relating it to prototypical members" (Langacker 1987: 14–17). Thus, Langacker's preference for prototype models is based on the factual assumption that linguistic categories can be represented more adequately in this way than by the criterial-attribute model.

Both accounts are superficially similar – they propose prototype models in preference to discrete models in semantics – while differing in important respects. Crucially, Langacker's view that linguistic categories may require special treatment because of "the organization and complexity of the linguistic data" (Langacker 1987: 17) seems opposed to Lakoff's assumption that they are like "other categories in our conceptual system" (Lakoff 1987: 58). Furthermore, Langacker's approach is primarily descriptive: in his view, the prototype model provides a more adequate representation of a range of linguistic phenomena than the criterial-attribute model. Lakoff believes that the prototype model is explanatory: that it shows how language and mind work.

The notion of "linguistic categorization" plays a central role in the remarks quoted above. As already mentioned (0.2.), it is ambiguous. In Taylor's formulation: whenever we use the same word to refer to various specimens of something, we categorize, or name "sameness in difference". Since words can also refer to linguistic entities, the term "linguistic categorization" covers not only categories in the world verbalized in a language, like DOG, but also linguistic categories, like WORD or LEXEME. To distinguish between these cases, in the latter one, which Taylor calls "reflexive" (1989: vii–viii), Rúa proposes to talk about "metalinguistic categories" (Rúa 2003: 46).

Let us notice, however, that this disambiguation does not seem to address the crucial issue. When Langacker mentioned the problem facing the linguist: "the organization and complexity of linguistic data", he did not mean linguistic categories like WORD or LEXEME, but rather linguistic phenomena, e.g. polysemic words or grammatical structures with a number of conventional uses. While it makes sense to use the term "metalinguistic categories" to refer to folk (e.g. WORD) or expert (e.g. LEXEME) categories ordering in some ways linguistic data, this description does not seem obviously applicable to the data. In his expo-

to provide some unique description of a class, but to locate the class in a taxonomy). The last one presupposes that "literal" uses of a word are rigidly tied to some definitional context (it identifies language use and the theoretical quest for representations of linguistic categories).

sition, Taylor disregards this point since he assumes (together with Lakoff) that linguistic objects are like non-linguistic objects:

> Just as a botanist is concerned with a botanical categorization of plants, so a linguist undertakes a linguistic categorization of linguistic objects. The second half of the book, in particular, will address the parallels between linguistic categorization in this second sense, and the categorization, through language, of the non-linguistic world. If, as will be argued, categories of linguistic objects are structured along the same lines as the more familiar semantic categories, then any insights we may gain into the categorization of the non-linguistic world may be profitably applied to the study of language structure itself. (J. Taylor 1989: viii)

Rúa takes Taylor to task for treating what she calls "metalinguistic categories" on a par with other kinds of categories. She claims that linguistic categorization proper involves objects which are "intrinsically" linguistic, rather than "additionally" linguistic. As she explains:

In simple terms, one thing is categorizing objects which have a concrete or abstract correlate in the world, and subsequently resorting to language in order to express the result of that categorization [...]; a different thing is categorizing objects which lack this correlate, or simply do not make sense in isolation from the system they belong to. (i.e. from language) (Rúa 2003: 32)

Consequently, Rúa postulates three types of "linguistic categories" (a superordinate, neutral term):

> (a) Metalinguistic categories (purely linguistic): they must be assigned a linguistic expression; (b) Semilinguistic categories: they are subdivided into *cognitive linguistic* (*bird*) and *perceptual linguistic* (*red*), since the latter type is highly dependent on sensory perception. Their linguistic expression is expected as a natural complement; (c) Extralinguistic categories (purely cognitive/perceptual): their linguistic expression is possible but not strictly required. (Rúa 2003: 33)

The criteria of Rúa's classification (whether a category must, should or may be verbally expressed) seem to be rather *ad hoc*. It is quite clear, for instance, that what would be an "extralinguistic" category in one language, could be a "semilinguistic" one in another, if conventionally expressed (rich evidence is provided by studies in the domain of colour perception and expression). But her point is consonant with Langacker's concern: "purely linguistic" categories – linguistic phenomena – may have unique properties which require special treatment. Still, the term "metalinguistic categories" is an unusual label for naturally, i.e. historically, developed linguistic categories or "natural categories of senses" (as opposed to reflexive metacategories). Rúa is aware of this problem: "there are problematic cases of difficult ascription (what kind of 'objects' are categorized under *over* or *hate*?)", she wonders (p. 33). It is legitimate to ask, then, in what sense linguistic phenomena – e.g. polysemic words – are "categories"? What is their "sameness in difference", in Taylor's expression?

1.2. Schematic networks

1.2.1. A resume of Langacker's position

Langacker's guiding principle is descriptive adequacy. In his treatment of linguistic categorization he points out two crucial aspects of phenomena, which must be taken account of: variability and conventionality (Langacker 1987: 369–373). Since symbolic units are generally variable both in form and meaning,[12] he thinks it is best to analyse their phonological and semantic pole as "complex categories". These categories are complex because "they group together, and treat as equivalent for certain purposes, a variety of distinct and sometimes quite disparate elements" (p. 369) As a result, "membership is commonly a matter of degree, resistant to strict delimitation, and subject to the vicissitudes of linguistic convention" (pp. 369–370).

Langacker argues for a nonreductive, usage-based model of symbolic meaning: even though a theorist rightly aims at a generalization, he should not eschew enumerating established senses covered by it, since they belong to a speaker's knowledge of linguistic convention. As Langacker says about a lexical item: "Even when all its attested values are plausibly analyzed as instantiations of a single abstract schema, or as extensions from a single prototype, there is no way to predict from the schema or prototype alone precisely which array of instantiations or extensions – out of all the conceivable ones – happen to be conventionally exploited within the speech community" (p. 370).

Specifically, Langacker opts for a "unified" account which "requires the listing of all conventionally established values of a lexical item, as a minimal description of the empirical data". The next step is "an analysis of how the category is structured, i.e. how the different senses are related to one another". There are two principal types of relationship to be accommodated in the model: "elaboration (the relation between a schema and its instantiations) and extension (the relation between prototypical and peripheral values)". The resulting network model "incorporates (as schemas) whatever generalizations can be extracted from specific instances and reflects the many categorizing judgments through which the complex category has evolved". Thus, Langacker's network model of a complex category comprises two kinds of categorization – by schema and by prototype – "as aspects of a unified phenomenon" (pp. 370–371).

The postulated compatibility of both types of categorization is represented by Langacker in the formula:

$$S > T = V$$

[12] The "formal and semantic polyvalence" mentioned by Taylor (1990: 522).

The conceptualizer (not represented) observes in the target (T) a configuration that satisfies the specifications of the standard (S) to some extent (V) – the magnitude of discrepancy between the standard and target. When T satisfies the specifications of S fully, then V = 0 (or more precisely, V falls below a certain threshold of tolerance). In such cases, S is referred to as a schema and the categorizing relationship between S and T (S→T) is one of elaboration or specialization: T exemplifies S in finer detail. When T is inconsistent with some specifications of S (V > 0), then S is referred to as a prototype, and the relationship between S and T (S--->T) is one of extension (p. 371).[13]

Langacker admits that even though it is sometimes difficult to distinguish them in practice (when V is close to the threshold on either side), both types of categorization are qualitatively different. Categorization by schema enjoys privileged status because it provides "full sanction" – it exemplifies conventional usage (cf. pp. 62ff.) or grammatical "well-formedness" – while categorization by extension provides only "partial sanction" and exemplifies nonconventional usage or grammatical "deviance". Langacker speculates that schematic relationships have special status because they represent the limiting case of S/T discrepancy (when V = 0). This is based on the general assumption that "qualitative distinctness and special cognitive salience often attach to an element that occupies the extremity of a continuous scale". Langacker concludes that discrete judgements of well-formedness can be "accommodated even in a model describing sanction and conventionality in continuous terms" (p. 372).

Langacker goes further in his attempts to reconcile both types of categorization. He claims that "categorization by extension typically presupposes and incorporates schematic relationships". If we have a concept X which is inconsistent in some respects with a prototype PT, it can still be assimilated to the category, if the conceptualizer observes some similarity between X and PT – relevant for his purposes – and is willing to overlook the discrepancies. In such a case, the situation comprises three elements: PT, X and their perceived similarity "which amounts to a schema (SCH) that PT and X elaborate in alternate ways".

Consequently, categorization by extension is to be depicted in the following way:

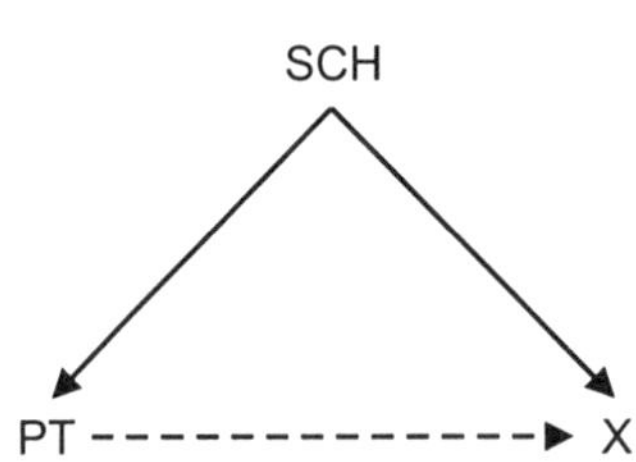

Figure 1: After Langacker (1987: 373)

[13] A solid arrow represents full schematicity, while a broken-line arrow represents partial schematicity (Langacker 1987: 69).

Langacker admits that neither the conceptualizer need be aware of the schema sanctioning the perceived similarity, nor the entrenchment of the extension ("repeated use", cf. p. 59) need raise the schema to unit status or cognitive salience. Still, "If we think of an extension as a 'horizontal' relationship, and schematicity as a 'vertical' one, we can say that the 'outward' growth of a lexical network by extension from prototypes is inherently associated with its 'upward' growth by extraction of schemas". Langacker concludes: "One is not impossible without the other, but they tend to co-occur as interrelated facets of the same expansive mechanism" (pp. 372–373).

This initial account is programmatic and highly abstract. Langacker provides an example: of a child learning the conventional senses of a lexical unit *tree* (pp. 373–388). In Langacker's notation, symbolic units are represented as [[TREE]/[tree]]. Square brackets denote unit status or entrenched cognitive routine (as opposed to round brackets which denote a novel use or "conception"). The name in capitals denotes the semantic pole, while the name in lower case – the phonological pole (cf. 57ff.). While discussing semantic phenomena, Langacker usually limits his description to the semantic pole.

Langacker asks the reader to imagine a child learning the conventional senses of the word *tree*, in his early experience first applied to ordinary deciduous trees: oaks, maples, and elms: "Their perceptual prominence and obvious gross similarities enable the child to extract a conception that embodies their commonality, while excluding the many properties that vary from one instance to the next". As a result, the child produces an abstraction – a low-level schema – which "presumably [...] emphasizes intrinsic, characteristic, and cognitively salient properties (e.g. shape, size, color, brachiation, leaves)". This schema – as the starting point for the evolution of a complex category – serves as "the category prototype" (p. 373).

Subsequently, the child encounters a pine and learns to call it a *tree*. The new symbolic unit derived from the original [[TREE]/[tree]] is represented as [[PINE]/[tree]]. The extension reflects the categorizing judgement of partial schematicity: [[TREE]--->[PINE]], since pines have needles as opposed to leaves. Langacker speculates that the child may conceive the schema (TREE') that embodies the commonality between [TREE] and [PINE] and neutralizes the difference in foliage type. If (TREE') becomes entrenched and achieves the unit status [TREE'], it may sanction other extensions (accommodating e.g. a palm to the category) and give ground to a higher-order schema [TREE"]. Since it is not certain, however, whether further extensions are derived from the PT [TREE] – which is cognitively salient because of its strongest entrenchment – or from the higher-level schema [TREE'] – which is more abstract, hence conflicts less sharply with the specifications of [PALM]) – in the model of this process depicted below there are broken-line arrows leading from both schemas:

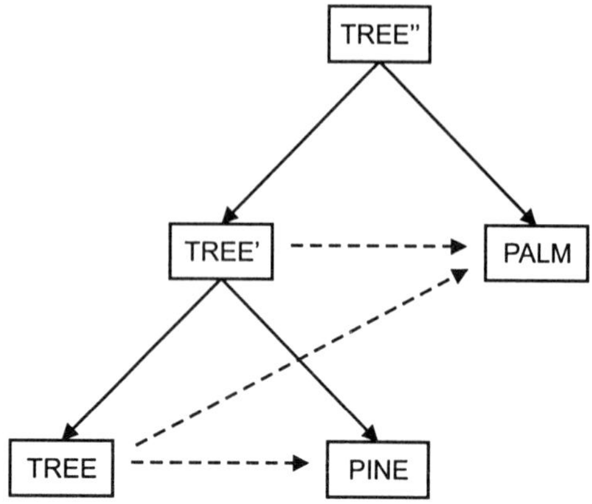

Figure 2: After Langacker (1987: 374)

Langacker comments that the "meaning of *tree* for the child at this point is not just the schematic [TREE'], nor is it just the prototype [TREE]; rather its meaning is given by the entire schematic network, any node of which can be accessed by the phonological unit [tree]" (p. 374).

Langacker points out that the schematic network is a dynamic structure: "changes in patterns of experience and communicative needs can alter the specific configuration of a network even for a mature speaker. Elms and maples may not survive as prototypical trees for a speaker who has lived for forty years in the desert". By a stretch of imagination, "there are speakers for whom the term *apple* now designates a fruit only by virtue of semantic extension, based on its similarity [...] to a computer logo". Langacker believes, however, that such a variation does not hinder effective communication due to "substantial overlap" (p. 376).

This story is supposed to show how the schematic network develops in principle. Langacker states that "much less hinges on the specific details of a network than one might think". This is so for two reasons: one can adopt a conventional usage without forming the postulated higher-order schema (i.e. noticing the similarity motivating a particular extension); besides, "the entrenchment and cognitive salience of such structures is in any case a matter of degree" (p. 377).

As concerns the structure of a lexical network, its nodes should not be conceived as "discrete containers" but rather as "'windows' on a common knowledge base". Each node "affords a different view by structuring this base in its own fashion, and by introducing supplementary specifications" (pp. 378–379). As we know, the relationships between nodes exemplify two types of categorization: specialization and extension (the former is treated as a limiting case of the latter). Since they are graded phenomena, one may talk about "elaborative distance" between a particular schema and its instantiation, and about the degree of S/T discrepancy in the case of extension. With greater distance – "especially when domain shifts restrict the similarity between standard and target to abstract configurational properties" – an extension is considered metaphorical, e.g. *tree* in Chomsky's *phrase tree* (p. 379).

Additionally, bi-directional relationships are possible. "If a perceived similarity motivates the extension of A to B, the same similarity can motivate the extension of B to A". Since this point shows Langacker's fidelity to phenomena, let me quote at length: "Often there are grounds for positing a particular direction of extension: speaker intuition, the obvious prototypicality of A or B, or general principles of semantic extension (e.g. it typically proceeds from concrete to more abstract domains). However, nothing guarantees that a nonarbitrary choice can always be made. The relationship A<--->B then indicates that the speaker perceives the similarity of each element to the other without attributing primacy to either one. By my own intuitions, various specific senses of *drive* are related to one another in this way (*drive a car*, *drive a ball*, *drive a nail*)" (pp. 379–380).

As concerns the privileged status of the nodes functioning as the category prototype and highest-level schema, Langacker says that the former is important "because of its developmental priority and notable cognitive salience", while the latter – "because it embodies the maximal generalization that can be extracted". Developmental priority of the prototype is supposed to define "the center of gravity for the category". Simultaneously, "not every complex category offers viable or unique candidates for the roles of prototype and schema at the 'global' level". Langacker points out two criteria distinguishing the global prototype: "it is substantially more salient that any other and functions as the apparent basis of more extensions". Since these conditions need not be satisfied, it is possible that "multiple prototypes of considerable local prominence will [...] arise in different portions of an extensive network". Similarly, there is no assurance that one can plausibly posit a single "superschema" for a category and that efforts to locate it would be worthwhile, since "it may well be only minimally entrenched and have very little cognitive salience" (pp. 380–381).

Towards the end of his exposition, Langacker mentions "semantic extensions that appear not to be based on any judgment of similarity". He cites the classic example of Middle English *bedes* – the extension from "prayers" to "beads". According to Langacker such extensions, based on cultural associations, can be treated as a special case of extensions based on resemblance. He points out that in the single relevant domain linking them – that of saying prayers – "both [PRAYERS] and [BEADS] evoke the conception of a one-to-one correspondence between prayers in a cycle and balls on a rosary; they contrast only by their choice of profile". Since this correspondence functions as a mediating schema, "the extension is quite comparable to those based on similarity", if one factors out profiling (p. 384).

Finally, Langacker comments on the notion of a lexical item: "To the extent that a semantic network with common symbolization approximates a coherent category, we can reasonably speak of a lexical item. Despite its convenience, however, this construct is more a descriptive fiction than a natural unit of linguistic organization. Not only is coherence inherently a matter of degree, but also the definition allows a single network to be divided into lexical items in multiple and mutually inconsistent ways. I regard this as a realistic characterization of the phenomena in question" (p. 388).

1.2.2. A discussion

Basically, Langacker offers a format for representing any meanings of a lexeme, whether they are conventionally sanctioned senses (his minimal requirement: the network should be capacious enough to contain all established senses, as found in a dictionary or elicited in one way or another), or nonce uses. Thus, he avoids the problem of how to identify distinct senses at the cost of eliminating the boundaries between lexical/encyclopedic knowledge and between semantics/pragmatics (see 0.3. for a critique). The format is based on schematic similarity, which is unproblematic in the case of specialization; in the case of extension one is required to find a similarity between a prototype and a novel use, apparently motivating the latter. This requirement puts no significant constraint on extension. As mentioned in 0.2., one can find similarities between any two entities. Moreover, the division of represented meanings into "units" (dictionary senses?) depends on definition, thus it is – to some extent – arbitrary.

At one level, this is clearly realistic. Words (like *star*) can be used in distant domains ("astronomy" ---> "showbiz") to designate something objectively unrelated to the original referent. As for definitions, a set of uses of a word can be classified differently, depending on the criteria of classification; cf. e.g. Geeraerts (2007). Consequently, it makes sense to have a highly flexible format, which allows to incorporate – compare, classify etc. – any relevant phenomena (the reason, I believe, why Langacker's account is very much "in principle"[14]).

But is it "descriptively adequate"? Let us focus first on a problem with metonymy, which is evident in Langacker's discussion of *bedes* (PRAYERS / BEADS). As commonly explained, the metonymic extension is motivated not by the schematic similarity between both concepts which Langacker finds (the cycle of prayers ---> beads in a rosary), but as a result of the functional (situational) salience of an aspect of the referent. It makes sense to call BEADS *prayers*[15] and a CUSTOMER a *ham sandwich* not because of some common schema one can de-

---

[14] The format is infinitely flexible because a "schema" of a highly general kind (e.g. ENTITY) can be extracted for any two uses of a word. That is why it plays no real role in the representation (and generation) of phenomena, as I will show below. Langacker fudges this issue by his "in principle" treatment: "Our inability to demonstrate directly and conclusively that a particular schema has been extracted [...] does not invalidate the claim that speakers do extract schemas" (1987: 377). But the question is: do speakers use (need) schemas, when extending a word's sense? And on the level of theoretical representation: what is the use of schemas which do not capture "essential" similarities, i.e. do not identify the higher level in a taxonomy.

[15] Cf. a similar extension in Polish: *pacierze ---> paciorki.*

tect in the bases of both concepts within a common domain[16] (a task which would probably pose a greater challenge in the latter case), but because in the situation a given aspect of the referent in question ("something used for saying prayers", "the one who ordered a ham sandwich") is found suitable for its identification. However, when one looks closer at the *bedes* example – cf. Queller (2008: 15–16) – even the standard metonymic explanation need not be required. Queller argues that in an original context of use (Middle English) the sentence below could have two readings:

(1) *She's counting her beads [bedes].*
(1) a. *She's saying her prayers.* (the standard sense)
(1) b. *She's counting her beads.* (the modern sense)

Once the possibility of a new reading is inferred in a context, it can coexist with the standard sense, because it does not lead to a communication breakdown.[17] Only when it is invoked out of the original context (e.g. "You have mislaid your *prayers*"), the semantic extension makes itself manifest and may become standard. This does not yet explain the actual social process of semantic shift but it clearly shows that apart from cognitive factors (schematic similarity, cognitive salience), other factors may be more relevant (contextual ambiguity of a given formal sequence).[18]

When we accept this possibility, Langacker's "schematic similarity" looks *post hoc* – a theoretician's device to represent the results of unexplored processes of extension. We may find a common schema for *star* as used in astronomy and show-biz, but the perception of similarity need not have been operative in the actual extension. As will be documented in 3.3. – on diachronic processes concerning Polish verbal prefixation – non-cognitive factors are clearly at play in semantic shifts.[19]

The *hysteron proteron* approach is even more striking in the case of the acquisition just-so story. It is completely wrong as a developmental account. As shown by Piaget (1966a, b) – cf. Donaldson (1986) – schemas are extracted not on the

[16] Finding a place for metonymy in Langacker's format based on schematic similarity is difficult, as shown by Tuggy's discussion (2007: 103–105). Tuggy's claim that a "conceptual unification of [metaphor and metonymy] is surely a desirable result" (p. 104) is unconvincing. One can conceptually unify anything with anything; the point is whether both phenomena have something essential in common.

[17] Cf. a possible double sense of the following sentence in modern Polish: "*Klepie paciorki*" ("S/he is saying her prayers / s/he is tapping her beads" – my example; all further examples, when no reference is provided, are mine). To be sure, both senses of *paciorki* are established, while in the context of prayer with a rosary normally only the former one is active. My point is to show that interlocutors can construe both of those readings in the same context without causing a communicative problem.

[18] This is a standard explanation of grammaticalization in diachronic linguistics as "reanalysis" and "extension", cf. Itkonen (2002).

[19] Non-cognitive in the sense: not based on a perception of similarity (metaphor) or functional salience (metonymy). Any act of language use is cognitive in some sense, but that unspecific usage would be uninformative.

basis of "perceptual prominence and obvious gross similarities", but in the field of action – when necessary to achieve one's goals. For a child, a tree could be similar to things affording related types of activity (e.g. climbing, aiming at, jumping from etc.). Distinguishing a tree as a tree would make sense only if it could be opposed to something in the context of an activity (e.g. a bush: "something to hide in when crouching" as different from "something to hide in when climbing"). The prototypical schema of a tree which Langacker has in mind (but which may have little to do with the actual type of trees in one's vicinity) would probably be first acquired during drawing lessons, when a child is taught what a "tree", "house", "doggy" look like.[20] Additionally, acquiring a linguistic category like TREE is not a matter of generalization, but – on the contrary – of limiting initial overgeneralization, or rather "syncretic" use, cf. Vygotsky (1962). To conclude, Langacker invokes a standard empiricist scenario of step-by-step generalization which is philosophically discredited since Hume and Kant, and replaced by more adequate psychological accounts at least since Vygotsky and Piaget (and earlier by the Gestalt school). As we have seen (0.2.), this account assumes from the start the existence of the category.

The acquisition story would not be of much importance, if we were not supposed to take it as an analogy to the process which we try to fathom, i.e. the development of a complex category.[21] Langacker's analogy is in itself paradoxical, because TREE in the acquisition story is a standard – classical – category. The analogy would be more adequate, if the child in Langacker's account learned to associate trees in the park, Chomsky's phrase trees <u>as well as</u> anything s/he could find similar in shape or function (or for any idiosyncratic reason) to the first referent (which means: virtually anything, as in fact happens, and as Vygotsky's examples from the "syncretic" stage amply demonstrate). To be sure, such "complex categories" are not "classical categories", for they do not really classify – they do not reflect a given practice or provide a stable insight into some referential domain.

Thus, Langacker's description of the <u>development</u> of a <u>complex</u> lexical category fits much better a theoretician's attempt at a <u>representation</u> of a <u>classical</u> referential category (i.e. of a category of objects in the world). Consequently, the following passage describes an analyst's attempt to provide a representation of a monosemic category rather than the actual development of a complex category: "If we think of an extension as a 'horizontal' relationship, and schematicity as a 'vertical' one, we can say that the 'outward' growth of a lexical network by extension from prototypes is inherently associated with its 'upward' growth by extraction of schemas. One is not impossible without the other, but they tend to co-occur as interrelated facets of the same expansive mechanism" (p. 373).

---

[20] "As is known today, image is not an element of thought, nor a direct continuation of perception: it is a symbol of an object; what is more, it does not appear yet at the level of sensorimotor intelligence (otherwise the solution of various practical problems would be much easier). Image can be treated as internalized imitation" (Piaget 1966a: 91).

[21] "For illustrative purposes, let us sketch a plausible (though simplistic) scenario for the evolution of a complex category" (Langacker 1987: 373).

Both networks discussed by Langacker (*ring* and *run*) are perhaps not extensive enough[22] to make that obvious but when one considers a fuller account, e.g. Tabakowska's model of KLUCZ [KEY] (1995: 51), which also comprises historically related forms, it is clear that a complex category consists of clusters. The category KLUCZ contains two opposing senses: OPENING and CLOSING, motivated by both salient functions of the key. There is little generalization apart from the extensions: "opening" ---> "providing access"; "closing ---> "denying access". There is, however, plenty of variation around salient cases (I will quote an English dictionary, which lists similar items):

> (1) an instrument for locking or unlocking, winding up, turning, tuning, tightening or loosening;
> (2) in musical instruments, a lever to produce the sound required; a similar part in other instruments for other purposes, as in a typewriter [and now a computer, mobile phone and so on – A.P.];
> (3) a system of tones related to one another in a scale; a scheme or a diagram of explanation or identification; a set of answers to problems; a crib translation. (*Chamber's Dictionary*)

The list is much more extensive, but the clusters relate mostly to shapes and functions (often in surprising or apparently conflicting ways).

Thus, lexical categories display family resemblances. As famously pointed out by Wittgenstein, one cannot define even such a relatively coherent lexical item as *Spiel*.[23] As for its English equivalent *game*, referentially it comprises e.g. "volleyball" and "animals good for hunting". Do they have a common schema? One of an extremely general type: "ACTIVITIES performed/ANIMALS killed for fun". This disjunctive schema (two schemas?) is obviously not a definition – at this abstract level it could referentially cover a good part of reality and (the crucial thing) it has no place in a taxonomy (except, perhaps, one borrowed from Borges). This clearly shows that the <u>development</u> of a complex category cannot be meaningfully compared to categorizing, while its <u>representation</u> does not primarily involve a search for common schemas (or definitions) but rather an identification of clusters.

The KEY example shows that an important part in extension process is played by the actual physical and functional features of a salient referent. Assuming that the key used to lock doors is prototypical (i.e. salient), *key* offers itself as a suitable name for a range of referents involving related activities, e.g. "winding up, turning, tuning, tightening or loosening". Thus, (in a set of cases) it may be the

---

[22] Since Langacker's schematic model is very much an account "in principle", rather than "in fact", his own examples (two in all, two pages long) are fragmentary: they are used to illustrate the model rather than to be treated as serious analyses; cf. Langacker (1988a: 51–53; 1988b: 135–136, repeated in 1991: 267–268).

[23] "How is the concept of a game bounded? What still counts as a game and what no longer does? Can you give the boundary? No. You can *draw* one; for none has so far been drawn. (But that never troubled you before when you used the word 'game')" (quoted in J. Taylor 1989: 39). To be sure, the label "family-resemblance model" makes little sense, assuming that a model should be based on principles reflecting insight into the structure of the reality modelled.

social availability (common experience) of the sense of action invoked by a prototype which drives extension: people will use a term which easily springs to mind when they do something similar.[24] To be sure, one would feel that a given activity is similar e.g. to "rummaging with a key in the lock", when actually rummaging with a tool in an object providing resistance. But the feeling that one engages in "a similar thing" can apparently drive extension process without a common scenario, as shown perhaps by both senses of *game*.[25]

The KEY example also shows, confirming Langacker's general remark and Geeraets' lexicographical observations (2007), that pointing out clusters is intuitive and depends on one's classificatory criteria. If one relies on "shape", one can assume perhaps that a musical *clef* represents the same type of extension as anatomical *clavis* (i.e. CURVED OBJECTS). If one relies on "function", one could place *clef* in the category OBJECTS PROVIDING ACCESS (like "translation crib" or Polish "cipher"[26]).

To conclude, Langacker's format is so flexible that the issue of "distinct" senses is dissolved (along with both distinctions mentioned), while the issue of relatedness of word uses (based on schematic similarity) may seem largely unproblematic, since there is no "reality check" built into the model. I will offer an assessment at the end of the chapter 1.4.

1.3. Radial categories

As opposed to Langacker, Lakoff does not provide a general discussion[27] of the structure of "natural categories of senses" (1987: 418).[28] He states, however, what a representation of such categories requires from an analyst:

---

[24] If so, then the similarity of shape or function (invoked in the metonymy explanation) could be perhaps relevant *post hoc*: while those objective features could be incidental or not actually operative in an act of extension, they would make its propagation more likely.

[25] I do not take into account the fact that the hunting sense involves a metonymy. In my context, the important thing is an objective difference between "playing volleyball" and "shooting pheasants", while the common name implies a commonality of sorts.

[26] In Tabakowska's model (1995: 51), "cipher" is described as "denying access", which is its primary function from the vantage point of a sender. From complementary points of view (of a receiver or interceptor), it "provides access". This social complementarity of perspectives could be an actual driving force of generalization (in the case under inspection, however, there is no "integration" of perspectives possible – we have a disjunctive schema or two schemas: "ENTITY WHICH PROVIDES/DENIES ACCESS"; thus, an analyst is forced to choose a preferred level of generality of his representation).

[27] To repeat his statement: "I generally prefer not to engage in methodological discussions and would rather just get on with my work" (1990: 39).

[28] Lakoff does not specify the meaning of this phrase. He uses it in his discussion of *window* – which, as he says, can mean either "opening", "frame" or "glass" – to point out the natural related-

> 1. One must provide a representation for the central subcategory and representations for each of the noncentral subcategories, since there are no general principles that can predict the noncentral cases from the central case.
> 2. A theory of *motivation* is required, since the noncentral subcategories are neither arbitrary nor predictable from the central subcategory.
> 3. A theory of the types of links between the central and noncentral subcategories is required.
> 4. [...] an adequate account of these links requires an experientialist theory of meaningful [*sic*] thought and reason. (Lakoff 1987: 379)

The first three points will reappear in the subsequent discussion. Here, let us return to the problem with the notion "category", as applied to a set of senses of a polysemic lexical item (this issue has a bearing on point 4.). As suggested, the problem is backgrounded (or fudged) by Langacker, when he says that complex categories "group together, and treat as equivalent for certain purposes, a variety of distinct and sometimes quite disparate elements" (1987: 369). The essential feature of categories – that they "treat as equivalent for certain purposes" a set of elements – may apply to sub-sets of a complex category (lexical items with one definition, clusters uniting closely related senses) but not to the whole, possibly with a single exception: all nodes of a semantic network are equivalent as tied to one phonological form.[29] Langacker cannot claim that they are also equivalent as historically related (like members of a family), since he openly excludes this criterion. Still, historical relatedness would be enough to define a lexical category only in extensional terms (by specifying a given "family-tree"). In intensional terms, one cannot provide a concept covering all members of a complex category by definition.[30] Thus, as used by Langacker, a "complex category" is apparently a misnomer.

In standard use, Lakoff's expression "natural categories of senses" would be probably understood diachronically as historically related families of senses (an extensional definition). However, since his declared goal is "psychological reality", the relatedness in question refers not to historical, but to psychological links. For Langacker, "cognitive reality" means something quite general: that a given model of linguistic usage should be in agreement with uncontroversial psychological assumptions. Lakoff, however, invokes a speculative notion of "image sche-

ness of meanings (it is a case of "active zones", as analysed by Croft and Cruse, see 0.4. above; a more general discussion is provided by Langacker 1991: ch. 7). Thus, it is *prima facie* baffling when Lakoff subsequently states that the notion "has been studied extensively in the domain of English prepositions", since in the former case the relatedness is extensional, while in the latter it is an intensional relation between lexical senses. Apparently, Lakoff does not distinguish referential vagueness (*window*) from polysemy.

[29] If one discounts the issue of homonymy, i.e. the existence of a set of formally identical but historically unrelated words.

[30] Additionally, as mentioned in 1.2.2., for Langacker a given conceptual delimitation of sub-sets (or "lexical items") is more or less arbitrary: "the definition allows a single network to be divided into lexical items in multiple and mutually inconsistent ways" (1987: 388). Thus, also sub-sets cannot be taken as fixed categories.

ma",[31] which in his model serves the role of the central or prototypical schema (an abstract definition, a relatively unspecified concept), while all nodes are related to it by various mental links. Thus, his model of linguistic usage is not supposed to be merely in agreement with some general psychological operations (e.g. abstraction, comparison); it is supposed to be a hypothesis about a real-life generation of meanings prior to language (linguistic convention merely provides labels for some results of independent psychological processes[32]). Thus, such categories are taken to be "natural" in the biological sense: as physiological processes which – at the level of the hypothetical "cognitive unconscious" – are transformed into spontaneously evolving semantic processes.

That account does not work either as a solution to the philosophical mind-body problem, or as a scientific hypothesis about independent semantic processes in the cognitive unconscious, or as an explanation of linguistic meaning in general. I will not pursue that point here (see e.g. McLure 1990; Pawelec 2005a; Zlatev 2007b, c), since we are primarily interested in the nature of Lakoff's model as a representation of polysemic senses of a lexeme – specifically, *over*. In this context, Lakoff offers an abstract schema (prototype), which is subsequently specified along a number of dimensions. A set of resulting schemas (images, concepts) give rise to further schemas via certain hypothetical mental transformations. Despite empirical rhetoric,[33] Lakoff's model is an *ex post* reconstruction based on a set of features (in that respect it is similar to the generativist approach) and mental transformations represented mostly in an imagistic way. Thus – in a striking opposition to Langacker's account – it is focused on "the underlying reality of language", rather than on its surface manifestations.

1.3.1. A resume of Lakoff's radial model of *over*

The model of *over* is "an extension and elaboration" of Claudia Brugman's thesis (Lakoff 1987: ix). In the context of the following presentation, two basic notions used by Langacker to describe spatial relations should be introduced, namely "trajector" (TR) and "landmark" (LM). A trajector is "the entity whose (trans)location

[31] Developed in some detail by Johnson (1987). Despite suggestions to the contrary by Lakoff and others, image schemas have a completely different function within his theory than Langacker's schemas in his network model, cf. Tuggy (2007) on schemas, and Oakley (2007) on image schemas. Tuggy summarizes the aspects of image schemas which draw Lakoff's attention: "their constant recurrence, their basis in bodily experience and thus their direct meaningfulness, their gestaltish nature (Lakoff 1987: 272), their 'preconceptual structuring' (292–293), their universality in human experience (302, 312), and their ubiquity in language use (272) [thus] for Lakoff, image schemas are 'central truths' (296)" (Tuggy 2007: 85).

[32] As expressed by Lakoff and Johnson: "A portion of the conceptual network of battle partially characterizes the concept of an argument, and the language follows suit" (1980: 7).

[33] I speak of "empirical rhetoric", because Lakoff never tries to explain how such processes could work. A number of researchers show that Lakoff's hypotheses are unsubstantiated or wrong (in fact or in principle), e.g. Sandra, Rice (1995); Rakova (2002); Zlatev (2003).

is of relevance", while a landmark is "the reference entity in relation to which the location or the trajectory of motion of the trajector is specified" (Zlatev 2007a: 8).

Lakoff (pp. 416–461) presents a radial model of twenty-two senses of *over* (primarily a preposition, but also a verb-particle and a verbal prefix).[34] The model represents spatial senses – additional "metaphorical" senses are discussed separately. The prototypical sense is represented in (1): the trajector (TR – the plane) crosses the region above an implicit, unspecified landmark (LM). The senses exemplified in sentences (2)–(7), in which the LM is specified, are treated as separate instances of the central sense.

(1) *The plane flew over.* (CENTRAL SCHEMA 1)
(2) *The bird flew over the yard.*
(3) *The plane flew over the hill.*
(4) *The bird flew over the wall.*
(5) *Sam drove over the bridge.*
(6) *Sam walked over the hill.*
(7) *Sam climbed over the wall.*

Lakoff claims that all these senses of *over* (exemplifying various types and configurations of TR and LM, according to three parameters: [+/– contact] between TR and LM as well as [+/– extendedness] and [+/– verticality] of the LM) should be represented in the model. He points out that there are two almost completely equivalent interpretations of these schemas: "on the minimal specification interpretation, only schema 1 exists in the lexicon; the other [sub-] schemas all result from information added by the verb and direct object"; the full specification interpretation, on the other hand, requires "a lexical representation for all these schemas; the more specific schemas are generated by schema 1 plus the general parameters we have discussed" (pp. 421–422). Lakoff opts for the full specification interpretation since meanings (2)–(7) function in his theory as links to further meanings, which – as he believes – could not be derived directly from the prototype. For instance, the meanings in (8) and (9), where one focuses on the end point of the TR's path, require an extended LM, as in (5) and (6) respectively.

(8) *Sausalito is over the bridge.* (by "end-point focus" from 5)
(9) *Sam lives over the hill.* (by "end-point focus" from 6)

Another group, exemplified in (10) and (11), is close in meaning to *above*. According to Lakoff, these meanings are related to (1) – TR is above LM – but they differ in two respects: they are static and they do not permit contact between TR and LM. Lakoff describes the meaning in (11) as derived through an image-

[34] Below, I generally follow Zlatev's more succinct presentation of the case (Zlatev 2003: 449–451). I will not use Lakoff's original abbreviations of spatial features, which make for a difficult reading.

schema transformation between an extended path and a one-dimensional TR (in this case, the powerline).

(10) *Hang the painting over the table.* (ABOVE SCHEMA, from 1)
(11) *The powerline stretches over the yard.* (a transformational link from 2)

Another group, exemplified in (12)–(19), expresses the notion of COVERING. This notion is claimed to be a variant of ABOVE SCHEMA, differing from it in two respects: the TR is at least two-dimensional (in ABOVE SCHEMA the dimensionality of the TR is not specified) and it need not be in contact with the LM (while ABOVE SCHEMA requires noncontact). Additionally, meanings (16)–(19), which require contact, are derived from meanings (12)–(15) through another image-schema transformation called "rotation" (TR is no longer vertically over LM).

(12) *The board is over the hole.* (COVERING SCHEMA, from ABOVE SCHEMA)
(13) *The city clouded over.* (from 1)
(14) *The guards were posted all over the hill.* (from 12)
(15) *I walked all over the hill.* (from 14)
(16) *There was a veil over her face.* (by rotation from 12)
(17) *The ice spread all over the windshield.* (by rotation from 13)
(18) *There were flies all over the ceiling.* (by rotation from 14)
(19) *The spider had crawled all over the ceiling.* (by rotation from 15)

Finally, there are two groups of senses where *over* functions as a verb-particle and a verbal prefix. In (20)–(21) the TR is described as "reflexive", since it plays the role of the LM.

(20) *Roll the log over.* (REFLEXIVE SCHEMA, from 1)
(21) *The fence fell over.* (from 20)

The example (22) represents "excess".

(22) *The bathtub overflowed.* (EXCESS SCHEMA, from 1)

Additionally, Lakoff discusses several metaphorical senses of *over*. To give an example, the excess schema, as instantiated by (22), represents a regular correlation in experience (the fluid which exceeds the capacity of a container is spilled and wasted). According to Lakoff, the schema may be applied to human activities (e.g. "to overdo something") on the basis of the metaphor AN ACTIVITY IS A CONTAINER.[35]

---

[35] Conceptual metaphors are conventionally typed in capitals. Since they involve a transfer between two conceptual categories, this usage may be treated as an extension of our convention to

1.3.2. A critique

Since Langacker's schematic model is very much an account "in principle" and his own examples are fragmentary, linguists and psychologists focused on Lakoff's radial model of *over*, which has been subjected to thorough criticism. I will report below a response by Vandeloise (1990). Further responses, since they develop alternative models of this lexeme, will be discussed in the next chapter.

Vandeloise takes issue with Lakoff's rejection of the "minimal specification interpretation". That rejection is given more emphasis in Lakoff's subsequent case study of *there* constructions, where he claims that abstract characterizations of a linguistic category need not have "any psychological reality" or play "any role in the grammar of language", hence "seeking common properties, as linguists are trained to do, does not always lead to the best analysis – even when one can find such" (Lakoff 1987: 536–537). Vandeloise points out that a search for generalizations is not "a professional distortion linguists should be careful about", since common features revealed in such analyses give substance to the abstract characterizations proposed for chosen categories – "substance, I believe, lacking from the image-schemata described by Lakoff" (1990: 417). Vandeloise states that both the minimal and full specification interpretation are admissible (while the former is clearly more desirable): "each lexical category can be analysed at different abstraction levels ranging from example enumeration (therefore polysemic) to a search for common features [...] ideally leading to a unique rule" (1990: 416). The traditional opposition between polysemic and monosemic characterizations of lexical units is thus presented as a matter of one's modelling strategy – presumably, chosen on the basis of one's goals and to be evaluated in reference to them. Vandeloise believes, however, that the search for an abstract description gives better insight into the structure of a lexical category and allows one to profitably reduce its polysemy. He treats Lakoff's appeal to "psychological reality" basically as rhetoric, which serves to mask arbitrary theoretical choices.

Vandeloise's analysis of the model's arbitrariness is too detailed to be reported here fully.[36] To give an example, Vandeloise questions the need to invoke in some cases the parameters ("features") introduced by Lakoff in his "full specification interpretation" (the examples repeated below for convenience):

(5) *Sam drove over the bridge.*
(6) *Sam walked over the hill.*
(7) *Sam climbed over the wall.*
(8) *Sausalito is over the bridge.* (by "end-point focus" from 5)
(9) *Sam lives over the hill.* (by "end-point focus" from 6)

---

capitalize categories/concepts. The same goes for image schemas, which are characterized as "preconceptual".

[36] I offered a fuller presentation of Vandeloise's objections in Pawelec (2005a: 123–130).

"Verticality" of LM in (7) – contrasting with LM's horizontal extension in (5) and horizontal/vertical extension in (6) – is not directly relevant for a successful characterization, since it does not explain why (7) – as opposed to (5) and (6) – cannot be used for "end-point focus" derivation. Vandeloise points out that in such cases – when a trajectory is replaced by its extremity, as exemplified by (8) and (9) – the physical path must allow the speaker the conceptualizaton of a continuous abstract movement towards the TR located behind/beyond the LM. Consequently, the crucial factor in (7) is not LM's "verticality" but the fact that it blocks vision (p. 424).

Similarly, an image-schema transformation between an extended path and a one-dimensional TR – as in (2) and (11) – is based on inadequate parameters. As Vandeloise points out: "For an immobile TR to be used with *over*, it must be conceived as a path, either because it carries electricity or vehicles, or because it permits an abstract and often visual movement of the speaker". Thus, TR's "unidimensionality" is not directly relevant. Additionally, LM's extendedness (contrary to Lakoff's description) may be not only horizontal, but also vertical and horizontal / vertical, as in the following examples (Vandeloise pp. 425–426):

(23) *The line stretches over the hill.*
(24) *The line stretches over the wall.*

So far, Vandeloise replaces Lakoff's spatial parameters with pragmatic restrictions. However, in the case of "no contact" he accepts the relevance of the parameter, while showing that it is justified not by image-schematic considerations proposed by Lakoff but linguistically "by relations of co-occurrence existing between different prepositions". Vandeloise points out that when a TR is higher than LM and in contact with it, the preposition *on* is normally used. Still, as shown by (6), *over* can also be used in such circumstances, when the TR is moving. The requirement of "no contact" in the extensions "TR -> trajectory" is justified by the fact that when a moving entity is replaced by an immobile entity and there is "contact", the preposition *on* imposes itself. Compare the sentences below (the first one repeated here for convenience):

(11) *The powerline stretches over the yard.*
(25) *The path stretches on the hill.*

Vandeloise concludes: "The contrast contact/no contact therefore plays a decisive role in the choice between the prepositions *on* and *over*; this constitutes a linguistic reason for distinguishing circumstances where TR and LM are in contact from those in which they are not" (pp. 426–427).

To sum up, Vandeloise shows that the image-schematic model of *over* is based on several spatial parameters (features) which have no direct relevance for the characterization of the category. This leads to "the abusive multiplication" of senses included in the model (p. 429). What is more, the model does not include crucial pragmatic and linguistic restrictions which can be detected when a theorist looks for a generalized description. It is ironical, perhaps, that a theory built under the banner of "psychological reality" should disregard cognitive motivations apparently shaping the linguistic data (and which, as seems more likely, may be revealed when looking for a "unitary" representation). Vandeloise's critique substantiates the claim that Lakoff focuses on some hypothetical "underlying reality of language" rather than on its surface manifestations (thus – among other things – he reverses the natural direction of the linguistic analysis).

1.4. Concluding remarks

As pointed out in 1.1., both models have a radically different status. Lakoff assumes that his model captures conceptual structure in the cognitive unconscious. Thus, it is a "hypothesis" about the functioning of mind/brain. The central image schema is developmentally primary, arises in bodily interactions with environment and is unspecific, while the subsequent (sub)schemas specify it in some respects, serve as links to further schemas and as a basis for mental transformations. That conceptual structure is then employed in various ways in semantic transfers (conceptual metaphor). Consequently, the model is potentially universalistic: its "English version" should be substantially correct for other languages, which can probably extend it at places (most likely in the latter part: conceptual metaphors are supposed to be shaped by culture as opposed to "bodily" image schemas). When discussing a network model of the Polish preposition *za*, I will try to show that such assumptions are wide of the mark (see 3.4.).

At this level of discussion, the only novelty for a linguist (as noted wryly by Vandeloise) is the use of drawings. Since, however, each schema is provided with a description (necessarily so: a picture on its own could represent any number of meanings; additionally, some of Lakoff's presumed meanings <u>cannot</u> be drawn[37]), that format might as well be translated into a standard "feature account" (of a rather shoddy kind[38]). This raises the question of its adequacy, since combinations of features lead to rampant polysemy. The model does not provide criteria to establish "distinct senses" (apparently, this status is awarded to main "schemas") and to distinguish them from more numerous sub-schemas. It is an unusual amalgam of "feature approach" and psychologically motivated rules.[39]

[37] For instance, those which have disjunctive specifications: [+contact] or [-contact].

[38] Once a set of features is proposed for a given lexeme, all combinations should be taken into account (if one invokes only some of them, a principled way of discounting others should be found).

[39] The latter may be valid in some form. However, a contrastive analysis of several prepositions in one language and a subsequent cross-linguistic analysis would seem necessary for the study of un-

Langacker offers a format for attested senses which is flexible enough to capture any meanings. Since he aims at an adequate description of available linguistic material, he is far from basing his account on any pre-linguistic structures, transformations or transfers (even though he does accept in general that concepts are prior to a linguistic expression and conventionalization). His "schemas" are constructed on the basis of actual lexical extensions as opposed to Lakoff's image-schemas, which are supposed to underlie such extensions.

As for the prototype, Lakoff's model develops from the centre in various directions (apparently, to reach attested senses). His choice of an unspecified schema as the category prototype (irrespectively of his mentalistic claims) seems to be required by the format: it would be a much more demanding task (if not an impossible one) to derive a set of divergent meanings from a more specific schema. Langacker avoids the problem of the category prototype. In his format any schema motivating extensions is a prototype: categories have as many prototypes as proposed extensions.

As we have seen, Langacker offers some comments about the "global" prototype (and the highest-level schema). The former is supposed to be important "because of its developmental priority and notable cognitive salience". Its developmental priority is supposed to define "the center of gravity for the category". Simultaneously, "not every complex category offers viable or unique candidates for the roles of prototype and schema at the 'global' level" (1987: 380–381). These remarks are based on the developmental just-so story, while the actual network models of lexemes display sets of clusters. If there is any centre, it is cognitively salient not because of its developmental priority (i.e. historical, following Langacker's analogy), but because it seems to motivate more extensions than other prototypes <u>from the contemporary vantage point</u>. The present-day perception of its salience need not reflect actual historical processes (the word form *key* brings first to mind the tool for locking doors – once this function of KEY disappears for some reason, e.g. when we use our fingerprints to lock and unlock doors, some other sense may take over this central position[40]).

Langacker's account may also be taken to mean (as long as one does not look at actual examples) that the "superschema", mentioned above, is similar to a definition. Only on this assumption does the following comment on its status seem to be relevant: "it may well be only minimally entrenched and have very little cognitive salience" (p. 381). Since we know now that such schemas are so general that they are totally uninformative (thus, a fortiori, not definitional), their detection is of no cognitive value.

---

derlying factors (to reduce the impact of linguistic contingencies, which are clearly most pronounced in the case of a single lexeme). Only from that general (as opposed to ethnocentric) perspective can one properly offer <u>universalistic</u> generalizations, as done by Zlatev (2003: 484ff.); cf. Zlatev (2007a).

[40] Langacker's jocular remark about "Apple logo" being, perhaps, the primary sense of "apple" for some language users goes in the same direction (1987: 376, note 7).

Consequently, the search for an adequate format to represent complex lexical categories has little to do with defining categories[41] (thus, it cannot provide arguments against "classical" definitions), or with the psychological issue of categorization (as, basically, a differential response in a situation). It is a properly linguistic task and should be treated as such (only when we have convincing representations of this kind, may they be shown to involve some psychological factors relevant for the issue of categorization). The widespread interest in network modelling suggests that the formats proposed by Langacker and Lakoff have a real potential to capture relevant linguistic factors at play in the extension of meaning (when placed against alternative accounts). I will try to identify this potential.

[41] Complex categories are not conceptual categories (they can be defined referentially, as a set of uses of one word form). Once we see this (Langacker does), the issue of defining them cannot properly arise (or else one must think that both senses of *game* discussed above occupy the same place in some taxonomy).

CHAPTER 2. THE STORY OF *OVER*

2.0. Introductory remarks

Lakoff's analysis of *over* has inspired several responses which aim at a better formulation of the model and/or of the assumptions underlying modelling of this type (in one variant or another). The first one is more Lakoffian in spirit that the original, i.e. it is based entirely on image schemas. The second one shows that an image schema linked to a word may get different interpretations within a phrase, thus it raises the issue of the influence of other words on the meaning expressed by a lexeme. The third one re-introduces into the discussion the distinction between semantics (senses of words in isolation) and pragmatics (rich construals in the context), which was questioned by Langacker. The analysis contains both Lakoffian and Langackerian elements and provides the most complete representation of the lexeme. It instantiates a more general "principled approach" to prepositional polysemy. The fourth analysis is of an entirely different kind: it shows that the assumption common to all previous attempts – i.e. that extensions are motivated by general cognitive factors[1] – may be inadequate, thus a new approach to meaning extension could be required.

Let me add that I recount below only a few episodes of the story, which is substantially richer and still developing. My presentations are significantly reduced (there is more internal dialogue between participants and the level of detail – and wealth of insight – defies summary). My aim is to give some idea of the style of argument in particular cases and of the direction of the debate.

2.1. A consistently imagistic model

Dewell's declared aim is to improve on the Brugman/Lakoff analysis "by relying more exclusively on image-schema transformations and eliminating some remnants of feature analysis" (1994: 351). His approach is inspired by the criticism of Vandeloise, according to whom Lakoff's model only "wants to be analogue",

[1] The third analysis by Tyler and Evans (2003b) is a partial exception, since they invoke "pragmatic", or situational, factors in meaning extension.

while ultimately "it must be replaced by an equivalent propositional representation" (Vandeloise 1990: 435). Dewell believes, conversely, that he can eliminate propositional content (specifically, features) from the model and offer an account in which all spatial variants of *over* "can be derived either directly or indirectly using nothing but natural, independently motivated image-schema transformations" (1994: 352). Dewell does not say why an imagistic representation should be preferred to a feature analysis. Apparently, he accepts Lakoff's general position that words follow prior conceptual structuring (which is imagistic[2] in nature) and is intent on removing some inconsistencies pointed out by Vandeloise. In this way, however, he does not face the more central point of Vandeloise's critique: that an analogue representation (relying on images) must be translated into a linguistic description to make sense.[3]

Dewell proposes to treat as central the schema exemplified by:

(1) *The dog jumped over the fence.*

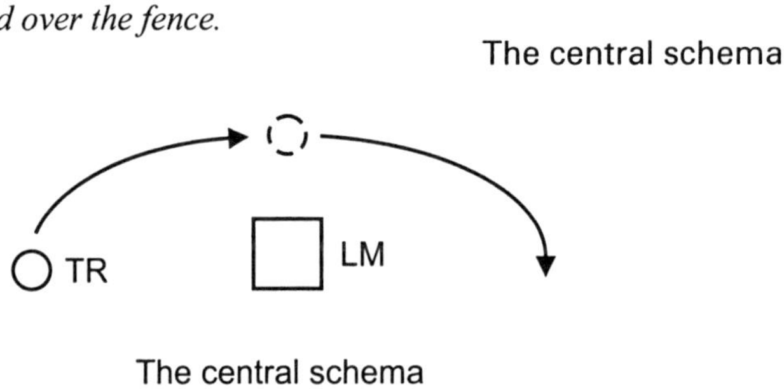

Figure 3: After Dewell (1994: 353)

Lakoff introduced it very late in his account, as "one of the most common instances" of his own central schema (1987: 433), in order to provide a link to "reflexive" and "excess" senses. Dewell argues that the "semicircular path" sense should be attributed central status, since it is a "recurring basic-level image schema grounded in experience", as reflected in common usage, e.g. "*step over, jump over, throw over, climb over* – all of which involve an arc-shaped path". As opposed to it, the flat-trajectory schema treated as central by Lakoff is exemplified in everyday life by apparently less frequent events, primarily by "birds and planes *flying over*"; such events, additionally, presuppose a contact with land, "however backgrounded [it] may be" (1994: 353), and thus – a curved path.

[2] To be sure, both Lakoff and Johnson repeatedly point out that image schemas are not images. However, the analysis of *over* makes it clear that the analyst thinks in terms of images (thus, Dewell's attempt makes sense in this context).

[3] This is based on the more general objection against empiricist "picture" theories of concepts (ultimately, versions of the "ostensive" definition, which assumes that an interlocutor already knows what meaning is pointed at). Since concepts may appear only in a field of meanings – a single concept is impossible – a picture cannot serve as an equivalent of a concept unless one adds some commentary. Consequently, one cannot rely on image schemas to explain the genesis of concepts.

In his analysis, Dewell assumes two "highly general" imagistic operations involving multiple TRs. The first one is the "multiplex-mass transformation", in which a "multiplex TR" (one made up of many individuals) is treated as mass (following Lakoff 1987: 428). The other one involves "a construction with a single predicate to describe multiple events with multiple TRs", e.g. "sheep jumping single file over a fence" or even "a swarm of fleas jumping over a LM in myriad directions simultaneously". Additionally, Dewell invokes specific "profiling" transformations which specify segments of the path in the central schema. Such segments, in order to be recognized as belonging to the schema, "must include the characteristic peak point of the arc" (1994: 354–355).

Dewell proposes four instances of this kind. The first one profiles the central region at the peak level, as exemplified by:

(2) *The plane flew over the hill.*

Another one profiles the downward trajectory, from the peak to the endpoint:

(3) *Sam fell over the cliff.*

The complementary upward segment is exemplified by:

(4) *The plane climbed high over the city.*

Finally, Dewell describes the "freeze-frame" at the peak, as in:

(5) *The plane should be over Baltimore by now.*

Apart from segments of the path, there are also "resulting-state" variants, in which the entire trajectory is present in the background. Dewell proposes two such cases. The first one is exemplified by:

(6) *Sam went over the bridge now.*

The endpoint of TR's path is profiled here; it becomes a separate sense, when the construal is not coded by a resultative construction, as in:

(7) *Sam is over the bridge now.*

This instance is to be distinguished from a closely related one, in which the path is not actually traversed by the TR but allows "subjective motion", i.e. an interpreter's "imagined movement along a path from a reference point to a location" (cf. Langacker 1991: 315–342), as in:

(8) *Sam lives over the bridge.*

The next group of senses is derived from the schema of "an extending TR, part of which remains at the starting location", e.g.:

(9) *She threw the rope over the limb.*

This type – in which the overall shape of the TR corresponds to the path taken by its leading point – is also subject to profiling, as for instance in:

(10) *We dropped the rope down over the edge.* (downward arc)

The "resulting state" variants are analogous to those discussed before:

(11) *The rope is hanging over the edge.* (downward arc)
(12) *That road leads over the mountains.* ("subjective motion")

The subsequent discussion is based on the assumption that the scene may be conceived not only from the side (the canonical two-dimensional perspective) but also from other vantage points. As a result, the distinctive elements of the arc schema (the semicircular path, vertical orientation) may disappear from view and new aspects may become prominent. Consider the sentence:

(13) *A line of soldiers marched over the ridge.*

When one views the scene from above, the separate arcs traced by marching soldiers are not visible, while the TRs – converted into one multiple TR and appearing as a plane via the multiplex-mass transformation (the "highly general" operations mentioned before) – reveal the shape of an edge extending horizontally. If a part of the planar TR remains at the starting location, we get an analogue of (9), as in:

(14) *He draped the sheet over the clothesline.*

TRs with leading edges may also move in several directions simultaneously, as with a fluid moving outward on a surface:

(15) *She poured the syrup out over the pancakes.*

In the "reflexive" sense, as in *roll over* or *fall over*, the immobile part of an extended TR functions as the LM, while the points on the moving part may be viewed as tracing a sequence of arcs reaching the rest position. When the semicircular path is backgrounded, the "covering" sense may become prominent, as in:

(16) *They laid a board down over the hole.*

This sense becomes independent, when the schema no longer includes the vertical axis implied by the canonical side-view but is oriented only in relation to the LM's surface:

(17) *They hung a curtain over the picture.*

According to Dewell, the vertical axis is still present in the background in the "covering path" senses, as in:

(18) *He rode his bike over the border.*

In this example, Dewell postulates "the notion of laying down an extended linear path with salient rolling wheels or stepping motions" (1994: 369). In other words, the central semicircular schema is present in the sub-movements of the TR (either the bike or the cyclist, or both) and not in its movement relative to the LM.

2.2. A three-level account

In his analysis, Kreitzer (1997: 292–293) points out some limitations of previous image-schematic models. He notes that there is "little principled constraint" in the derivation of postulated extensions (similarity links, instance links, transformational links). There is also little "independent motivation" for the image schema transformations proposed by Dewell, since one would have to show that they apply to a variety of prepositions in the language and – more importantly – that there is cross-linguistic evidence for their operation.

Kreitzer believes that a more constrained analysis is possible when one distinguishes different levels of schematization inherent in the linguistic expression of spatial scenes.[4] On the lowest conceptual level, he postulates nondecomposable "component level schemata", e.g. surfaces, lines, points (according to Kreitzer, image schema transformations occur at this level). The next level represents spatial relations expressed by prepositions which may be decomposed at least into the following elements: TR, LM, and also PATH, when the relation is a dynamic one. Such "relational level schemata" are subsequently integrated at the third level – the linguistic "phrasal level" – to produce "integrative level schemata" (pp. 293–294, 301).

---

[4] Kreitzer follows Talmy; cf. Talmy (2000: 177–254).

The crucial constraint results from the assumption that it is the relational level schemas which represent the "senses" of a preposition – and thus, the basic level of "granularity" of the prepositional model. As a result, the polysemy of *over* may be drastically reduced. While Lakoff treated the uses of *over* derived by image schema transformations as separate senses of the word, Kreitzer takes them to be merely extensions of "the application of one particular sense". The interpretation of *over* in utterances is supposed to occur "via conceptual transformations of the components of spatial scenes (image schema transformations), and via the integration of multiple relational and component level schemas [*sic*][5] (image schema integration)" (pp. 295–296).

Kreitzer's approach may be illustrated with an example taken from Dewell:

(1) *The plane climbed high over the city.*

For Dewell, this use of *over* profiles the upward segment of the TR's trajectory (cf. 2.1.(4)). Kreitzer argues, on the contrary, that the dynamic path schema is coded by the verb, while the relational schema for *over* is static. Additionally, there are two possible construals of this scene on the integrative level:

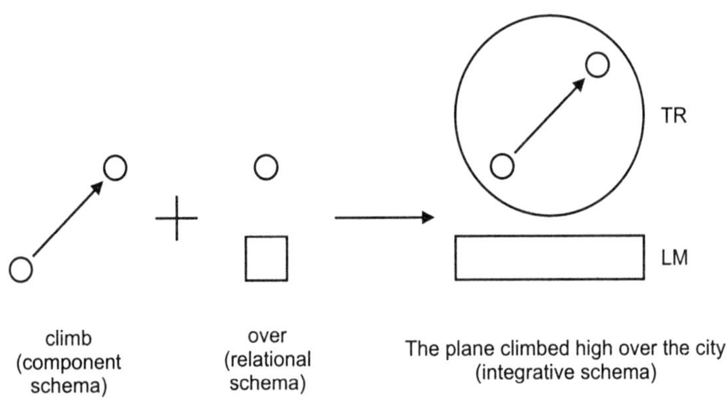

Figure 4: After Kreitzer (1997: 299)

[5] The problem with alternate spelling of the plural is noted by Tuggy (2007: 111, note 1). This is actually a more general problem of the shifting boundary between American and non-American English (as also exemplified in the present work).

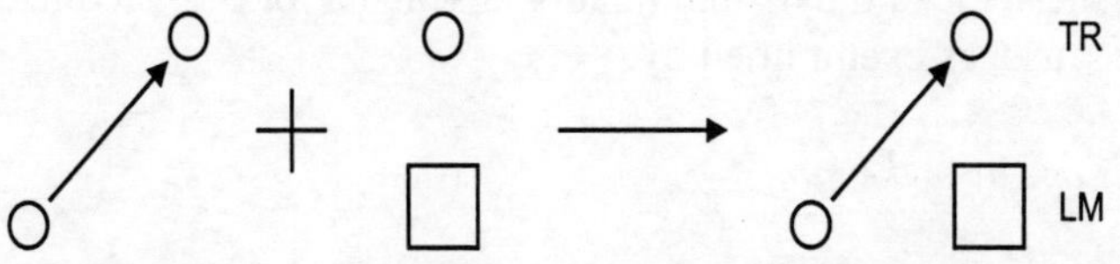

Figure 5: After Kreitzer (1997: 299)

In the first construal, the whole action takes place at a static location within the boundaries of the LM. In the second one, it is only the endpoint of the path schema which stands in the static relation coded by *over*.

The difference between the static and the dynamic sense of *over* is illustrated by two construals of the following sentence:

(2) *The clouds moved over the city.*

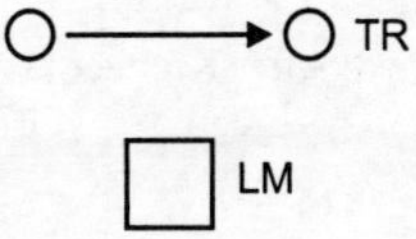

"The clouds moved over the city" : construal 1

Figure 6: After Kreitzer (1997: 305)

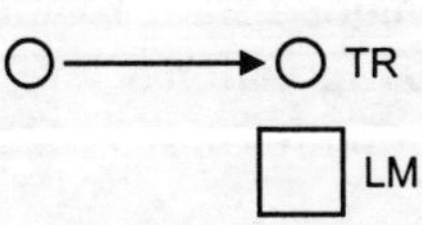

"The clouds moved over the city" : construal 2

Figure 7: After Kreitzer (1997: 305)

In the first construal, the path is a component of a dynamic relational schema – it is the path schema which stands in relation to the LM. In the second one, the relational schema is static (p. 305).

Apart from the static and dynamic relational schema for *over*, Kreitzer postulates one more sense, as exemplified by:

(3) *The clouds are over the sun.*

This static relational schema consists of two component level schemas: the TR occludes the LM, as viewed from a deictic centre (p. 313). The schematic relation coded by *over*3 is represented below:

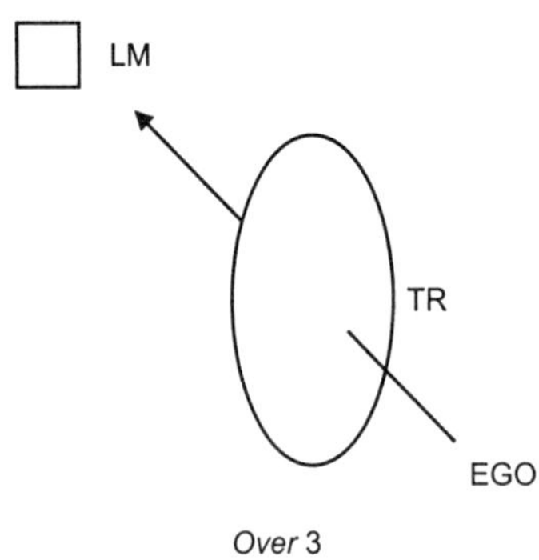

Figure 8: After Kreitzer (1997: 305)

To sum up, Kreitzer proposes three distinct senses – or relational level schemas – for *over*: a static one defined on the vertical axis (*over*1), a dynamic one defined on both the vertical and horizontal axes (*over*2), and a static one defined egocentrically (*over*3). Kreitzer believes that *over*1 is historically central and speculates that *over*2 could be derived "in a process of conventionalization, whereby an integrative level schema consisting of a static relational level schema and a dynamic path schema is reanalyzed as a relational level schema" (p. 323). He does not propose a hypothetical derivation for *over*3.

2.3. A principled polysemy framework

Evans and Tyler, in a book (Tyler, Evans 2003a) and a series of articles (Tyler, Evans 2003b; 2004a, b, c), developed a prototype approach to polysemy of English prepositions which they call a "principled polysemy framework". They note that previous attempts to model polysemy of such items failed "to distinguish what is coded by a lexical expression and the information that must be derived from context, background knowledge of the world, and spatial relations in general" (2003b: 97). The charge is based on the assumption that formal linguistic expression underspecifies for meaning, hence the recovery of a message – as postulated by cognitive researchers (e.g. Fauconnier 1994, 1997; Fauconnier, Turner 2003) – requires "conceptual integration of linguistic and nonlinguistic prompts, guided by various global cognitive principles" (Tyler, Evans 2003b: 97). To use general labels discussed before, Evans and Tyler criticise previous analyses for disregarding the boundaries between linguistic and encyclopedic meaning and between semantics and pragmatics. They also notice that their predecessors have not pointed out convincing criteria for "distinguishing between distinct senses within a network versus interpretations produced on-line" and for "determining the primary sense associated with a preposition" (p. 98). Their declared aim is to propose "principled" solutions.

With this goal in mind, Evans and Tyler attempt to improve on previous analyses of *over*. They begin by criticising Lakoff's "full-specification" model along the lines developed by Vandeloise (1990) and Sandra, Rice (1995).[6] Subsequently, they discuss Kreitzer's analysis, which they call a "partial-specification" approach.[7] As they say, Kreitzer assumes that a linguistic articulation of a spatial scene requires three distinct levels of schematization: the component level, the relational level, and the integrative level. The component level contains such conceptual primitives as LM, TR, path, verticality, extendedness of LM or contact between TR and LM.[8] The components combine to produce schemas at the relational level, which Kreitzer takes to be "the basic level of 'granularity' representing a sense of a preposition" (p. 100).

Evans and Tyler point out some problems with this account. Since Lakoff's radial representation has been abandoned, the senses do not share a common TR /LM configuration. Specifically, *over*3 is unrelated to the other senses.[9] What is more, Kreitzer only partially addresses the contribution of sentential context and background knowledge. For instance, following his assumption that *over* has both a static and a dynamic sense, he proposes two construals of the following sentence (cf. 2.2. (2)):

---

[6] This article develops the issue of arbitrariness of network models (in the context of their "psychological reality"), as signalled by its title: "Network analyses of prepositional meaning: Mirroring whose mind – the linguist's or the language user's?".

[7] A strange label, since Kreitzer's analysis is by far the least polysemic (3 senses as opposed to 14 identified by Evans and Tyler and 22 by Lakoff).

[8] Strictly speaking, contrary to this exposition LM and TR are not "primitives", since they make sense only on the relational level. Kreitzer talks about "surfaces, lines, and points" (1997: 301).

[9] Actually, Kreitzer admits both points. He says: "There does not seem to be a single common schema that could account, in a constrained way, for the application of *over* in various contexts"; and he states that *over*3 is defined in egocentric rather than absolute terms, as opposed to *over*1 and *over*2 (1997: 323).

(1) *The clouds moved over the city.*

As we have seen (cf. Fig.6 and 7 in 2.2.), in the first construal the clouds originated outside the city, moved over it and beyond. In the second one, they were outside, moved directly over the city and stayed there. According to Kreitzer, the first construal results from *over*2, while the second one represents an integration of the verb *move* (containing "path" as a component) and *over*1. However, Evans and Tyler describe yet another construal: the clouds move only within the city boundaries:

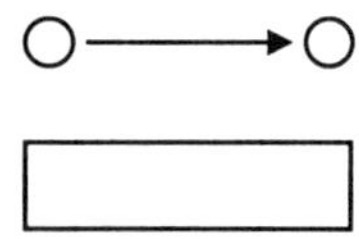

"The clouds moved over the city" : construal 3

Figure 9: After Tyler, Evans (2003b: 103)

Following Kreitzer's account, this sense should be represented as an integration of *move* and *over*1. As a result, there are now two construals with the same image-schematic representation. Since Kreitzer's model provides no means to distinguish between them, Evans and Tyler conclude that the problem results from the assumption (shared by Kreitzer and Lakoff[10]) that the final construal of spatial scenes is coded entirely by formal linguistic expression. To fix it, they postulate a higher level of integration – which they call a "conceptual" one – at which we are able to interpret ambiguous linguistic cues thanks to our knowledge about the world (the process they call "complex conceptualization"). The final problem is that neither Kreitzer nor Lakoff explain how they determined the primary sense of *over*.

Evans and Tyler attempt to find principled solutions. First, they propose two criteria for distinguishing senses of prepositions. In order to be recognized as a distinct sense, a given instance must involve a meaning which is either not purely spatial (following the assumption that the primary sense of prepositions is normally spatial), or based on a spatial configuration different from other senses in the network. Additionally, one must be able to locate instances of the sense which are context-independent, i.e. cases in which one could not infer the sense from another sense and the context. Consider the following sentences:

(2) *Joan nailed a board over the hole in the ceiling.*
(3) *Joan nailed a board over the hole in the wall.*

[10] Dewell also acts on this assumption.

In both cases, the spatial relation between the TR and LM is different from the "above" meaning. Apart from that, there is a (partly) nonspatial sense – that of "covering" or "obscuring from view" (the first criterion). Evans and Tyler argue that this sense cannot be always derived from the context and the "above" sense (the second criterion). Consider the following sentence:

(4) *The tablecloth is over the table.*

In this scene, the TR is higher than the LM. Viewing the scene from the standard vantage point, one can infer that the table is covered and partly obscured from view. Evans and Tyler believe that such inferences are not possible in (2) and (3), since the relations between the TR and LM do not correspond to the "above" meaning. They point out that in (2) the spatial relation would be typically coded by *below*, while in (3) by *next to*. They conclude: "unless we already know that *over* has a covering/obscuring meaning associated with it, there is no ready contextual means of deriving this meaning" in sentences (2) and (3) (p. 106).

Next, Evans and Tyler try to tackle the problem of the primary sense. They note that Lakoff and Kreitzer proposed different primary senses: Lakoff opted for the dynamic "above and across" sense,[11] while Kreitzer for the static "above" sense. Evans and Tyler argue – while claiming to build on Langacker's suggestions (cf. Langacker 1987: 376[12]) – that "there are at least four types of linguistic evidence that can be used to narrow the arbitrariness of the selection of a primary sense [...]. The evidence includes (i) earliest attested meaning; (ii) predominance in the semantic network; (iii) relations to other prepositions; (iv) and grammatical predictions" (p. 108). It is important to underline at this point that a primary sense is what Langacker calls "the sanctioning sense" (Langacker 1987: 157), i.e. the sense serving as the basis for extensions. That explains the following careful formulation by Evans and Tyler concerning point (i): "Given the very stable nature of the conceptualization of spatial relations within a language, one likely candidate for the primary sense is the historically earliest sense" (p. 108). In other words, the search is for the earliest sense perceived to be conceptually alive, i.e. still motivating other senses. In the case of *over* it is, according to Evans and Tyler, "higher" (from Sanskrit *upan*) and "above" (from Old Teutonic *ufa*), i.e. the configuration in which the TR is above the LM. As concerns the second criterion, "predominance" applies to the sense whose meaning components occur most frequently in the network. Evans and Tyler point out that among 14 distinct senses of *over* they identified, 8 directly involve the TR being located higher than LM. As for the relations with other prepositions, the sense which distinguishes

[11] At a more specific level, Lakoff's "central schema" differs also from Brugman's choice – Lakoff's dynamic configuration does not contain an extended LM (the LM is implied); cf. Vandeloise (1990: 436, note 7).

[12] As we have seen, Langacker does not consider diachronic evidence relevant for the structure of the network. Still, his developmental story does strongly suggest the possibility of a diachronic interpretation of his model.

over from *above*, *under*, and *below* "involves the notion of a TR being located higher than but potentially within reach of the LM". As concerns point (iv), since the primary sense gives rise to a chain of extensions, for any of them "we should be able to find sentences whose context provides the implicature that gives rise to the additional meaning associated with the distinct sense", as already shown in reference to examples (2)–(4) above. Sentence (4) is taken to provide grammatical evidence for the claim that the sense involving the configuration "the TR higher than the LM" is likely to be primary, since it allows to infer the "covering" sense in a suitable context (p. 109).

In Evans and Tyler's conception the primary sense takes the form of a "protoscene" – "an idealized spatio-functional configuration". It is derived by abstracting away "rich detail" from individual conceptualizations of spatial scenes. The protoscene for *over* is described in the following way: "It consists of a schematic TR, which is the locand (the element located, and in focus), and is typically smaller and movable; a schematic LM, which is the locator (the element with respect to which the TR is located, and in background), and is typically larger and immovable, and a conceptual configurational-functional relation which mediates the TR and the LM. In the case of *over*, the TR is conceptualized as being proximate to the LM, so that under certain circumstances, the TR could come into contact with the LM. The functional aspect resulting from this particular spatial configuration is that the LM (or the TR) is conceptualized as being within the sphere of influence of the TR (or the LM)" (p. 110).

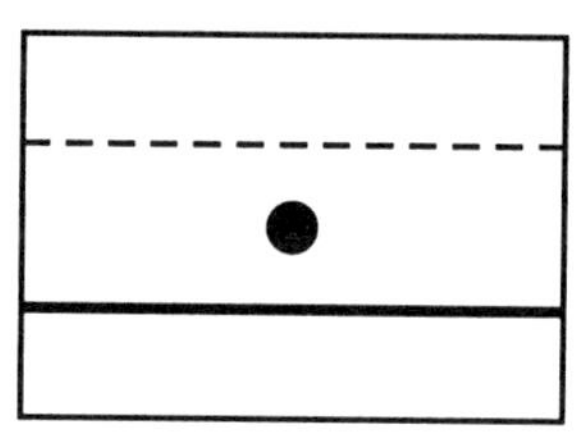

The protoscene for *over*

Figure 10: After Tyler, Evans (2003b: 111)

The dot stands for the TR, the bold line portrays the LM, while the dashed line signals the proximal part of the scene to show that the TR is within potential contact with the LM. In this way Evans and Tyler represent the contrast with the preposition *above* (the TR not within the reach of the LM).

The semantic network for *over*, proposed by Tyler and Evans, contains 14 distinct senses (including the protoscene):

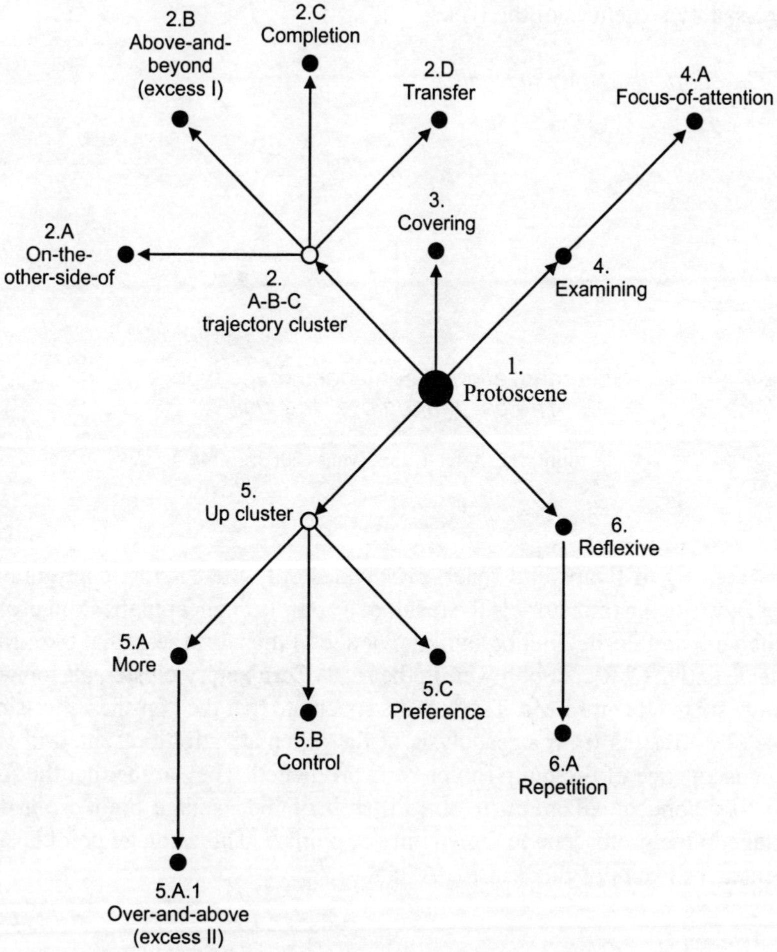

Figure 11: Based on Tyler, Evans (2003b: 125)

Each distinct sense is represented as a black dot, with the protoscene occupying the central place. In some cases, there is a chain of senses: a conventionalized sense gives rise to another one (4.–4.A, 6.–6.A). There are also two "clusters of senses" in the network (marked by a circle). They arise when a complex conceptualization (as opposed to a conventionalized sense) is submitted to "multiple reanalyses", which generate several distinct senses.

The first such cluster is derived from the arc schema which Dewell took to be the central sense of *over* (cf. Fig. 3 in 2.1.). In the present analysis, *over* does not code dynamic senses. The arc schema is treated as a representation of the scene expressed by sentences of the type:

(5) *The cat jumped over the wall.*

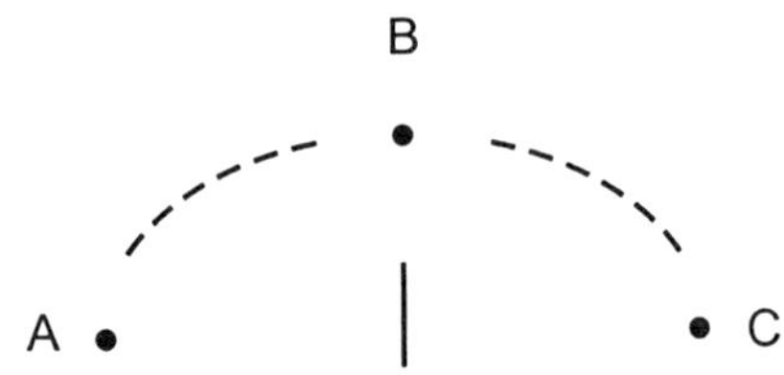

Schematization of sentences of the type:
The cat jumped over the wall

Figure 12: After Tyler, Evans (2003b: 114)

According to Evans and Tyler, *over* codes only the TR/LM configuration at point B, while the trajectory is the result of a complex conceptualization prompted by the verb and fleshed out by our knowledge of the world, e.g. that the LM is an obstacle and the TR cannot hover. In the A–B–C trajectory cluster, all four senses involve such TRs and LMs. The authors speculate that the "on-the-other-side-of" sense (2.A) results from a reanalysis of the schematization presented in Fig.12: the consequence of the jump (point C) is privileged. They argue that the A–B–C trajectory conceptualization involves a shift of the vantage point from default offstage in the protoscene to the vicinity of point A. This vantage point is evident in sentences exemplifying sense 2.A, e.g.

(6) *The cat is over the wall.*

Tyler and Evans do not comment on the fact that a complex conceptualization of sentence (5) may involve almost any vantage point: located close either to A or C, or even B for someone standing on the wall. They merely state that the "experiential correlation" required for sense 2.A (privileging of point C in the trajectory – locating the TR there) cannot be construed without a vantage point close to point A. They speculate that "through the use of *over* in contexts where on-the-other-side-of is implicated, this meaning has come to be conventionally associated with *over* as a distinct sense" via the so-called "pragmatic strengthening" (pp. 127–128).

The next sense of the cluster is exemplified by:

(7) *The arrow flew over the target and landed in the woods.*

This "above-and-beyond" sense (2.B) is derived from general knowledge about aiming at a target. The spatial configuration is the same as in the protoscene but the LM is construed as the target. When the TR misses the LM, it goes above and beyond it, or too far. This reanalysis of the A–B–C trajectory produces the "excess" sense. Since Tyler and Evans find an alternative route to this sense in the network (cf. 5.A.1), 2.B is named "excess I".

Another reanalysis of the A–B–C trajectory takes its endpoint C as representing the completion (2.C), while the path is backgrounded:

(8) *The cat's jump is over.*

Tyler and Evans argue that the TR's location is reanalysed in such a way that it does not represent a spatial relation (as in (6)) but an aspect of the process (motion). This is reflected syntactically: *over* is not a preposition here (which mediates a TR/LM relation) but an "adprep" (profiling some aspect of a process).

The final sense in the cluster is exemplified by:

(9) *Sally turned the keys to the office over to the janitor.*

This "transfer" sense (2.D) results from reanalysing A–B–C trajectory (movement) as a process of transfer (hence *over* is an adprep, again).

The "covering" sense (3.) is exemplified by:

(10) *Frank quickly put the tablecloth over the table.*

In (10) the TR is not only above the LM, but it also covers it as a result of two changes relative to the protoscene: the TR is untypically large, while the vantage point is not default offstage but as represented in the figure below:

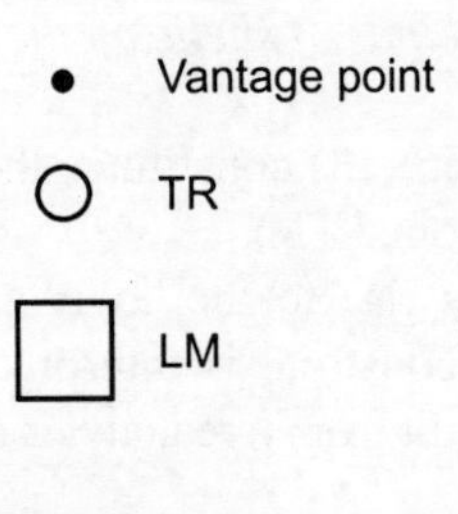

The covering sense

Figure 13: Based on Tyler, Evans (2003b: 133)

This is a distinct sense since the TR, as we have already seen, need not be located higher than the LM (cf. examples (2) and (3) above).

The next two senses also require a shift of the default vantage point. In scenes involving the "examining" sense (4.) the vantage point is that of the TR, whose line of vision is directed at the LM, as in:

(11) *Mary looked over the manuscript quite carefully.*

The examining sense gives rise to the "focus-of-attention" sense (4.A), as in:

(12) *The little boy cried over his broken toy.*

According to Tyler and Evans, the meaning of *over* in (12) could be paraphrased by *about.*

The "up" cluster (5.) contains four senses. All of them arise from construing a TR as being vertically elevated, or up, relative to the LM, as represented below:

The up cluster

Figure 14: After Tyler, Evans (2003b: 137)

As for the motivation of this extension, Tyler and Evans point out that in everyday life the use of *over* often involves situations in which the TR moves up. Additionally, an upward orientation is treated as positive and superior in human experience (cf. Lakoff, Johnson 1980: 14–21).

The "more" sense (5.A) results from an experiential correlation of vertical elevation and quantity, as exemplified by:

(13) *Jerome found over 40 kinds of shells on the beach.*

The number mentioned in (13) constitutes the LM, which is exceeded by the actual number (the unmentioned TR).

The "more" sense gives rise to the "over-and-above" sense or "excess II" (5.A.1), when the "more" construal is interpreted as "too much". The authors think that this sense may result from a reanalysis of scenes involving containment, as in:

(14) *The heavy rains caused the river to flow over its banks.*

When the TR (the level of water) moves up, it exceeds the capacity of the LM (the banks). The "excess II" sense seems to be linked with the idea of a "natural capacity" as opposed to the notion of "missing the target", which grounds "excess I". Evans and Tyler point out that it is often difficult to ascertain which of them is involved in a complex conceptualization. They make a more general remark concerning this point: "our network should be thought of as a semantic continuum, in which complex conceptualizations can draw on meanings from distinct nodes as well as the range of points between nodes, which provide nuanced semantic values" (p. 153, note 31).

The "control" sense (5.B) is exemplified by:

(15) *She has a strange power over me.*

Evans and Tyler derive it from an experiential correlation between physical control and the "up" position (the winner is standing, while the loser ends up on the ground) and also the relative size of the controller (who is, usually, physically bigger than the controlled).

The "preference" sense (5.C) results from construing that which is higher as more preferable. It is exemplified by:

(16) *I would prefer tea over coffee.*

The authors attribute it to a correlation in experience between "up" and greater quantity – conventionally preferred to a lesser quantity. Alternatively, being up implies positive states, which are preferable to those implied by being down.

The "reflexive" sense (6.) results from a reanalysis of a process in which two salient positions occupied by a single entity are integrated (via summary scanning) into a TR – LM configuration, as in:

(17) *The fence fell over.*

Since *over* profiles a process, it is coded as an adprep.

Finally, the "repetition" sense (6.A) adds an iterative component to the meaning of *over*, as in:

(18) *After the false start, they started the race over.*

Evans and Tyler speculate that the repetition sense may result from iterative application of the reflexive sense. However, as they pointed out earlier, while discussing "excess I" and "excess II" senses of *over*, one could imagine alternative routes of motivation (e.g. an iterative application of the A–B–C trajectory).

2.4. The case of (*all*) *over*

The analysis carried out by Queller (2001, 2008) and taken up by Taylor (2006) differs from previous accounts. Both authors focus primarily on the meaning of the phrase *all over* to argue for a highly "granular" approach to the polysemy of *over* – an approach of a radically different kind than Lakoff's (and those presented above).

Queller refers back to Lakoff's discussion of *all over*, who posited two subschemas for it:

(1) *There were flies all over the ceiling.* (multiplex covering)
(2) *The spider had crawled all over the ceiling.* (multiplex covering path)

Lakoff derived the first sense from the basic image schema for "covering" via a mass-multiplex transformation: the TR is to be conceived not as a single, continuous entity covering the LM, but rather as a group of individual entities which are distributed over the LM conceived as a set of small regions containing at least one entity each (Queller dubs this notion "sectoral coverage" – 2008: 5). The multiplex covering schema, in turn, gives rise to the multiplex covering path schema, "in which the points representing the multiplex entity [...] are joined to form a path [...] which 'covers' the LM" (Lakoff 1987: 428–429).

Queller shows that subsequent researchers tended to eliminate the subschemas postulated by Lakoff from their models. As we have seen, Kreitzer (1997) postulates that distinct senses of *over* should be sought on the "relational" level, while image schema transformations (like the ones instantiated in examples (1) and (2)) influence only construal operations on components of a full relational schema. For Tyler and Evans (2003b), these subschemas do not represent distinct lexical senses, "but rather a contextual implicature based on real-world knowledge of what 'covering' of a surface by less typical sorts of TRs like a swarm of flies or a spider's path would look like" (Queller 2008: 7).

Contrary to those accounts, Queller argues that the "multiplex covering" schemas do represent distinct senses. He points out that (*all*) *over* is frequently used with various verbs to denote "chaotic dispersal": "*daub/dribble/drip/dump/pour/scatter/smear/spatter/spill/splash/splatter/spread/sprinkle TR (all) over LM*" (p. 8). It seems clear that in such collocations the sense in question is prompted by the verbs. However, the same sense can be expressed by stative/resultative constructions with *all over*, in which there is no overt reference to an action:

(3) *There are crumbs all over the floor.*

The "chaotic dispersal" sense of *all over* becomes all the more evident when "crumbs" in (3) are replaced with a TR normally forming a regular design, as in:

(4) ? *There are tiles all over the floor.*

This sentence could be felicitous only on the assumption that the tiles do not cover the floor as its design, but are rather scattered randomly over its surface. Such examples suggest that "covering" may be not at issue here. Queller points out that it would take a relatively few crumbs to justify (3). What is more, the "sectoral coverage" of the LM need not be the case: the crumbs could be placed only on a small portion of the floor's surface and possibly elsewhere. Queller concludes that the notion of "chaotic dispersal" best captures the data in question: "in typical uses of *all over* the distribution of the TR has little regard for the boundaries of the LM surface"; additionally, it "also captures the non-topological, subjective sense of a loss of control that results in things ending up where they don't belong, creating a 'mess'" (p. 9).

A similar argumentation may be invoked for some idiomatic uses of *all over*, e.g.:

(5) *George has guilt written all over his face.*

If one construes the meaning of the phrase as involving "covering", analogous uses based on this construal should be fully acceptable. However, this is not the case. Queller states that native speakers find the variants in (6) decidedly odd, compared with "prototypical instantiations involving words like *guilt*" (p. 10):

(6) ? *He had rage/amazement/indifference written all over his face.*

This fact becomes understandable when we construe the emotion to be expressed as "chaotically dispersed" across the face. Guilt serves as the best example because we typically try to hide it behind a facade. When it nevertheless gets through, we attribute that to a loss of control leading to a messy situation. The emotions mentioned in (6) are not typically construed in that manner, since they normally cannot (rage) or need not (amazement, indifference) be contained.

The "chaotic dispersal" sense of *all over* is evident in the following idioms:

(7) *This paper is all over the place.*
(8) *The data are all over the map.*

What is more, the "coverage" interpretation of such sentences would be positively misleading. An interpretation of *all over* in (7) as implying an exhausting presentation of a subject would be opposite to the real meaning: that the paper is chaotic to the point of incoherence. Similarly, (8) does not express "full coverage" but a lack of structure in the presentation of the data. Both examples represent "a schema involving the evaluation of a summarily scanned path as chaotically dispersed" (p. 11) (cf. "multiplex covering path" schema in Lakoff's model).

In his discussion of *all over*, Taylor (who consistently quotes corpus data or results of google searches) focuses first on the contribution of *all* to the meaning of the phrase. As we have seen in (7) and (8), *all* does not seem to have a quantificational sense there (consistent with the compositionality principle) which would suggest that the coverage is in some way total.[13] Taylor provides additional evidence against the quantificational interpretation of *all*. First, it can often not be dropped from the phrase, suggesting that *all over* functions as a unit, e.g.:

(9) ? *Oh, God, I thought, she can see the lipstick over me.*

Second, it cannot be added to quantify some sentences with *over*:

(10) ? *I held my hand all over my face for a few moments before speaking.*

Such a use would not be felicitous even if a physical covering of the face took place (when we replace "my hand" with "both my hands"). Third, *all* does not readily contrast with other quantifiers, e.g.:

(11) ? *Oh, God, I thought, she can see the lipstick* [*half, partly, somewhat, mostly*] *over me.*

Taylor points out that such phrases with *over* are possible and they do seem to involve some quantification, as in:

(12) *She pulled the sheet half over her head, to be ready to jump out, and she waited.*

Finally, following Lakoff's characterization of the covering sense of *over*, which involves a TR extending across the boundaries of the LM (1987: 426), *all* in its quantifying sense would be redundant, since the coverage is (in one way or another) full by definition. But of course, as shown by Queller, the notion of "covering" does not provide an adequate interpretation of *all over*.[14]

---

[13] Contrary to Lakoff's characterization which invokes the idea of "sectoral coverage", i.e. sectorally distributed full coverage (1987: 428).

[14] It is curious, perhaps, that Taylor does not follow the question of *all*'s contribution to the phrase (he seems satisfied with the conclusion that *all over* functions as a unit not with the compositionally predictable sense of "complete covering", but rather with the "chaotic dispersal" sense). But if it is not quantification, what is it? Perhaps a comment by Dewell could serve as a promising point of departure. He noticed that in "*There is paint all over the wall*", the TR "would be considered a continuous covering layer without *all*, which suggests scattered splotches" (1994: 373). Thus, in this minimal pair, *all* introduces the sense of discontinuity. If *over* suggests "continuous coverage"

Subsequently, Taylor suggests that *all over* treated as a unit has a particular distribution of uses (to be determined by further studies). He notices that several examples – as (9)–(12) above – contain references to human body (either as a TR or a LM). In other cases, *all over* occurs with some geopolitical entity as a LM (e.g. "*all over the country/the world/Britain/Europe*"). These properties, he suggests, contribute to the "semantic profile" of the expression.

All over not only has a distinctive pattern of uses but it may "combine with other items to produce expressions which also have their distinctive values" (Taylor 2006: 68). Thus, the process of "idiomaticization" is recursive, as exemplified by sentences with *all over the place*:

(13) *Why somebody's left an old choc-ice on the floor, and it's run all over the place.*
(14) *There is no way that a farrier can shoe a horse that is so angry or frightened that it is rearing and leaping all over the place.*

While in (13) the phrase designates a contextually defined region (and could be replaced by *everywhere*), in (14) it carries the idea that the action of the horse is impossible to predict (which makes the substitution inadequate). As we have seen, this notion of randomness, lack of pattern or structure was present in (7) above, discussed by Queller.

Taylor points out that a new idiom like *all over the place* can be creatively extended. In this case, the "slot" provided by *place* can be filled by other lexical items. We have already seen *all over the map* in (8) above. Additionally, Taylor quotes examples with *all over the show*, *all over the shop* and *all over the paddock* (an Australasian variant), which may all carry the ideas of randomness, unpredictability or dispersal.

Finally, Taylor provides some evidence to show that Queller's interpretation of *written all over (one's face)*, as exemplified in (5)–(6), is not waterproof.[15] Some corpus examples do not conform to the idea that a subject is unable to contain emotions which are visible all over his face:

(15) *As William and Harry boarded the 10.30am BA flight, excitement was written all over their faces.*
(16) *The Conductor was sitting with satisfaction clearly visible all over his face.*

Taylor suggests that a more general interpretation based on the notion of THE FACE AS INTERFACE (where emotions are made manifest and can be "read") would be more adequate.

---

of some kind (a big splash?), perhaps *all* distributes this effort on the whole area? This contribution would involve quantification.

[15] Actually, Queller admits as much: "An internet search for phrases like *pleasure (was) written all over his face* will yield exceptions to the generalizations outlined here" (2001: 80, note 2).

2.5. A discussion

Dewell's account is most Lakoffian in spirit. His discussion may be used to point out an essential arbitrariness of the imagistic analysis. Dewell intuitively posits a curved path as the central image schema/meaning of *over*. He says that this image is "maximally distinct" from schemas for *above* and *across* (invoked jointly by Lakoff to characterize his central sense). Dewell is subsequently at pains to see an arc in *prima facie* flat trajectories. Thus, planes have to land at some point (and the horizon is oval, anyway), while the clothesline stretching across the yard is attached to poles at each end (1994: 355–356, 359). Since most of the uses of *over* do not involve actual paths, Dewell invokes mental scanning ("subjective motion") in his proposed shape. Thus, when a plank is over a hole in the floor, its leading edge is imagined as having traversed a curved path. The most ingenious of all is, perhaps, the proposed image for crossing the border on a bike (the semicircular path is traced by "salient rolling wheels or stepping motions" (p. 369)).

Dewell does not notice that his account assumes what it sets out to prove. One can always imagine arcs, if one needs them. Whether Sam lives across the bridge or over the bridge, one can represent the hypothetical mental trajectory either as flat or semicircular, depending on one's assumptions. When an actual curved path is expressed by the "wrong" preposition – "Sam walked across an arched bridge" – one can always say that the physical arc is less important than the mental "flat trajectory". Once one realizes that a given expression can be imagined to represent an infinite number of configurations within some general constraints, then it becomes clear that the focus of an analyst should be on those constraints.[16]

Kreitzer accepts Lakoff's image-schematic approach, while his declared aim is to reduce the rampant polysemy of the model by suggesting that "distinct senses" appear on the "relational" rather than "component" level of analysis. That solution merely shifts the problem. The question remains: why should one accept the three spatial relations pointed out by Kreitzer rather than the twenty-two pointed out by Lakoff?[17] The issue of the "division of semantic labour" among various elements of the sentence (primarily, between *over* and the verb), which is supposed

[16] In particular cases, Dewell notes constraints on the use of *over* which, however, are not visual. For instance, Lakoff's argument (1987: 423–424) that "end-point focus" is possible only for extended LMs was questioned by Vandeloise (1990: 424), who pointed out that what really counts is whether the LM blocks vision or not (thus, "Sam lives over the wall" is impossible, because the wall blocks vision). Dewell (citing Brugman) noticed that the only relevant restriction is pragmatic: whether one can actually take the route (1994: 358). Thus, the sentence is felicitous, if the LM is the Berlin Wall or a prison wall which can be traversed. We will see in Vandeloise's account of "length/ width" (4.2.) that pragmatic explanations take precedence over perceptual or objective explanations (Lakoff's features). In hermeneutical terms, they are more "originary".

[17] Or fourteen, as identified by Tyler and Evans. Or one, as suggested by Szwedek: prepositions "have a single, schematic meaning" (2007: 256). The basic question concerns what is "in" a word out of context, or the nature of the semantic perspective.

to take place on the "integrative" level (and which Kreitzer is the first to raise), is potentially more important. In this context, Kreitzer suggests that when the verb codes ascension (*climb*), *over* is apparently static (i.e. it codes the relation "TR above LM"). When the verb is general in meaning (*move*), *over* may be either static or dynamic, depending on the construal: if the TR crosses the boundaries of the LM, *over* is dynamic; if it moves to stay within LM's boundaries, *over* is static. Like Dewell, Kreitzer does not notice that a possibility to imagine some spatial configuration is not relevant in a linguistic analysis, unless it is linked to some constraints on the use of a lexeme. The distinction between the static and dynamic sense of *over* is gratuitous, if one does not try to show its formal relevance.

Evans and Tyler offer the fullest account, combining several elements from previous models and taking a position on most issues raised before. As concerns their method, the crucial question to be asked is whether their approach offers genuine insight, actually solving some vexing problems (as the label "principled polysemy framework" promises), or whether it is syncretic. They begin their analysis by pointing out that Kreitzer's scenario mentioned above may also include the TR actually moving <u>within</u> the boundaries of the LM, thus his model has no means to distinguish two dynamic construals. On this basis, they advocate a further level of integration, which fuses the semantic structure provided by words with general knowledge.[18] This is a curious argument: Evans and Tyler's "conceptual" level of integration also does not allow to distinguish <u>all</u> possible construals unless one knows what could be actually meant. If in the sentence "The clouds moved over the city" we replace "clouds" with a TR adopting any trajectory (e.g. a figh-ter jet), then the physical relation could be plausibly construed in several other ways. Without any context, one can more or less specify possible trajectories of clouds in relation to the city (thus, general knowledge seems useful), while one cannot really know how a jet could behave. To be sure, we can all imagine several possible trajectories (having seen war films etc.), but since none is more likely that others,[19] we normally would not have any preferences. Thus, it is irrelevant in the context of a linguistic description of a lexeme what scenario one actually imagines or can imagine <u>as long as</u> such alternatives do no have formal consequences.[20]

When Evans and Tyler distinguish "lexical concepts" from "cognitive models", we seemingly return to the structuralist distinction between the dictionary and encyclopedia (or properly linguistic and extra-linguistic knowledge) rejected

[18] Evans develops this approach, which he calls now "LCCM theory", i.e. "theory of lexical concepts and cognitive models", e.g. 2007. I will treat both accounts as sketches of the same model.

[19] As opposed to the clouds scenarios: Evans and Tyler's case is clearly the least likely, since clouds do not respect city boundaries, and one cannot really know, if the boundaries have been crossed. In general terms, a "cognitive model" cannot solve the problem of the background – one cannot translate a life-world into conceptual structure. Cf. e.g. Searle (1999), Dreyfus (1992).

[20] The "imagistic" interpretation of language had been repeatedly criticised before the advent of CL. Cf. Richards' argument against T.E. Hulme's "imagism" (1965: 129–132) or Jonas' criticism of Arnheim's account of "visual thinking" (1974).

by Langacker. However, the account remains Langackerian, since both elements are integrated at the "conceptual" level and cognitive models define the "semantic potential" of a lexeme.[21]

One wonders what Tyler and Evans actually mean at some other junctures. For instance, they propose a unitary "protoscene" for *over*, thus their model seems monosemic; cf. Lewandowska-Tomaszczyk (2007: 153). At the same time they claim that "this representation alone is inadequate" (2003b: 112), and they offer a radial model with fourteen senses. Subsequently they add that "our network should be thought of as a semantic continuum, in which complex conceptualizations can draw on meanings from distinct nodes as well as the range of points between nodes, which provide nuanced semantic values" (p. 153, note 31). This may be a realistic characterization of phenomena but in a "principled approach" one would expect a theoretical defence.

In their account of how to identify the central sense of *over*, Tyler and Evans offer four principles. The first two ("etymological priority" and "frequency of occurrence") are formulated at such a level of generality that they seem hardly useful (the authors do not raise the question of their arbitrariness). According to the third one, the central sense should be clearly different from related prepositions. Evans and Tyler propose "the notion of a TR being located higher than but potentially within reach of the LM" (p. 109). Why not Dewell's arc? They assume that *over* is static, thus they make the arc (A–B–C trajectory) the basis for cluster 2. One may wonder in what way this choice is "principled". The final principle concerns "grammatical predictions". In their formulation: since the primary sense gives rise to a chain of extensions, for any of them "we should be able to find sentences whose context provides the implicature that gives rise to the additional meaning associated with the distinct sense" (p. 109). But these are not grammatical predictions in any formal sense – this is their "method" of deriving "distinct senses". Thus, one may ask if the sum of four apparently arbitrary principles (at least, at the present stage of formulation) is any less arbitrary?

The last – highly granular – approach actually provides some answers to issues which were raised in the previous accounts (but not followed) and radically changes the perspective. The question of "granularity" looks very different when is it transferred from the general level – how many senses does a word have? – to the more specific level of the meaning of a word in various phrases. Thus, in the sequence: *over*, *all over*, *all over the place* the meaning of a given unit at each subsequent level of complexity need not be fully compositional (i.e. not predictable from the senses at a lower level). Since this process is recursive (cf. Harder 2006), as Taylor points out, a specification of senses at the word level seems premature and not instructive (certainly so in the cases when phrasal meanings are not predictable – "idiomatic").

---

[21] Cf. Evans (2007: 21ff.). A real opposition to Langacker's view appears possibly at the next stage: when the semantic potential becomes actual "meaning" (the semantics – pragmatics distinction), pp. 27ff.

In this way, the issue of the "contribution" of particular elements to the meaning of the whole gets in focus. As we have seen with *all over*, no clear-cut answer is provided, since the "emergent" sense is explained not on the basis of global cognitive principles (which perhaps could make such attribution possible) but rather situational logic – "situated rationality". If we accept Queller's pragmatic account based on "reanalysis and extension" (or "abduction", cf. Itkonen 2002), then *all over* is reinterpreted as a whole: the "covering" sense of the phrase is replaced by the "chaotic dispersal" sense due to a situational change of perspective. As noticed, an alternative explanation is suggested by Dewell. In the contrastive context: "There is paint over the wall" (a continuous splotch) vs. "There is paint all over the wall" (many smaller splotches) *all* seems to introduce discontinuity. According to a partly compositional interpretation, since *all* could not introduce in this context the standard sense of "complete" covering (splotching does not normally allow of such a possibility), it distributed the effort[22] inherent in splotching across the LM. However, one can safely assume that some other situational scenarios motivating this extension could be presented. This example is consonant with Saussurean view that form and meaning should be treated as units – that they cannot be decomposed (cf. 4.1.). Contrary to Saussure's methodological approach, it reveals the significance of pragmatic, situational factors.

---

[22] I suspect that Dewell's arc primarily expresses a surmounting of an obstacle. Thus, the prototypical sense (chronologically) would be dynamic. This guess follows Werner and Kaplan's "physiognomic" conception of language (1963), emphasizing correlations between body postures and linguistic senses. And it accords well with the hermeneutical view that pragmatic explanations are more "originary" than perceptual or objective ones, as confirmed by Vandeloise's analysis presented in 4.2.

CHAPTER 3. THE STORY OF *ZA(-)*

3.0. Introductory remarks

The Polish *za(-)*[1] will be analysed below primarily in two roles: as a preposition and a verbal prefix – and also cursorily as an adjectival or adverbial modifier – since all those cases are described as belonging to "the same extended network of senses".[2] Such is the claim put forward in the most comprehensive cognitive analysis of *za(-)* known to me, which was presented by Tabakowska (2003: 158). Tabakowska (to appear) extended that account, answering some objections to her first article raised in an earlier version of this chapter. The most detailed network model of the preposition can be found in Przybylska (2002: 339–387).[3] Dąbrowska discusses the verbal prefix (1996: 482–489), while Bacz focuses on the *za* + GEN uses of the preposition (2004: 441–448).

The choice of *za(-)* is motivated by several factors. First, in a range of its usage it is an equivalent of *over*, thus it may potentially provide cross-linguistic evidence of some kind. Second, as a preposition it enters into valence relations with various nominal cases, thus raising with greater force the question of a semantic "contribution" of particular lexical items or their mutual interaction in the grammatical co-text and referential context (cf. Halliday, Hasan 1976). Finally, as a verbal prefix it played a part in the development of the Polish system of verbal aspect. Since network models are usually synchronic,[4] while their diachronic confirmation is sometimes postulated,[5] *za-* may provide interesting evidence in that respect. Both issues clearly require that cognitive investigations be placed against more traditional linguistic approaches.

---

[1] A more convenient alternative version of spelling would be "ZA" in capitals – the convention used for categories or concepts, cf. Tabakowska (to appear).

[2] It may also function as a "derivative formant", but this role will not be exemplified in the network, cf. Tabakowska (to appear: 1).

[3] She also published an extensive treatment of Polish verbal prefixes (not including *za-*), see Przybylska 2006.

[4] As mentioned (1.2.2.), Tabakowska presented a diachronic application of Langacker's network model for the Polish lexeme *klucz* ("key") and related words (1995: 50–51). The issue of the status of network models in the context of the synchrony/diachrony distinction will be raised in chapter 4.

[5] E.g. Tyler and Evans (2003b) in their search for criteria allowing to identify the prototypical sense. In the present case, Tabakowska states: "A necessary prerequisite [...] of a more comprehensive study would involve the diachronic development of prefixed forms" (2003: 158).

Tabakowska mentions two traditional approaches to prepositional semantics.[6] The co-textual (descriptive) approach which focuses "either on the semantics of nominals within prepositional phrases (PP) or on the features of verbs in adverbal prepositional complements" and the structuralist approach which looks for "an overall system of semantic oppositions" (2003: 156). On the one hand, she points out that the cognitive approach is close to the structuralist polysemic interpretation[7] of particular prepositions; on the other hand, she opts for a co-textual analysis which shows that "semantic differences arise from the interaction of the meaning of the preposition itself with that of the case marking on the PP nominal and the semantics of the verb, whenever the PP functions as an adverbal prepositional object" (pp. 156, 159). In the cognitive framework, the latter approach takes a "conceptualist" form: it is the conceptualizations prompted by relevant features of the verb and the noun in the PP (or LM) which influence the meaning of the preposition. In our specific context, "it is precisely the semantic and pragmatic properties of LM that are decisive of individual senses of *za*" (p. 159).

Tabakowska does not comment on an apparent divergence between the descriptive and the structuralist method: the latter searches (ideally) for a single abstract representation of an item within a system of postulated oppositions, while the former accepts all intuitively distinct senses (e.g. as listed in dictionaries).[8] She notices, though, that when constructing a semantic network of senses for a given preposition, individual components of meaning should be carefully kept apart, and mentions the problem "as to which particular senses should indeed be considered as 'distinct'" (p. 159). This complex of methodological issues must be kept in mind.

3.1. A network model of the preposition *za*

Tabakowska starts her analysis (2003: 159–161) by presenting four uses of *za* listed as separate entries ("homophones") in dictionaries:

---

[6] I will treat Tabakowska's articles (2003, to appear) as the framework for the following presentation, while referring to Przybylska (2002), Bacz (2004), and Dąbrowska (1996) when appropriate.

[7] As repeatedly mentioned, the monosemic interpretation is the standard goal of structuralist models, while some analysts allow that a lexeme may have more senses (see the next note).

[8] Cf. Vandeloise's statement concerning the relationship between these two approaches: "As far as polysemy is concerned, I believe that each lexical category can be analysed at different abstraction levels ranging from example enumeration (therefore polysemic) to a search for common features in circumstances allowing the use of the preposition, ideally leading to a unique rule". He adds that he reached this goal in his analysis of French prepositions "except for *devant* for which I would rather suggest two rules" (1990: 416).

(1) a. *(siedzieć)* *za* *drzewem*
(to sit) behind tree-INST
"to sit behind the tree"
b. *(iść)* *za* *drzewo*
(to go) beyond tree-ACC
"to walk beyond the tree"

(2) *za* *dnia*
by day-GEN
"by daytime, during the day"

(3) *za* *duży* *dom*
too big house

The last case is a lexeme traditionally classified as a modifier (adjectival or adverbial), which expresses the notion of excess. It is convenient to deal with it first because it is conceptually simplest (and does not formally belong to the class under investigation).

In this context, Tabakowska refers to Weinsberg's structuralist study of spatial prepositions.[9] That author defines two semantic oppositions he takes to be valid for all instantiations of the preposition *za*: (1) the location of TR (in his terminology: "the entity that is localized") outside the LM region, and (2) the (spatial) foregrounding of LM with the simultaneous backgrounding of TR (p. 161). Tabakowska notices that the first feature – the TR is situated outside the LM – is too powerful to be useful, since it characterizes several other Polish prepositions.[10] It fits, however, the more general meaning of the compound preposition *poza* (*po* + *za*: "(all) over-and-beyond"),[11] as below:

(4) *(przebywać)* *poza* *domem*
(live / stay) (all) over-and-beyond house-INSTR
"(stay) beyond the house, out of the house"

It also accounts for the meaning of the modifier *za*: "the LM is conceptualized as a certain pragmatic norm (which is left unspecified), which the TR is considered to have metaphorically gone beyond" (p. 161). In our example (3), the house (TR) is described as having crossed the acceptable limit of size (LM).[12]

[9] Weinsberg (1973). Cf. Przybylska's discussion of his account (2002: 78–81).

[10] E.g. *przed*: "in front of", *przy*: "near(by)", *nad*: "above", *pod*: "below", etc. However, the force of Tabakowska's objection is unclear, since it is the conjunction of features which serves as a characterization of a particular item in the structuralist analysis.

[11] For an analysis of *po(-)*, see Tabakowska (1999).

[12] Bacz (2004: 447) points out that "Tabakowska's discussion and her semantic networks of the Polish *za(-)* do not include the use of *za* in emphatic expressions with the particle *co* (what) and a nominal in the nominative case, as in: *Co za dzień!* – NOM (What a day!), *Co za gospodyni* – NOM (What a hostess). It could be speculated that the presence of *za* in these phrases is motivated by their emphatic character. Emphasis implies excess, and the notion of excess, which can be visualized as going over (beyond/behind) a limit, has been well shown [by Tabakowska] to be inherent in the meaning of *za(-)*". In her new discussion, Tabakowska mentions the axiological character of such

Tabakowska postulates that the area where the TR is to be located (its search domain) must be limited to the zone situated behind or beyond the LM. In the examples (1) a., b. this schema (in the default readings) involves spatial orientation relative to the observer: [13] the arrangement between the "proximal" LM and the "distal" TR is established from the vantage point of the speaker. Tabakowska states that this particular instantiation of Weinsberg's second feature is "the simplest conceptually" and exemplifies "the category prototype" (p. 162). The difference between the two variants (*za* + INST; *za* + ACC) is that between the static and the dynamic senses: the former is used to locate a TR behind or beyond a LM, while the latter expresses the movement of a TR to a location behind or beyond a LM (in simpler terms, the former phrase is an answer to the question "Where?", while the latter one to the question "Where to?").

Tabakowska points out that the static/dynamic opposition is exhibited by other Polish prepositions and apparently results mainly from the meaning of the verb (the ACC marker co-occurs with verbs of motion). She draws the following conclusion: "In view of its systematic character, this general opposition is not directly relevant when distinguishing between the individual senses of *za*, and it becomes significant only in the cases of structural gaps" (p. 160). Let us notice, at this stage, that the question whether the static or the dynamic senses of prepositions are cognitively primary looms large in other cognitive analyses.[14]

The remaining PP – *za* + GEN as in (2) – expresses the notion of duration and, according to Tabakowska, "constitutes one of the category-peripheral extensions" of *za* (p. 165). I will return to her interpretation in due course.

The sense of (1) a., b. is one of the two schemas considered prototypical for *za* by Tabakowska. In the other one, the spatial orientation along the proximal-distal axis (Weinsberg's second feature) is conceptualized not in relation to the location of the observer but relative to the LM, which may be "conventionally seen as having an inherent 'front' and an inherent 'back'" (p. 162):

(5) a. *(drzewo)* *za* *Jasiem*
(tree) behind John-INSTR
"the tree behind John"
b. *(przesunąć się)* *za* *Jasia*
(move over) behind John-ACC
"(move over and stand) behind John"

---

uses (to appear: 3). In CL, the axiological aspect was taken into account by e.g. Krzeszowski 1993, 1997.

[13] "Egocentric" orientation in Kreitzer's analysis (2.2.).

[14] E.g. Przybylska (2002: 576–577). Tabakowska's conclusion is shared by Szwedek: "we can only say that prepositions are *open* to static/dynamic, and possibly other interpretations, in the sense that they can appear in such contexts" (2007: 259; emphasis in the text). Szwedek, as noticed, expressly rejects polysemic interpretations of prepositions of the type exemplified in Lakoff (1987): "[such explications] are in reality paraphrases of the context contributing nothing to our understanding of the preposition *over*" (Szwedek 2007: 260).

The LM may also be "conceived as having an ad hoc 'front' and 'back'" (p. 162) due to the sequential scanning of the elements placed along a line, irrespective of the overall orientation of the relevant space":

(5)	c.	*(krok)*	*za*	*krokiem*
		(step)	after	step-INSTR
		"step by step"		

The scanning may be performed over physical or abstract motion: "TR and/or LM are conceptualized as moving along a line marked by their spatial ordering" (p. 162):

(5)	d.	*(iść)*	*za*	*radą*
		(go)	after	advice-INSTR
		"follow advice"		

In metaphorical extensions of the use exemplified in (5) d. "what precedes is conceptualized as the cause of what follows" (p. 163), e.g.:

(5)	e.	*(czuć)*	*ból*	*za*	*najlżejszym*	*poruszeniem*
		(feel)	pain	after	slightest-INSTR	movement-INSTR
		"feel pain at the slightest movement"				

According to Tabakowska' account, the observer-oriented prototypical schema exemplified in (1) a., b. gives rise to two most frequent extensions, as evidenced by dictionary uses. One is defined by Weinsberg as "passability": the LM, conceptualized as a boundary separating TR from the observer, "may be crossed by [the TR] moving ahead over its upper surface" (p. 164):

(6)	a.	*(mieszkać)*	*za*	*granicą*
		(live)	over	border-INSTR
		"live abroad"		
	b.	*(wyjechać)*	*za*	*granicę*
		(go)	over	border-ACC
		"go abroad"		

In the other one – called by Weinsberg "the sense of a curtain" – the LM "blocks the view of an area so that it cannot be seen by the observer" (p. 164):[15]

(7)	a.	*(schować coś)*	*za*	*murem*
		(hide something)	behind	wall-INSTR
		"(hide something) behind the wall"		

[15] This and previous quote from Weinsberg (1973: 57) in Tabakowska's translation.

	b. *(schować się)*	*za*	*mur*
	(hide oneself)	behind	wall-ACC
	"hide behind the wall"		

If "the view" is extended to cover metaphorical "seeing", it may mean lack of access (p. 165):

(7)	c. *tęsknić*	*za*	*dziewczyną*
	pine	after	girl-INSTR
	"miss the girl"		

In this example "some unspecified secondary LM blocks the TR's metaphorical access to the specified primary LM (girl)".

Tabakowska argues that since time is conventionally conceptualized as a linear sequence of units, it is "natural to think of an entity (TR) as an object 'getting over' one or more such units (LM) along the time axis" (165) (a temporal extention of the "passability" sense as in (6)):

(8)	*(Jan przyjdzie)*	*za*	*dwie godziny*
	(John will come)	behind	two hours-ACC
	"John will come in two hours' time"		

John (TR) moves metaphorically over two hours (LM) to finally find himself on the other side of (= behind) it (the ACC rather than the INSTR case is explained by the "dynamic component").

The exclusively temporal *za* + GEN structure, exemplified earlier in (2), is explained in the following way: "The (temporal) search domain for the TR is defined by the (temporal) extension of the LM; the relation is conceptualized as holding only for as long as the TR remains 'hidden behind' the LM. As its subsequent emergence is implied by the underlying conception of the passing time, the 'curtain' is only temporarily drawn – the partiality that might possibly explain the use of the GEN marker on the LM nominal" (p. 165).

In her analysis, Bacz offers an alternative account (2004: 445–446). She points out that in Tabakowska's explanation of (2) the observer must be located outside the line of passing time ("as if he were watching a passing train"), if he is to conceptualize the required arrangement: an unspecified TR event as temporarily hidden behind the temporal LM (a day – a unit of the passing time). Thus, the schema proposed for (2) differs from the one postulated for time expressions with *za* as exemplified by (8), in which the speaker/viewer is located on the time line. In the interpretation put forward by Bacz, "the barrier separating the speaker/observer from the TR event is not the time period evoked by the GEN nominal, but the end limit (the final moment) of that period". In other words, the end limit of a primary

LM1 period (from the vantage point of someone located on the time line) serves as a secondary LM2.

In her rejoinder, Tabakowska admits that both interpretations are equally plausible (or "equally implausible"), while claiming that in most uses of the *za* + GEN construc-tion the "end limit barrier" is not really relevant, e.g. "*Za dnia policjant, wieczorem kulturysta*" ("By day a policeman, by night a body-builder") (to appear: 8–9).

Bacz also questions Tabakowska's hypothetical explanation of the GEN marker. She points out that limited duration ("partiality" underlying some uses of GEN) can be also seen in (8), in which the ACC marker is used. Consequently, she proposes that the *za* + GEN construction can be explained by the case's potential to express reference points, as with Polish "dates in non-prepositional GEN expressions, such as *piątego maja*-GEN (on the fifth of May)" (Bacz 2004: 444, 446).

As suggested by Tabakowska (to appear: 9) – the *za* + GEN construction could be then explained as a metonymy, signifying the full structure "*za początkiem/ przed końcem dnia* ('*za* beginning-INSTR before end-INSTR day-GEN')".

It should be noticed that the amount of attention given to *za* + GEN construction partly results from the fact that the case is *prima facie* awkward for linguists of cognitive persuasion, since it is exemplified only by temporal uses, which are treated as extensions of more basic spatial uses within the cognitivist paradigm. That specific problem is mentioned by Przybylska, who treats *za* + GEN as "a separate category, unrelated by any semantic links to contemporary categories set up by *za* + ACC and *za* + INSTR" (2002: 386). The problem resurfaces in general cognitive treatments of prepositions because some of them do not seem to have spatial senses, cf. Tyler, Evans (2003a).

The final category-peripheral extension mentioned by Tabakowska also involves a reference point interpretation:

(9) *(kupić)* *dom* *za* *milion*
(buy) house for million-INSTR
"to buy the house for a million"

(10) *(wziąć)* *dziewczynę* *za* *rękę*
(take) girl by hand-INSTR
"take the girl by the hand"

In both cases the primary LM1 in the PP serves as a reference point, which allows access to an entity (the secondary LM2 – the direct object): in (9) the object of purchase is available only after the obstacle has been removed (i.e. the money paid); in (10) "the girl becomes accessible via her body part" (2003: 166).

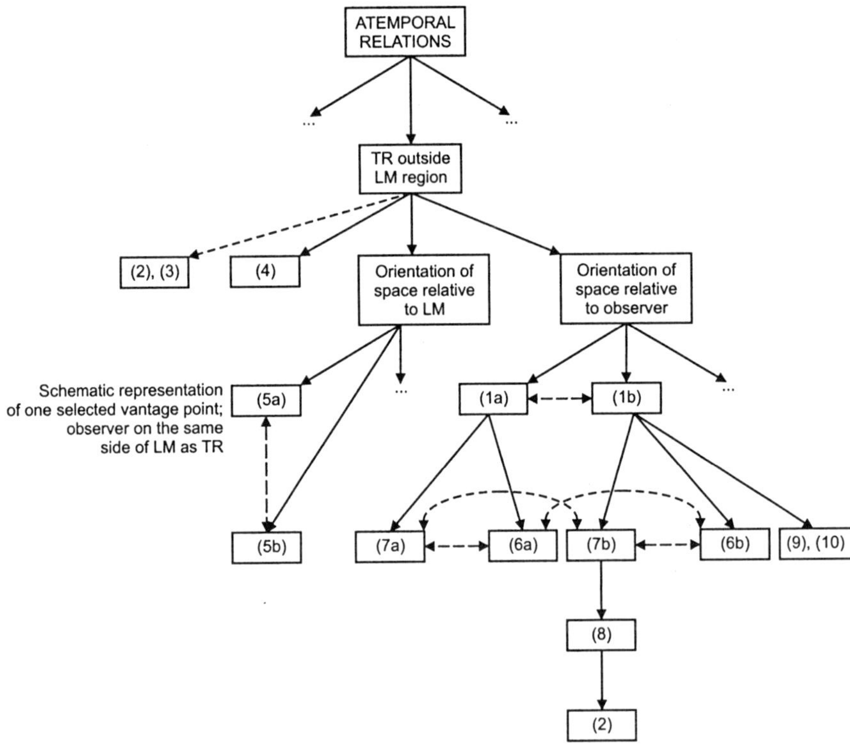

Semantic network of the preposition *za*

Figure 15: Based on Tabakowska (2003: 167)

3.2. A network model of the verbal prefix *za-*

Tabakowska assumes that "general principles of verbal prefixation may be revealed through a systematic comparison of the semantics of the category of verbal prefixes with that of prepositions, following the assumption that verbal prefixes originally developed from adnominal elements, which then later turned into lexemes defined as prepositions" (2003: 157). More specifically, her aim is to substantiate the hypothesis that individual senses of the *za-* perfectives[16] constitute a network of interrelated nodes, which find their counterparts in category nodes described for *za* (p. 166). Thus, this attempt seems based on a diachronic hypothesis

[16] Tabakowska limits her model to perfectivizing uses of *za-*, as does Dąbrowska (1996).

that the evolution of verbal prefixes and prepositions from adnominal elements preserves some basic senses of *za* and / or runs in parallel.

Tabakowska points out that an analysis of prefixes adds a new level of complexity: "teasing apart the individual components of the overall meaning of [...] clauses proves difficult because of the complexity of interactions between the meaning of the prefix, verbal semantics and the semantic features of LM" (p. 166).

In Tabakowska's account the category *za-* develops around the "dynamic" prototypes exemplified in (1) b. and – when the space is oriented relative to LM – (5) b., as in the following example:

(11) *zaskoczyć* *kogoś*
za-jump somebody-ACC
"surprise somebody"

Originally, she explains, the phrase meant "to steal from behind (the LM)", thus implying that the LM has a "back" and a "front".

In most cases of the prototypical use the vantage point of the observer is adopted and transitive verbs are used. In the example below the primary LM1 (direct object) is made to "go round" an unspecified secondary LM2 (a potential oblique object):

(12) *zagiąć* *drut*
za-bend wire-ACC
"bend the wire (over something)"

The sense described earlier as "passability" (exemplified in (6) a., b.) is taken to be one of the main two extensions from the prototype. The notion of a passable boundary extends to "an abstract boundary separating non-being from being" which is supposed to explain the occurrence of *za-* with intransitive inchoative verbs:

(13) a. *zapłonąć*, *zakwitnąć*, *zaśpiewać*, etc.
za-burn (to begin burning) *za*-blossom (to begin blossoming) *za*-sing (to begin singing)

In this context, Tabakowska comments on the seeming paradox (remarked on by other authors) that the inchoative sense co-occurs with the sense of completion. She suggests that "the paradox can be resolved if the analysis includes the semantic contribution from primary or secondary LM", as in:

(13) b. *zajechać* *(aż)* *do wsi*
za-go (Intens.PART) to village
"go into the village"

The sense of completion is to be interpreted as the crossing by the TR of the boundary between "non-village" and "village" (LM conceptualized as a bounded region).

The sense of "going beyond a boundary" is extended to cover the sense of "exceeding a norm" (cf. (3) above), which is to be evident in both intransitive and transitive verbs with *za*-:

(13) c. *zaspać*
za-sleep
"oversleep, sleep too long"

d. *zaczytać* *książkę*
za-read book-ACC
"wear the book down by reading"

The other main extension from the prototype involves the sense of "curtain" (cf. (7) a., b.) which is relevant when the TR (the agent) is conceptualized as placing a barrier (a LM2 which may be left unspecified) so that it blocks access to an entity (the primary LM1 – direct object):

(14) a. *zastawić* *stół* *(szafą)*
za-stand table-ACC (wardrobe-INSTR)
"to block access to the table with a wardrobe"

The "curtain" may be literal, as above, or metaphorical, as below:

(14) b. *zabronić* *palenia*
za-forbid smoking-GEN
"to forbid smoking"

Tabakowska follows Dąbrowska's suggestion (1996: 483) that "blocking access" implies "protection", which further implies "securing for future use", as in:

(14) c. *zapisać*, *zachować*, *zapamiętać*, etc.
za-write, *za*-store, *za*-remember
"write down" "store away" "store in memory"

The notion of "curtain" is taken to be compatible with that of "covering": something (the specified LM1) is covered with something else (a secondary LM2 which need not be specified), so that it cannot be seen (accessed, etc.):

(14) d. *zamalować* *ścianę* *(farbą)*
za-paint wall-ACC paint-INSTR
"to cover the wall with paint"

If the primary LM1 is conceived as a container, then the notion of "covering" implies filling in:

(14) e. *zapełnić* *koszyk* *jabłkami*
za-fill basket-ACC apples-INSTR
"to fill the basket with apples"

By a further extension, what cannot be seen any more, does not exist any longer; hence, it makes room for something else (a use reminiscent of (9) above, "where the thing metaphorically covered with something else makes room for it and ultimately becomes replaced with it"):

(15) *zastąpić* *masło* *margaryną*
za-step butter-ACC margarine-INSTR
"to replace butter with margarine"

The final extension (considered analogous to (8)) evokes the image of an entity moving metaphorically over a LM (possibly unspecified) and "finding itself on the other side of it". Since many linguists take this schema to be definitional for the "pure perfective", the semantic contribution of the prefix may be seen as being limited to its grammatical meaning, i.e. "a natural end of a process". With transitive verbs, the "natural end" is imposed by the contours of the LM:

(16) a. *zaśpiewać* *piosenkę*
za-sing song-ACC
"sing (up) a song"

With intransitive verbs, the temporal limit of the action results from a limited duration of a particular action type:

(16) b. *zaszczekać*, *zażartować*, *zasalutować*, etc.
za-bark *za*-joke *za*-salute
"to give a bark" "to crack a joke" "to give a salute"

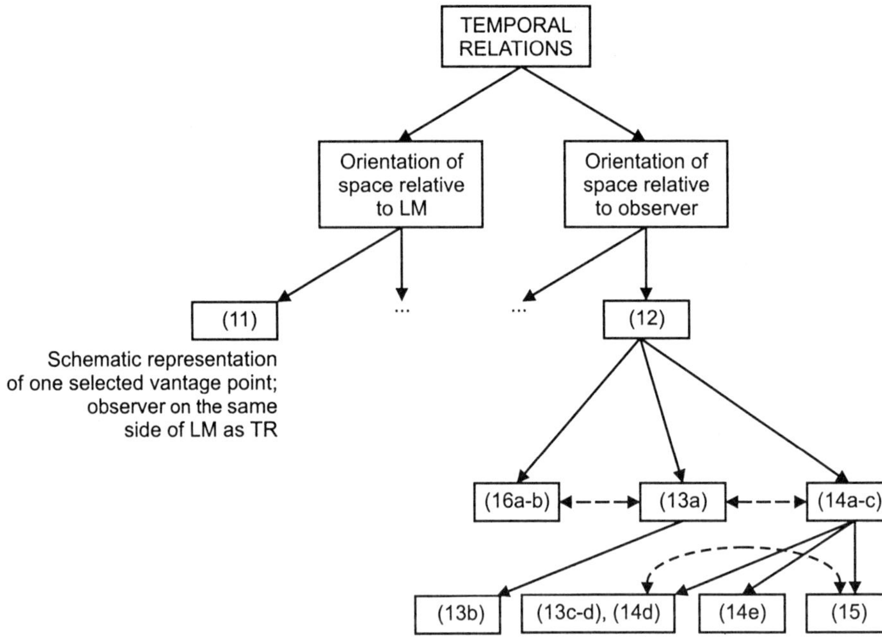

Semantic network of the verbal prefix *za-*

Figure 16: Based on Tabakowska (2003: 172)

3.3. Some diachronic observations on the verbal prefix *za-*

As noticed in the previous section, Tabakowska assumes that "general principles of verbal prefixation may be revealed through a systematic comparison of the semantics of [verbal prefixes and prepositions], following the assumption that verbal prefixes developed from adnominal elements, which have later turned into lexemes defined as prepositions" (2003: 157). More specifically, her aim is to substantiate the claim that "the distinct senses of the *za-* perfectives [...] constitute a network of interrelated category nodes which correlate with the category nodes described for the preposition *za*" (p. 166)". I concluded that, *prima facie*, her attempt is based on "a diachronic hypothesis that the evolution of verbal prefixes and prepositions from adnominal elements preserves some basic senses of *za* and/or runs in parallel". In this section, I will show that this interpretation is not tenable.[17] I will compare Tabakowska's readings with some of the historical meanings of verbs with the prefix *za-* from *Słownik Staropolski* ("The dictionary of Old Polish") as chosen and interpreted by Janowska, Pastuchowa (2005).[18] The discussion below will mostly take the form of a running commentary to Tabakowska's presentation as reported in 3.2., while I will group her examples according to my proposed readings.

In the example (11) above – "*zaskoczyć kogoś*" – an unmentioned TR is supposed "to steal from behind (of LM)" (in the literal sense of physical movement). The Old Polish verb carries a more general sense, which is also standard in modern use: "to cause (in most cases) an undesirable situation by a premature or unexpected action" (Janowska, Pastuchowa 2005: 190). If we look for the hypothetically original physical sense pointed out by Tabakowska, we should probably place it in the context of other verbs of movement with *za-*, in which the prefix had the meaning "to move <u>towards</u> someone (possibly with bad intentions), block someone's passage", e.g. "*Zastąpić*: 1. To <u>stand</u> (on a public road) blocking someone's passage; metaphorically: 2. To ambush" (p. 191; my emphasis). Consequently, the original meaning of "*zaskoczyć*" would be that of a TR unexpectedly blocking a LM's passage from <u>any</u> direction rather than moving from the LM's behind.[19]

The verb "*zajechać*", which appears in (13) b.: "*zajechać (aż) do wsi*", is perhaps another example of this type. Tabakowska explains its meaning in reference to the notion of passability ("to go so far that one crosses the boundary" of the village). In Old Polish, its first meaning was "to ride on a public road towards someone to block the passage" (Janowska, Pastuchowa 2005: 184). In this respect, it was similar to e.g. "*zajść*" ("*za*-go"), "*zabiec*" ("*za*-run") (p. 175). The original meaning of this verbal group ("to move in some fashion as to stand in the way of someone") is evident in present day uses of "*zajechać*", e.g.

(17) a.	*zajechać*	*komuś*	*drogę*
	za-drive	someone-DAT	way-ACC
	"to cut someone off on the road"		

[17] In her rejoinder, Tabakowska says that "the analyst's adherence to a diachronic interpretation might in fact be an imputation on the part of the critic". She seems to vacillate, however, between searching for a legitimate place for diachronic data in network models and relying exclusively on synchronic criteria (e.g. statistical distribution). Importantly, the status of "general principles of human cognition" is uncertain in that dichotomy. Since they are taken to influence the directionality of development – Sweetser (1990) remains the most important statement of this position – Tabakowska mentions "cognitive chronology" (to appear: 3). The issue of the cognitive "diachrony within synchrony" will be taken up in chapter 4.

[18] Additionally, Janowska (2007a, b).

[19] In her rejoinder, Tabakowska points out that the physical sense of movement "might have disappeared before the historical stage in the development of Polish to which [Janowska and Pastuchowa] refer" (to appear: 8). She does not take up, though, the issue of the directionality of movement, which remains in question. Thus, we face a clear-cut divergence between a "hypothetical reconstruction [...] based – intuitively – on the attested regularity in category development" (Tabakowska, to appear: 8) and a hypothetical reconstruction based on an interpretation of the actual historical material.

The example above refers to dangerous overtaking: a TR moves ahead of a LM2 to block its passage (LM1).[20] One can feel that the original meaning still reverberates in (17) b. (in which there is no obvious boundary to cross), especially when placed against (17) c.:

(17) b. *zajechać* *pod* *dom*
za-drive under house-ACC
"to stop at the house" (in a vehicle)
c. *podjechać* *pod* *dom*
pod-drive under house-ACC
"to stop by the house" (in a vehicle)

"*Zajechać*" suggests a more ostentatious arrival – possibly related to the original notion of blocking the passage. If this interpretation of (17) b. is correct, then the idea of crossing a boundary evident in (13) b. results from the meaning of the preposition "*do*" ("(in)to").

The sense of verbs of movement presented above probably gave rise to a more general sense: "to forbid something by some action", e.g. "*zapierać*" ("*za*-push") – "to forbid entry". This meaning is present in *verba dicendi*, e.g. "*zapowiedzieć*" ("*za*-tell"), "*zakazać*" ("*za*-order"). It is possible that also "*zabronić*" (cf. (14) b. above) followed this pattern (cf. p. 176 – the authors say, though, that one cannot state with certainty whether "*zabronić*" followed or initiated that pattern). Let us notice that the notion of placing a barrier (the sense of "curtain") is present already in the verb "*bronić*" ("to forbid" in Old Polish). Consequently, the prefix *za-* is pleonastic: it puts an additional emphasis on the meaning of the stem.[21]

If this chain of development is correct, we get a different picture of meaning extension from the network model presented above. The starting point is not an abstract spatial schema "a TR behind/beyond a LM" but a concrete (and dynamic) notion of "a TR moving in order to block a LM". The "blocking movement" is extended to a "blocking action" and to a metaphorical blocking – "forbidding

[20] Tabakowska points out that (13) b. contains an intransitive use, while (17) a. a transitive one, thus they may well illustrate two different senses. Subsequently, she invokes the example "*zajechać komuś drogę*" in a methodological context, i.e. that of identifying "distinct senses", to show that the phrase does not yet have such a status, since it may designate not only "dangerous overtaking", but also blocking passage from the front; to appear: 5. She does not comment in that place on the possible continuity of meaning between "blocking" as in (17) a. and "ostentatious arrival" as in (17) b. In another part of her article she does oppose "*zajechać*" to "*podjechać*" but in two different co-texts; as a result, a comparison of the "contribution" of both prefixes is difficult, cf. to appear: 7. Apart from historical considerations (analogy to common constructions which designate "blocking passage"), my case rests on the following argument: since transitive *zajechać* (*drogę*) may take place from any direction, then the actual spatial configuration is secondary to the fact that passage is blocked; since "blocking passage" is a/the central sense of *za(-)*, it may well appear in both transitive and intransitive uses. If my interpretation is correct, example (13) b. does not represent "passability" but a "curtain" of sorts.

[21] One can assume that pleonastic uses are "iconic": "more form" of a given kind implies "more content" conventionally linked with it. Cf. e.g. Tabakowska, Ljungberg 2007; Pawelec 2007c.

by some action". In other words, the cognitive vision of conceptual development from the concrete (interpreted as "spatial relations") to the abstract (interpreted as "relations in nonspatial domains") is reinterpreted in view of the historical data presented here as going from concrete human activity (i.e. involving physical movement) to more "abstract" action (i.e. involving more complex social relations).

The meaning of passability, even if contestable in (13) b., is clearly present in (13) c.: "*zaspać*" ("to oversleep"). In Old Polish, however, it was much more limited than today and can be attributed (without certainty) to only a few examples (pp. 176–177), e.g.

(18)	*zabić*	*za*	*żywe*
	za-hit	behind	live-ACC

"to drive the nail till it reaches flesh"

Thus, my interpretation above is apparently corroborated by statistical data: the "curtain" sense readings are much more likely in Old Polish material. In present-day Polish the statistical distribution is clearly different, since the "passability" sense is no less central than the "curtain" sense (one source of the likelihood of *hysteron proteron* interpretations based on contemporary intuitions).

The situation is different with the inchoative sense exemplified in (13) a., since the prefix *za-* "imparted the inchoative meaning [to the verb] throughout the history of the Polish language" (p. 177) and Old Polish material offers numerous incontestable examples, e.g. "*zajeść*" ("*za*-eat") – "to have only a bite". The extended interpretation of "passability" proposed in such cases by Tabakowska sounds plausible but rather too abstract: "The notion of a passable borderline easily extends to stand for an abstract boundary separating non-being from being: the passage from the former to the latter is instantiated as a passage from non-action to action" (2003: 168). Janowska points out that in Old Polish the inchoative sense was expressed usually by *za-* and *roz-*, while most prefixes could serve this function (2007a: 57). If so, then the sense of passing "from non-action to action" was common to all such cases, while the choice of a particular prefix had to be motivated in some other fashion. One can assume that each prefix expressed the inchoative sense in its own way and the abstract meaning is the result of bleaching (thus, Tabakowska's interpretation captures the outcome of a more complex process or provides its general schema).

The extended senses of "curtain" – "covering" as in (14) d. and "filling in" as in (14) e. – are richly represented in Old Polish material, e.g. "*zakopać*" ("*za*-dig"), "*zalać*" ("*za*-pour"), "*zasypać*" ("*za*-strew") (Janowska, Pastuchowa 2005: 177). One may wonder, however, if the chain of extension from "blocking access" to "protection" and "securing for future use" (first proposed by Dąbrowska), as in (14) c, is the best conjecture.[22] One of the examples provided by Tabakowska certainly had a different meaning: "*zapamiętać*" ("*za*-remember") meant originally "to lose from memory, to forget". In Old Polish, there were two verbs with the prefix *za-* with the same meaning (and a similar derivation): "*zapamiętać*" and "*zapominać*" ("*za*-remember"). In both cases, the negative sense suggests the notion of passability ("going too far", "crossing the limits of memory"). In a historical process, due to "a division of linguistic labour", "*zapamiętać*" reversed its meaning, perhaps following the pattern of "*zatrzymać*" ("*za*-keep") – "not allow to escape".

To conclude, what one can see in the historical material is not an instantiation and extension of abstract schemas but rather a propagation of particular co-textual patterns, involving both meaning and form. This can be better shown in reference to the example (15), which Tabakowska explains in the following way: "By a further extension, what cannot be seen any more, does not exist any longer; hence, it makes room for something else (a use reminiscent of (9) above, 'where the thing metaphorically covered with something else makes room for it and ultimately becomes replaced with it')" (2003: 171).

It is likely that in Old Polish the verb *zastępować* ("*za*-step") evolved from the verb (the stem) with PP: "*stąpić za kogoś*" ("to step *za* somebody-ACC"; "to replace, to represent somebody"). Such a pattern of development (as shown by Janowska) is clearly discernible in a group of verbs (carrying the meaning "attack") with PP in which the preposition "*na*" ("on") occurs, e.g. "*iść na coś*" ("go *na* something-Acc"), "*jechać na coś*" ("ride *na* something-Acc"), "*paść na coś*" ("fall *na* something-Acc"). Such verbs appeared also with a variety of prefixes, e.g. "*nad-*" ("over-"): "*nadjechać*" ("*nad*-ride"); "*przy-*" ("at-"): "*przyjść*" ("*przy*-go"); "*w-*" ("in-"): "*wpaść*" ("*w*-fall"). Janowska argues that when the stems lost the semantic value of "attack" (due to specialization), the prefix "*na-*" was the natural choice to take over that meaning, since "*na*" appeared in the PP in most cases. As a result, other prefixes in such contexts fell into disuse, while "*na-*" in the meaning of "attack" began to appear in new derivations, e.g. "*nalatywać*" – "*na*-fly"; "*naskoczyć*" – "*na*-jump"; "*nalegać*" – "*na*-lie". With the passage of time, the new forms became lexicalized and "*na-*" in this sense is no longer productive (Janowska 2007a: 108–109).

Janowska and Pastuchowa (2005: 178–179) believe that a group of Old Polish verbs with the prefix "*za-*" and the meaning "to replace somebody in some activity" had a similar origin, e.g. "*zajść*" ("*za*-go" – "to replace the defendant in court"), "*zasadzić*" ("*za*-place", originally "sit" – "to place a successor in one's post"). Thus, the use of the prefix "*za-*" in "*zastępować*" would indeed be closely linked with the use of the preposition "*za*" (as Tabakowska assumes in her analy-

[22] It could be hypothesized that this cluster of senses is motivated by associating aspectual *za-* with the sense of culturally salient verb-stems denoting "preservation for further use", e.g. "*zakisić*" ("*za*-pickle").

sis), but because of a primarily syntactic rather than conceptual affinity.[23] If the chain of developments sketched above is correct, then this link can be placed in the following hypothetical sequence:

1. a number of verbs of motion followed the pattern "Verb + '*za*' + ACC" to express what one could classify as a specific variant of the general meaning "to replace somebody in some activity";
2. the verbs acquired various prefixes (presumably, to mark the aspect or express a particular manner of "replacement" signified by the stem), while still being followed by PP with "*za*";
3. when the stems started to lose the semantic value "to replace (in some way)", the prefix "*za-*" (as analogous to "*za*" in PP) was attributed the meaning of "replacement" and other prefixes fell into disuse;
4. the prefix "*za-*" in this sense was possibly used in new derivations which became lexicalized, while it is no longer productive in this function.

We can now try to point out some differences between the cognitive and the diachronic explanation of the prefix "*za-*" in the sense of "replacement". The former treats this semantic value as an extension of a basic dynamic sense of the preposition, relying on the following reasoning:

1. The sense of curtain: a TR covers LM1 with LM2;
2. Hence, LM1 disappears from view;
3. As a result, LM2 replaces (stands for) LM1.

Thus, a fairly abstract schema of a physical action is reinterpreted as a much more abstract schema of any kind of action. If this scenario is taken to describe actual developments, a thinking subject – when faced with a new situation – apparently must make such mental leaps in order to express a more comprehensive view with the formal tools at hand. The latter analysis paints a different picture. At the point of departure we have several specific social activities, which require/allow someone to take the position of someone else.[24] In such contexts, articulated by "Verb + *za* + ACC", the clause expresses the required meaning, while in other contexts, it may mean something else, cf. "idzie za niego" ("(she) go *za* he-ACC" – "she marries him"). Thus, the sense is extracted from the situation. Only when some formal pattern develops, a mental generalization co-occurs. If there are any

[23] To be sure, one cannot really disentangle "conceptual" and "syntactic" motivations. CL shows in great detail the conceptual aspect of syntax as an "end-state" (i.e. when some forms are intuitively stable in some conceptual roles). Here, I inspect the genetic aspect of syntax: when it actually takes on some conceptual roles.

[24] Contrary to Tabakowska's suggestion (personal communication), I think that such forms articulated first a replacement of humans, and only subsequently of objects. Pragmatically, the notion of replacement seems to presuppose a system of social roles, which one can take up. To be sure, objects may also "play" different roles but this usage seems to be based on an analogy with human roles.

mental leaps in this scenario (which is doubtful), they follow verbal forms as used in some context.

The final extension considered by Tabakowska covers the purely aspectual use of the prefix.[25] In this role, "*za-*" evokes the image of a TR "finding itself on the other side of (a LM)", and thus expresses "a natural end of a process" (2003: 171).

The historical material shows that the development of the aspectual (perfectivizing) function of prefixes is a complex and still unravelled story (Janowska, Pastuchowa 2005: 235–239; Janowska 2007a: 64–68). For our purposes it is enough to point out that at first the perfectivizing function of prefixes was not obligatory: in some cases verbs with prefixes had clearly imperfect meaning (one can also find such cases in contemporary Polish). Usually, prefixes did perfectivize but it is often impossible to say if in a given case they were purely aspectual or carried some meaning of their own.[26] Still, the prefix "*z-*", which was and still is by far the most productive in this function, was predominantly used perfectively. There is no detectable general pattern why a particular prefix took on this role with a particular stem. The only exception is a group of verbs in which prefixes were added pleonastically: the prefix carried a similar meaning to the stem (e.g. "*zjednoczyć*", "*ogrodzić*"). Consequently, it is not surprising that in numerous cases a given stem was perfectivized by several different prefixes. The abundance of (apparently) synonymous verbal forms contributed to the reduction of verbal polysemy, claims Janowska (2007a: 67–68).

One can assume, then, that it was – to some extent – a matter of chance which one of several prefixes retained the purely perfectivizing role (while the remaining derivatives were used to express some specific meanings). In such cases, there was no need for the perfectivizing prefix to be semantically motivated: it was the one which was not employed for other purposes.

In the last section of her article Tabakowska points out some advantages of cognitive modelling. She claims that "an understanding of [extension mechanisms] enables us to analyse a good numer of old (or lexicalized) derivatives whose earlier transparency has now been obscured through the process of grammaticalization" (2003: 174). For instance, the imperfective *bić* ("beat") and the perfective *zabić* ("*za*-beat: to kill"), which are now classified as separate lexemes, are clearly related (the construction with "*za-*" being motivated either by the notion of "complete covering" or "going beyond").

The historical material, however, does not confirm the assumption that the construction of *zabić* was "transparent", i.e. motivated by one of the senses ascribed to "*za-*".[27] In Old Polish, the sense "to kill" was expressed by several dif-

[25] "Purely aspectual" does not mean "semantically empty" but "highly schematic".

[26] "We cannot say with any certainty if in Old Polish, for instance, the spatial meaning of '*na-*' ('on') in the derivate '*napisać*' (*na*-write) was still felt or not" (Janowska, Pastuchowa 2005: 238).

[27] Cf. Janowska, Pastuchowa (2005: 178); Janowska (2007a: 110–111); Janowska (2007b: 118–119).

ferent verbs, e.g. *bić* ("beat"), *gładzić* ("stroke"), *gubić* ("lose"), *tłuc* ("whack"), *siec* ("cut"). In such cases the basic sense referred to a type of activity, which was (metonymically) extended to cover its result (such a combination of senses is still present in the case of *bić*: 1. "beat"; 2. "kill" pigs). These verbs took on various prefixes which apparently played only the aspectual function, e.g. *wybić*, *ubić*, *zbić*, *dobić*, *zabić*; *pogubić*, *zgubić*, *zagubić* etc. In the process of semantic specialization (reduction of polysemy) two prefixes acquired the anihilative sense: "*za-*" – e.g. *zadusić* ("*za*-strangle"), *zadźgać* ("*za*-poke"), *zastrzelić* ("*za*-shoot") and "*u-*" – e.g. *ubić* ("*u*-beat"), *udusić* ("*u*-strangle"), *usiec* ("*u*-cut") – of which the former is still active. The case of *zabić* is thus analogous to *zastąpić*: the prefix took over the meaning conveyed by the stems and became productive in this sense.

Finally, Tabakowska's reconstruction is based on contemporary data. As a result, it leaves out those semantic values which have gone extinct. In this context, the ablative sense[28] of "*za-*" is of particular importance, since it is opposed to the adlative sense taken to be prototypical by Tabakowska.[29] Thus, for instance, *zabiec* ("*za*-run") could mean both to "run away" and to "run towards someone". The historical material contains several examples of this kind. What is more, some other prefixes also expressed both ablative and adlative senses ("*po-*" and to some extent "*od-*" and "*z-*").[30]

It is possible, then, that historically the adlative schema for "*za-*" was <u>not</u> prototypical. One can speculate that since the presence of widely divergent (or even opposed) senses conveyed by the same form was felt to be awkward and the ablative constructions fell into disuse (in a historically opaque process), the adlative sense gained the upper hand and developed in various directions; cf. Janowska, Pastuchowa (2005: 180).

3.4. A discussion

As Tabakowska wryly notes, *za* as a preposition is representative of "a category which has been most frequently, and most excessively, discussed within the framework of cognitive linguistics" (Tabakowska 2003: 156). The analysis of *over* by Brugman/Lakoff can be seen as the best known example and the paradigm of

---

[28] TR moving away from LM (as opposed to approaching it in the adlative sense).

[29] In her rejoinder, Tabakowska questions the view expressed by Janowska and Pastuchowa (2005: 174) that ablative uses of *za-* are unknown today. She claims that when one takes into account the vantage point and perspective, the phrase *zabrać (coś komuś)* ("*za*-take something somebody-DAT") still displays that sense (to appear: 7–8). One may raise the question, however, whether that sense is contributed by the verb or the prefix.

[30] Janowska, Pastuchowa (2005: 174, note 84).

a popular genre, which is only fragmentarily documented in the present study.[31] The popularity may be attributed to the belief that prepositions – because of their basically "spatial" or "localist" semantics – provide an excellent testing ground for the cognitive postulate that language should be explained in reference to perception, and specifically to "our intuitive understanding of space" (Tabakowska 2003: 158). What is more, "because of their enormous semantic potential and wide syntactic distribution, these items make an ideal lexical class for postulating and testing theories of lexical representation and processing" (Rice 1996: 136).

I have left out of this presentation psychological issues of language processing, as they are secondary to my topic (even though they provide important empirical evidence concerning claims about "cognitive reality" of network models).[32] It is safe to say, however, that evidence of this kind (coming from psychological testing and computer modelling of spatial lexical categories) is, at best, inconclusive. Thus – as was my assumption throughout – the adequacy of such models should be judged primarily on the basis of linguistic criteria.

One should mention, however, two practical applications of network analyses which are quite widely discussed and may prove to be of significance in an overall assessment of this venture, namely in lexicography and foreign language teaching.[33] As for the former, network format is employed by an Internet graphical dictionary (visuwords.com) and seems to be a potentially attractive alternative to standard dictionary entries, since it helps to visualize at a glance the overall structure of a lexeme and subsequently to explore internal relations step by step.[34] The pedagogical potential is perhaps best represented by a "textbook for guided self-learning" of phrasal verbs (Rudzka-Ostyn 2003), which gives an "insight into the networks of metaphorical meanings of each particle" (back-cover).

The pedagogical aspects are closely connected with the cross-linguistic perspective. I have already noted that in a range of its usage *za* may be an equivalent of *over*. For instance:

(19) a. *Sam drove over the mountain.*
b. *Sam pojechał za górę.*
Sam *po*-drove *za* mountain-ACC.

(20) a. *The bird flew over the mountain.*
b. *Ptak przeleciał nad górą.*
Bird *prze*-flew *nad* mountain-INSTR.

---

[31] See e.g. Taylor (1988); Pasich-Piasecka (1993); Kochańska (1996); Kalisz, Kubiński (1998); Cuyckens (1999); Tabakowska (1999).

[32] See e.g. Sandra, Rice (1995); Zlatev (1998, 2003).

[33] In lexicography, see e.g. Geeraerts (1990, 2007); in pedagogy, see e.g. Kurtyka (2001); Queller (2001); Tyler, Evans (2004c).

[34] Geeraerts describes a dictionary format based on the notion of alternate structuration of entries inspired by prototype semantics (1990).

(21) a. *Sam lives* *over* *the mountain.*
b. *Sam mieszka* *za* *górą.*
Sam lives *za* mountain-INSTR.

(22) a. *Sam lives* *behind* *the wall.*
b. *Sam mieszka* *za* *ścianą.*
Sam lives *za* wall-INSTR.

Even a cursory analysis reveals that Lakoff's image-schematic model of *over* could be profitably cross-checked against Polish usage. The comparison is not quite straightforward, however (as we have already seen in Tabakowska's analysis), because of the Polish verbal aspect in Past Tense – (19) b., (20) b. – and the case system. Still, as is shown by the difference in translation between (19) b. and (20) b., the vertical LM in the latter sentence is preceded by *nad* ("above") and not *za* (since the path is profiled, rather than its end-point). The difference between (21) a. and (22) a. is not reflected in the translation: *za* does not require the possibility of traversal (the reason *over* is not used), but merely the blocking of vision.[35]

Consequently, what Lakoff announces as a universalistic hypothesis about conceptual processes is in fact an ethnocentric description in a network format of some constraints on the use of a lexeme. This (foregone) conclusion suggests a reversal of perspective: rather than view a set of uses of a lexeme as symptomatic of independent "imagistic" processes (an approach based on the possibility of a continuous "imagistic" extension[36]), one should treat linguistic material (in a given language) as consonant with some pragmatic (i.e., at some level, also perceptual) motivations. Only cross-linguistic comparisons, and further empirical work, may justify universalistic claims.

As concerns Tabakowska's analysis, it differs markedly from the models of *over* presented above not only because it is offered in the Langackerian format, but primarily because it is not programmatic: it is an attempt to represent a conceptual unity of the whole range of linguistic material, as attested by dictionaries.[37] Moreover, this attempt goes back to and confirms the results of an older structuralist analysis by Weinsberg, who pointed out two central senses of *za*, glossed as "curtain" and "passability".[38] The cognitive innovation is to actually

[35] To be sure, most if not all such relations can be construed differently when other prepositions are chosen in translation (as they well may be, since the meaning of original sentences can be interpreted in alternate ways).

[36] The limitations of which and, ultimately, futility have been best demonstrated by Dewell's valiant attempt (2.1.).

[37] The case of *(all) over* – involving corpus research or at least actual usage – is a natural empirical continuation of this approach. As its partial character strongly suggests, it involves the risk of an exponential growth of "nodes".

[38] This historical continuity suggests that Vandeloise's defence of an ideally unitary approach – against Lakoff's "full specification" approach (when one disregards the actual context of that debate) – receives further validation.

link various uses of *za* to those central senses, as their instantiations, and to show that they also apply in other morphosyntactic categories, i.e. the verbal prefix and adverbial modifier.[39] Thus, Tabakowska's analysis incontestably offers greater insight into the structure of ZA and better shows a conceptual unity of this category than a structuralist account based on features. Additionally, this approach allows to represent with unprecedented clarity differences in conventional construal of contrastive cases (when *za(-)* is opposed to other prepositions or verbal prefixes). What is perhaps most impressive is the author's persistence to reveal a relatedness between the central senses and *prima facie* unconnected specimens of *za*, e.g. "*wziąć za rękę*" ("to take by the hand") or "*kupić za milion*" ("to buy for a million").

As I have tried to suggest,[40] following some glimpses into the diachronic material concerning *za-*, Tabakowska's interpretations are sometimes congruent – at a more schematic level – with historical developments, while in other cases they provide competing accounts. How is one to decide whether a "hypothetical reconstruction [...] based – intuitively – on the attested regularity in category development" (Tabakowska, to appear: 8) is more or rather less convincing than a hypothetical reconstruction based on fragmentary, largely contextless[41] historical material? As in all such (hermeneutical, interpretative) cases, there is only one (not terribly helpful) answer: we should follow what helps us make better sense of our material. As soon as one notices that one's data are always implicated in one's theoretical assumptions,[42] the problem shifts onto the level of the strengths and limitations of one's framework, when confronted with alternative approaches.

As already noted, the hermeneutical perspective does not offer any help at this "objective" level. It is not a method, thus (ideally) it does not take sides in debates between methodologies. The evidence presented in 3.3. does not serve to prove that a diachronic approach is more powerful than a cognitive one in general (if such a comparison could make sense), or as a way to illuminate synchronically intuited relatedness of senses (our topic). Both approaches reveal something,[43] while diachronic observations are useful in the task of establishing the proper limits of CL (my declared task).

Throughout this study, I have been trying to show that CL, despite invocations to conceptual processes and structures moulding language, is essentially agenetic:

---

[39] However, the centrality of both senses does not seem sufficiently transparent in the diagrams of both semantic networks.

[40] "Suggest" is the word: my aim was to show that from the diachronic perspective one can offer alternative explanations. To generalize, all evidence is sketchy and intuitive at some point. In hermeneutical (interpretative) ventures one cannot really prove the validity of one's approach; one can only try to develop the best case.

[41] Often, also co-text is missing: many specimens are gleaned from judicial records in Latin, containing single Polish expressions.

[42] As evidenced – at the simplest level – by the choice of one's data. More importantly, such choices are always guided by what one finds relevant: by the criteria of analysis presupposed in one's approach.

[43] And both have their limitations. I will repeat here yet again that limitations should not be viewed as negative: one can see something only because one adopts a specific vantage point.

it does not take into account the genesis, development and actual use of language. Thus, its approach is static.[44] As a result, CL can encompass – on a single plane of analysis – conceptual "motivations" underlying linguistic units and their relatedness. This is *prima facie* paradoxical, since "motivations" belong to genetic (dynamic, processual, diachronic) accounts, while "relatedness" is captured *post factum* (from a static, synchronic perspective). The paradox dissolves once we see that the relatedness in question reflects not actual motivations at work (historical, situated, contextual), but "cognitive" ones, based on presumed mental powers and conceptual structures of a "generic" human being.

This interpretation is not meant to belittle CL's achievements. Quite the opposite: within this basically asocial and agenetic paradigm, researchers have been able to show at a much greater detail than any alternative approach that "grammar is meaning", that there are no "empty" forms, that everything in language is interrelated and motivated (i.e. not arbitrary). My point concerns the status of "motivations" invoked in CL as *a posteriori*: as *hysteron proteron* explanations, reversing (or by-passing) the natural historical order of development. From this point of view, Tabakowska's insightful analysis captures the results of a contingent and perhaps largely impenetrable historical process, in which forces of different kinds are involved (as suggested in the diachronic section). The strength of this kind of analysis is a transparent presentation of the whole range of attested material as a possible instantiation and extension of two central senses. This is a real achievement: as an interpretation,[45] it captures in the fullest form available present-day intuitions concerning the relatedness of attested senses. The limitation is linked to the strength: a transparent presentation is possible because the messy background is largely lost from view. Specifically, the "motivations" invoked in the analysis – the possibility to imagine plausible scenarios linking apparently unrelated senses – rely on contemporary intuitions (they are to make sense to today's language users).

Can one go any further within these limits? One does not know beforehand, but a possible avenue is suggested by the case of *(all) over* (it also seems implied by Tabakowska's remarks concerning the "contribution" of various elements in a sentence). Since words form "idiomatic" (i.e. compositionally unpredictable) phrases, one could try to represent in the network not only intuitions concerning single lexemes (as disentangled from larger wholes), but also intuitions concerning higher-level units, exemplifying "recursive" processes. In this way, the interplay between form and meaning could be (to some extent) captured in the model.[46]

---

[44] An insightful formulation of this charge may be found in: McNeill 2005. I will briefly present his approach in 5.1.4.

[45] All semantic analyses are "interpretations". Network models "interpret" linguistic data (dictionary senses or corpus specimens) as related – at some level of granularity, on the basis of some criteria – to central senses (distinguished in one way or another). All such interpretations may be contested and replaced by a "more transparent" account.

[46] A step in this direction is made by Kardela (1993) in his attempt to represent collocations within the framework of Langacker's grammar.

CHAPTER 4. COGNITIVE "DIACHRONY WITHIN SYNCHRONY"?[1]

4.0. Introductory remarks

In the Introduction, I posed a basic question concerning network models: what phenomena (at what level of reality) are they models of? Do they represent psychological reality (putative semantic structure stored in the mind, which underlies an actualization in the context), historical reality (a diachronic social process of meaning extension), or logical reality (relatedness of ideas)? Or some combination of these? The first two options presuppose a developmental account of the relatedness in question.[2] This assumption was famously rejected by Saussure in his attempt to establish linguistics as a discipline on solid foundations. I have already hinted at his view, when "the unity of the sign" was mentioned (1.0.). It is time to see in greater detail what his position involves and to what extent it shapes contemporary approaches to language.

4.1. Saussure: synchrony vs. diachrony

What are the grounds for a linguist to focus on language as a state? First, since a succession of historical developments "does not exist insofar as the speaker is concerned",[3] a linguist "can enter the mind of speakers only by completely suppressing the past" (Saussure 1959: 81). Saussure clearly assumes that the "reality" of language is in the present state of the mind of its speakers and that it must be

[1] The phrase was used as the title of a collection of papers on cognitive historical linguistics: Kellermann, Morrissey (1992).

[2] One may postulate that the structure is there all along. This Platonic "solution" (ridiculed by Plato in *Parmenides*) underlies e.g. Chomsky's "nativism". In that way Chomsky limited the developmental problem to the issue of "activation" of particular cognitive structures, but he did not even try to work out what that issue involved, as manifested by his lack of interest in Piaget's arguments during the famous Royaumont debate, cf. Piatelli-Palmarini (1995); Rosner (1995, 1996). Piaget saw clearly the danger of divorcing structures from their developmental background (1972: 175). Alternatively, one can assume that the structure is purely formal (as in logic) or conventional and arbitrary (Saussure), thus backgrounding the issue of genesis.

[3] This statement is reminiscent of Bréal's view quoted in 0.4.

captured without reference to past states. He also argues that the opposition between the synchronic and the diachronic view "is absolute and allows no compromise", since individual changes become operative only when integrated into the system (p. 83). Second, the system of language is based on the synchronic notion of "value", as illustrated by a comparison with chess:

> Take a knight, for instance. By itself is it an element in the game? Certainly not, for by its material make-up – outside [...] the game – it means nothing to the player; it becomes a real, concrete element only when endowed with value and wedded to it. Suppose that the piece happens to be destroyed or lost during a game. Can it be replaced by an equivalent piece? Certainly. Not only another knight but even a figure shorn of any resemblance to a knight can be declared identical provided the same value is attributed to it. We see then that in semiological systems like language, where elements hold each other in equilibrium in accordance with fixed rules, the notion of identity blends with that of value and *vice versa*. (Saussure 1959: 110)

This analogy shows that a material entity (a knight in chess or a phonic sequence in language) gets a specific meaning only in a field of relations with other elements: there are no atomic meanings. Once it acquires its identity, the material shape is secondary – it can be replaced by something else – as long as the system remains operative.[4] Thus, value and identity of elements are inextricably linked.

In this way we get to the notion of "the unity of the sign". Let me quote once again the passage concerning the delimitation of units, this time in a more extensive version:

> Without language, thought is a vague, unchartered nebula. There are no pre-existing ideas, and nothing is distinct before the appearance of language [...]. The characteristic role of language with respect to thought is not to create a material phonic means for expressing ideas but to serve as a link between thought and sound, under conditions that of necessity bring about the reciprocal delimitations of units. Thought, chaotic by nature, has to become ordered in the process of its decomposition. Neither are thoughts given material form nor are sounds transformed into mental entities; the somewhat mysterious fact is rather that "thought-sound" implies division, and that language works out its units while taking shape between two shapeless masses. (Saussure 1959: 112)

Thus, language is "the domain of articulations" – each unit is an "*articulus*", a member, a subdivision in a larger sequence (pp. 112–113). From this point of view, Saussure argues that the nature of material used for symbolizing is secondary (whether phonic or gestural, as in sign languages), since "what is natural to mankind is not oral speech, but the faculty of constructing a language, i.e. a system of distinct signs corresponding to distinct ideas" (p. 10).

---

[4] Presumably (as minimal requirements in the chess context), the new material entity must differ in form from other elements and the changes cannot be too numerous. If we apply this perspective to language, we can see that formal oppositions – crucial in a genetic context – lose some of their importance in further history, once they are integrated in the system. Thus, few formal prompts may go a long way in communication (as is evident in various real-life situations).

Let us take stock of the argument so far. The claim that historical vagaries of a language (abundantly exemplified by the author) do not exist for the speakers may mean this: language is operative, because each unit has a place in the system; previous states are different systems; mixing them up would cause chaos. Saussure's idea makes sense in the context of his chess analogy. If we change a single rule, however slight, we may get a very different game. Consider "off-side" in soccer: abolishing this rule could entirely change the strategy and the dynamics of a football game. More importantly though (and this is the main point), one can play a game only if all players abide by the same rules.

However, Saussure's analogy between language and a game breaks down at two points. The more obvious one concerns the nature of both types of activity: games are competitive, while language is based on cooperation. One cannot compete without clear rules, while one can cooperate with very little agreement, or even without any agreement, as long as a given kind of behaviour is perceived by both sides as advantageous (Harris 1988: 119–120).[5] The more far-reaching objection concerns the nature of rules: they are always embedded in the wider unarticulated background of the activity in question (Wittgenstein 2000: 20, cf. C. Taylor 1995: 165–180). From this fundamentally diachronic perspective, the system of rules is secondary to practice, of which it is a partial articulation. In the (clearly extreme) case of competitive games, one may think that rules are completely arbitrary. But they must have evolved to satisfy the underlying need "to have a good game" of sorts and this very need – in particular circumstances – underlies all attempts at a reform of rules.[6]

Thus, the chess analogy ultimately leaks (as is true of all analogies). It conveys the general idea that language is a system, in which everything hangs together.[7] And that its users have a sense of what the system allows. This sense – speakers' intuitions about correctness and incorrectness of particular "moves" – is the actual object[8] of the discipline as defended by Saussure: "*Synchronic linguistics* will be concerned with the logical and psychological relations that bind together coexisting terms and form a system in the collective mind of speakers". And as opposed to: "*Diachronic linguistics* [which] will study relations that bind together suc-

[5] The notion of "cooperation without rules" is developed in game theory ("the prisoner's dilemma" etc., cf. e.g. Becker 1986) and it is the founding insight of the idea of a "spontaneous order" (e.g. Hayek 1978). For this approach in diachronic linguistics, see Keller (1994).

[6] As e.g, in volleyball: if one can win points only after one's serve, while virtually all attacks are successful, then a game is stalled: sets may last forever. In itself, this makes the game attractive for viewers but in an era of TV transmissions it causes problems (many games change their rules to become "good games for television").

[7] Which is clearly overstated, when one bears in mind the extent of "redundancy" in language (e.g. most words do not really die out – they survive in odd phrases or may be revived for some reason). Thus, a biological "organismic" analogy, suggesting continuous presence in some form of no longer functional structures, may serve as an antidote to the limitations of the "chess" analogy.

[8] As tirelessly pointed out by Itkonen. Intersubjective intuitions (concerning what is perceived as socially acceptable) must be distinguished from individual introspections (which concern one's inner psychological states), see. e.g. Itkonen (1981); cf. Sandra, Rice (1995).

cessive terms not perceived by the collective mind but substituted for each other without forming a system" (1959: 99–100; emphasis in the original).

Saussure's argument serves well to make tangible some crucial points about language. First, it is a social normative activity: one must normally follow "the way things are done". In other words, language is fundamentally about successful social coordination (in relation to some challenges, tasks etc., which must be taken into account at some point). Second, the material side of language reflects systematic (ideal, conceptual) divisions, because it originally took part in their constitution.[9] Thus, conceptual or articulated thought is not prior to language. Before language, thought, or some mental state, is a situational whole ("nebula"). Only when "decomposed" thanks to systematic "delimitations", it gets articulated. It acquires a (relatively) independent identity. At this stage one may talk of "pairings" between material and conceptual chunks (as in "nomenclaturism"), while primarily language is a structured system of differences.

In this way we get to the most difficult point: "in language there are only differences *without positive terms*" (p. 120; emphasis in the original). The "pairings" specify "significations", i.e. concepts which may refer to something in the world. However, this most obvious function of linguistic units ("descriptive", cf. Bühler 1965) is founded on their more basic differentiation. They may get to mean something only when integrated with existing units as opposed to them in some respects within a system of such oppositions: "In language, as in any semiological system, whatever distinguishes one sign from others constitutes it" (p. 121). Consequently, Saussure defined the "linguistic point of view" as an attempt to capture the system of oppositions which underlies but is not directly influenced by all uses and vagaries of a language. As pointed out by a commentator: "[the whole array of Saussurean concepts] has a common aim: to separate the linguistic point of view from any direct relationship with the 'real' world" (Normand 2004: 104).

Is such a program viable? It clearly divorces language as a synchronic system of oppositions which can be accessed only through intuitions of its users from the life (and history) of the community, which engages in linguistic activity. Thus, it proposes to treat the system of differences as separate from the activity of differentiation, which underlies it. In other words, Saussure treats articulation formally as "delimitation" of units, which have a material and conceptual side; a linguist is not to be interested how concepts are related to reality, but only how they are related among themselves. For Saussure, linguistic articulation is a formal structuration[10] within the linguistic system rather than an articulation of ideas, which, in turn, articulate reality. However, formal "value" of linguistic "units" may be captured only because we understand ideas expressed in some referential situations

---

[9] Nevertheless, detecting the actual "units" of language is a difficult task, since they are subject to temporal contingencies, may be invisible, appear at various levels of complexity etc.

[10] To repeat, "formal" refers both to sounds and concepts. Saussurean vision of language is "formalist" because it divorces the linguistic system from the task of expressing reality (cf. 5.2.).

(not in some abstract realm of ideas[11]), and we can understand ideas because we live in a reality that makes some sense to us. Thus, in order to delimit the proper "object" of linguistics, Saussure divorces language from the forces which underlie its generation and the real-life background without which linguistic "value" cannot be assessed.[12]

Whatever one may think of Saussure's agenda, it is an openly linguistic one and it is realized to some extent by all protagonists in my account, also generativists and cognitivists. The former take up the idea of an abstract system of oppositions: a differential system of features is used to define particular lexical units.[13] The latter, since they aim at "psychological reality" of some kind, push formal oppositions (and clear-cut boundaries) into the background, but they clearly show the necessary interconnectedness of concepts. *Pace* Taylor, CL is not obviously more Saussurean than TG, while Langacker's theory is Saussurean not because it is "symbolic",[14] but because he shows that the generativist view of abstract atomic features as underlying linguistic concepts is simplistic: a concept – as a profile against a base – is part of a system, in which everything is connected.[15] Before we try to assess what kind of reality is captured in network models, let us inspect an attempt to overcome Saussure's strictures on diachrony within synchrony.

4.2. Logical diachrony: the case of "length, width, and potential passing"

The analysis in question was undertaken by Vandeloise (1988) to show that an attribution of the complementary pair of terms *length* and *width* to particular entities cannot be reduced to an abstract "objective" formula concerning their shape, since it crucially involves pragmatic factors ("potential passing"). Thus, it is primarily a conceptual study – a search for an adequate description of the conditions of use of

---

[11] There is no denying that our ideas may get very abstract. But they are generated and understood only because they refer to something, some referential domain (e.g. complex numbers or the hierarchy of angels).

[12] For instance, the functional opposition between *bus* and *coach* expresses a differentiation in actual practice (service within/between towns). When the practice is reshaped, the linguistic value of that pair may become "intuitively" inadequate.

[13] This is also true for Chomsky: syntactic units form a comparable differential system.

[14] For Saussure the "pairings" are secondary: a result of a systematic differentiation of two spheres; "symbolic" in CL is nomenclaturism pure and simple.

[15] There in no sense in "mentalistic" CL – the sense motivating Saussure's conception – that the "conceptual system" is genetically anchored in the "system of linguistic units". Quite the reverse, it is assumed that concepts are available prior to linguistic expression. Cf. 5.l. for evidence to the contrary.

both terms – rather than a lexical one (aiming to represent a distribution of words in use, in some range of their senses).

Vandeloise begins with the pragmatically simplest situation: entities conceived as truly linear have no width ascribed to them, while their length is evaluated along their actual shape (e.g. a piece of string). The latter is also true for paths (e.g. roads), which, however, "have a width, evaluated along a direction perpendicular to their length" (p. 406).[16] Let us call this formulation "Rule 1" (R1). At the next level of complexity, mobile entities (e.g. moving cars) have their length evaluated parallel to their direction of movement, and their width – perpendicular to it (R2). At the third level, that of immobile multidimensional entities, especially relatively symmetrical ones (e.g. a house or a table), the assessment may depend on the vantage point of an observer.[17] Their length/width is evaluated along a parallel/perpendicular direction to the general orientation of an observer (R3).[18] The final rule is independent of the former ones. It is used in geometry because of its objective character: it is independent of movement of the object and of the speaker's position. According to this "metric" definition (R4), the "length/width of an entity is its greatest/smallest non-vertical extent" (p. 408).[19]

Vandeloise mentions two problems ("constraints") with an application of the rules (pp. 409–410). First, some types of objects cannot have length. For instance, vertical objects whose height is the greatest dimension, e.g. doors or narrow windows. In such cases, what would be normally called *length* is more naturally labelled *height*. Second, as concerns width, it can be always assessed provided the entity in question has a significant extension along this dimension (this constraint holds true for all dimensions).

Subsequently, Vandeloise points out an apparent paradox: why is it that speakers believe that "length" and "width" are "monosemic", while one needs four rules to describe their application? In order to solve the paradox, he invokes the notion of "pragmatic bridges", i.e. some facts concerning human functioning in the world which go "beyond simple formal similarity or direct proximity" (pp. 410–411). For instance, even though the statement "X is *behind* Y" may be used in reference to two different situations (1. X cannot be seen because it is behind an obstacle; 2. X cannot be seen because it is behind the observer), both uses are linked by X's inaccessibility to perception (pragmatic bridge). The transition from R1 to R2 is explained by the fact that roads allow movement: the length of a road and a car moving along it is assessed along the

[16] I will not quote the author's precise definitions in full.

[17] Normally, a house is attributed intrinsic dimensions: *width* relates to its front, while *depth* to its internal extent (p. 426, note 6).

[18] General orientation is also a complex notion (p. 427, note 7). Vandeloise will invoke it in his discussion of a pragmatic transition from R2 to R3 (p. 417).

[19] Since real life is more complex than geometry, several dimensions may compete for an evaluation of actual situations according to R4. In such cases, a choice must be made whether to follow R2 or R3 (p. 409).

same direction. The transition from R2 to R4 is explained by aerodynamic (i.e. objective) properties of moving entities: a moving object (evaluated according to R2) offers less resistance, if its objectively longer dimension (R4) is parallel to movement.

The bridge between R2 and R3 (i.e. between an evaluation of mobile objects on the one hand and immobile objects from an observer's vantage point on the other) is the most complex one (pp. 412–418). Vandeloise begins his account by an attempt to explain why R1 applies to linear entities and paths and not to multidimensional objects. He points out that the latter can be scanned along several directions, while the linear objects only along their actual shape. Similarly, a road is naturally assessed along the direction of movement it affords. Nevertheless, Vandeloise rejects as inadequate the most straightforward pragmatic bridge between roads and linear objects: "while roads are paths imposed on mules and donkeys, linear objects impose paths on the line of vision (pp. 413–414). He notices that in functional contexts, e.g. when sewing, the thread may be assigned different lengths, because for some tasks a simple thread is used, while for others – a double one. Consequently, "there is not a univocal relation between a multipurpose object and its length but rather there is a univocal relation between its length and its different functions" (pp. 414–415). This rule holds not only for actual but also for potential functions, when one assesses an entity which is not actually in use (or whose function is unknown).

In Vandeloise's account, "function" of one kind or another is conceived as some actual, regular or (more generally) potential movement (i.e. a trajectory of a given kind). Thus, the bridge between R1 and R2 (the analogy between scanning and actual movement) can be expressed in a more generally pragmatic way than before: in both cases potential movement (as functionally required) is involved.[20] In other words, potential passing as a criterion of evaluation of length /width subsumes both the perceptual and concrete functional explanations. This account has prepared the ground for the bridge from R2 to R3. Moving objects like cars actually pass the observer. When we deal with immobile objects like houses, their length is assessed relative to the observer's potential movement (beside them rather than through them, as with paths; that is why "general orientation" is important). In this way R3 is shown to subsume R1 and R2 (all are covered by the criterion of potential passing). Vandeloise concludes: "Synchronically, this complex network of relationships [i.e. rules and pragmatic bridges] is fairly representative of what speakers feel length/width have in common" (p. 418, emphasis mine).

---

[20] This explanation allows to conceive of "width" not merely as "perpendicular" to movement, but as "proportional to the easiness of the passing" (p. 415). To repeat, both "scanning" (R1) and "movement along a path" (R2) remain valid explanations but they are generalized – taken to represent pragmatically motivated potential movement.

Vandeloise speculates that, from the diachronic perspective, there must have been the "first access to the semantic pole of a word, [involving] a simple portion of this network". That portion the author dubs "historical impulsion" of a lexical category. He points out that in the case of many words "impulsions lose their prominence", being then "of little interest for a general theory of the lexicon". However, in other cases some constraints on their present usage may be treated as "traces of their evolution". Specifically, there is a node in the network (labelled "logical impulsion") "such that synchronic evidence shows that a development from this node to the other nodes of the network is more likely than other developments". On the methodological level, "developmental approach must explain, as far as possible, some seemingly arbitrary aspects of the distribution of spatial terms [the author's field of investigation] and most notably their selection restrictions" (p. 418).

I will not recount here Vandeloise's speculative ideas concerning the logical order of development (or "logical diachrony") of his "complex category" (pp. 418–424). Of interest in the present context are his remarks concerning the discrepancy between logical diachrony – which aims to describe "the *systematic* evolution of the distribution of words" (p. 425, emphasis in the original) – and actual diachrony (or history). He invokes the homonymous French adjective *large* ("wide"), which also means "generous" (lat. *latus* and *largus*, respectively), and points out that if one overlooks etymological information as well as some synchronic clues formally differentiating both senses, one could relate them to the same (logical) impulsion "and... succeed!".[21] Thus, logical diachrony merely predicts that the extension from *large* as "wide" to *large* as "generous" is likely and could actually occur in other languages. To make things more complex, however (as Vandeloise adds), in French the perceived relation of both senses may have influenced a phonological fusion of forms.

Vandeloise's paper is not only a *tour de force* in its own right but also a most illuminating contribution to the task at hand, i.e. to an assessment of the status of network models. Actually, Vandeloise also takes his exposition to be an argument for a specific interpretation of "complex networks", but, I believe, for the wrong reasons.[22] Crucially, his own analysis of "length/width" does not aim at a representation of a lexical category (as it happens, a monocentric one), i.e. of a particular distribution of lexical items in use. "Length/width" in his analysis are related not to a range of actual senses of both items[23] but to the conditions of

[21] As he comically confabulates: "a wide table bears more food than a narrow one; generous men in paintings always have *un large sourire* and open their arms *largement* on a huge belly" (pp. 424–425). As already noticed, "folk etymologies" testify to the fact that confabulation is an effective force in history.

[22] Probably because he accepted at face value Langacker's rhetoric about a possibility of a unitary schema for a complex category and interpreted such a schema as a definition of a kind. As we shall see below, Vandeloise's notion of "complex category" is different from Langacker's.

[23] This range is quite homogeneous (LENGTH/WIDTH are "monocentric" rather than "polycentric" categories). Still, one can find phrases – e.g. "to speak at length": (1) for a long time; (2) after

use of both concepts in various situations. He is concerned to find out why people conceptualize a set of different entities in some of their dimensions as either LONG or WIDE. His aim is to connect various referential applications of both concepts (and not just words; it does not matter whether LENGTH is expressed by *length*, *long*, *lengthen*, *lengthwise*[24]). To repeat his conclusion: "this complex network of relationships [of rules and pragmatic bridges between them] is fairly representative of what speakers feel length/width have in common" (p. 418). In short, Vandeloise asks[25] what LENGTH/WIDTH really mean when invoked in discourse.

One cannot ask, however, what KEY (a complex lexical category) really means, as it comprises entities of different kind. The question to be asked is about the relatedness of those entities. In order to begin answering it, one must have some idea how to identify the entities in question (the "level of granularity" issue) and which entity/ies should have priority in the order of explanation (the issue of "central" or "prototypical" sense/s).

As for the latter issue, Vandeloise offers "logical impulsion", i.e. "such [a node] that synchronic evidence shows that a development from this node to the other nodes of the network is more likely than other developments". It is important to realize what kind of venture Vandeloise has in mind. Its point of departure is the presence of "some vestiges [...] of [a category's] evolution", i.e. things which seem problematic or arbitrary in present usage ("seemingly arbitrary aspects of the distribution of spatial terms and most notably their selection restrictions"). The "logical" approach seeks to explain synchronic arbitrariness by suggesting a putative developmental sequence, and the "logical impulsion" is proposed as its most likely starting point (p. 418).

As we have seen, "logical" is equivalent to "systematic" and offered as an alternative to "historical" explanations. Vandeloise suggests to proceeds from R1. This starting point is openly opposed to R4 which is normally offered as a general definition of the category, because R4 is divorced from reality. For instance, it does not take into account the fact that linear objects are normally not attributed "width"; or that the length[26] of a solid object – a modern building's facade – would be assessed as a straight line, even if the facade in question consisted of many

---

a pause – in which other senses may appear. In short, Vandeloise aims to show pragmatic "unity" of a homogeneous conceptual category, while the point of network models is to represent conceptual "relatedness" of a widely heterogeneous (polycentric) lexical category.

[24] I do not know whether the verb and the adverb could actually appear in all relevant contexts and whether they follow all rules mentioned. I aim to show that Vandeloise offers a conceptual analysis of a unique kind. In linguistics, the aim is normally to relate some actual distribution to a given unit. In the more usual semasiological approach, one relates a lexical unit to a range of its senses; in the onomasiological approach, one relates a conceptual unit to a range of its lexical articulations.

[25] An analogy to this venture is provided by Socrates asking about the "definition" of justice, or its "true meaning". For Vandeloise (as different from Socrates), the "true meaning" of a concept is what pragmatically unites its different referential applications.

[26] Or width, if its dimensions are taken to be intrinsic (e.g. a house).

indented facets;[27] or that a particularly wide vehicle could actually have a shorter length than width. From the vantage point of R4 such facts would be arbitrary.[28]

Thus, when we have a complex of referential uses (the distribution of LENGTH/ WIDTH), one of them – the case of linear objects and paths – seems best suited for the role of "logical impulsion", because a visual following of a linear curved object (scanning) or an actual following of a path seems the only sensible way to assess the length of such entities. To be sure, R4 also "imposes" itself in the case of unsymmetrical rectangles, but it cannot be applied to clearly related objects, e.g. triangles – where "width" is opposed to "height" – nor probably to most polygons. R4 may be discounted as the candidate for "logical impulsion" because it is static and best suited to a narrow range of abstract shapes; it obviously cannot deal with actual usage (as we have seen in the previous paragraph). It is the dynamic character of R1 – manifested also in the case of static objects – which makes it perhaps the best candidate for that role.

What actually concerns us, however, is the applicability of "logical impulsion" to the problems underlying network modelling. Vandeloise introduces this notion to account developmentally (via pragmatic bridges) for what may seem arbitrary in various referential uses from the objective perspective. Language users do not see problems of that kind: they apply both words intuitively as "monosemic" (p. 410). Vandeloise notices a paradox, however, since an application to different entities is based on four different rules. In order to solve it, he proposes a "complex network" of pragmatic bridges as "fairly representative of what speakers feel length/width have in common" (p. 418).

This is a curious argument. In standard terms, *length/width* are monosemic. They are not like "a key in the lock vs. the key to the future". Outside the domain of prototype semantics, problems with referential application (e.g. *die*, *lie*, *bachelor*, *mother* etc.) are not normally taken to influence the monosemic status of a word, as most forcefully stated by Wierzbicka (1990b) (cf. Antas 2000: 157ff.). One may not know whether the pope can be called a "bachelor" (and hedge this use with "technically") but this does not make *bachelor* a polysemic word – merely a referentially vague one.[29] Generally speaking, people do not need a defini-

[27] This is a real problem when measuring the circumference of a bounded region. Depending on the scale of measurement (centimetres, metres, kilometres), "straight lines" underlying the measurement of length look very different. As a result, the circumference in centimetres of e.g. Poland would be several times greater than when measured in kilometres (even if in "objective" calculations they are equivalent).

[28] Generally speaking, since "objectivist" treatments often reflect a rationalistic, "emancipatory" attitude, one could imagine that the common way of assessing length in the case of the wide vehicle would be branded as reactionary or that a reform of "unenlightened" usage in such cases would be proposed. One could easily cite real life examples from other domains. On the subject of "measures and life", see Kula (2004).

[29] This is true of all words, as demonstrated by Labov's experiments with "cups" and "vases" (cf. 0.2.).

tion[30] to use a word. They feel a word has one meaning as long as they cannot meaningfully oppose it to another one, e.g. *bachelor* as "a young unmated male of some species". That is why a "complex network" of pragmatic bridges does not solve any actual paradox. A monosemic word (i.e. a concept) like *length* is a pragmatic perspective on reality which provides a set of related answers, depending on the circumstances of application (cf. McLure 1990). In history, this concept does not change its identity (i.e. it is not transformed into another one) but rather develops in a set of oppositions to (most obviously) "width", but also "height", "breadth" and other notions, against which it helps to articulate unprecedented circumstances.

From this (hermeneutical) point of view, "logical impulsion" cannot be primary, as it does not involve a meaningful opposition (there is no opposition between "length" and "width" in the case of linear objects and in the case of paths the role of "width" is purely nominal[31]). Consequently, Vandeloise's assumption that "logical impulsion" could be the same as "historical impulsion",[32] if it were not for historical contingencies, is wrong. The same goes for his claim that in language acquisition the child first gets access to "a simple portion of this network" (p. 418).[33] What is the role of "logical impulsion", then? It is a brilliant methodological device: it serves as the most primitive pragmatic perspective on a concept's application, which allows extension to pragmatically less clear-cut situations.[34] As such, it helps to reveal the pragmatic unity of a concept's range of application. This result is real and precious, as it shows that people probe reality applying and, in consequence, developing concepts at their disposal (it does not show how it happens, though).

When one turns from monosemic words (i.e. concepts, monocentric categories) to polysemic words (complex, polycentric categories) that pragmatic description of conceptual development is deeply suggestive and provides a crucial point of departure. A monosemic word is a set of pragmatically consistent "takes" on different states of affairs, revealing reality as something or such-and-such. Following Vandeloise's insights, one may speculate that the opposition "long/wide" (assuming that nouns are derivative) relates primarily to features open to access or allowing access on the one hand, and limiting access or hidden on the other. One

30 As shown by Vandeloise's attempt, providing a definition covering all referential uses of a concept is obviously a vertiginous task. Since language users apply concepts on-line in unprecedented circumstances, it seems safe to assume they do not rely on rules and pragmatic bridges (a "psychologist's" or a "linguist's" fallacy).

31 It gets some pragmatic sense in Vandeloise's reinterpretation as "proportional to the easiness of the passing" (p. 415).

32 "In a systematically evolving language, logical impulsions should parallel historical impulsions" (p. 418).

33 In the present case, the child should learn to use the concept LENGTH for linear objects. As I have tried to show after Vygotsky (1.2.2.), the child – to understand the concept in some vague sense – would first have to reduce the initial overgeneralization in the syncretic stage.

34 R1 is clearly more pragmatically primitive than R4, as it relies only on scanning as opposed to physical measurements. I did not recount Vandeloise's argument concerning R2 and R3 as too complex.

can imagine walking in a tunnel with extended arms as an approximation of this stance: one fathoms "length" while moving forward, and "width" is what blocks or limits the passage (it is "proportional to easiness of the passage" in Vandeloise's formulation). When this stance towards reality is applied to linear objects – e.g. threads – the proper opposition to "length" (the dimension which allows to do the work at hand) is "thickness" (*grubość* in Polish), which offers resistance. When one observes a moving object, its "length" is normally its side, and "width" its front, reflecting one's point of access to such objects. With stationary objects, the access is by walking past them. The metric definition is a de-humanized or purely "objective" version of this stance: the accessive dimension is reduced to greater size. Since the observer is removed from the picture, we can see now why so much in actual usage seems arbitrary, when viewed in metric terms.

A polysemic word is a set of formally and genetically related "takes" on a variety of situations, which are not felt to be pragmatically unified. A given stance is (partially) applied to a pragmatically different domain to take hold of something felt to be related. When *key* ("in the lock") is used to bring to mind "something providing access", the referential situation importantly changes. One no longer invokes a tool adapted to a particular social role, but – first – another tool used in a different role, which is felt to be functionally related (i.e. inviting a similar stance). A cluster of this kind invites a generalized use: "whatever helps one get there"; and as adjective: "the feature without which the job cannot be done". Such general ideas may be "reached" from various directions, while words carrying such abstract senses retain their history of usage.[35] To sum up, the use of a word to articulate a different situation is crucial in the process of transforming its identity: when meaningfully placed in an unusual context, it contracts relationships with words which have articulated the new domain so far. At the same time, the impulse to generalize, abstract, express analogies and connections at a higher conceptual level is evident in all domains.[36] The Saussurean system of syntagmatic and paradigmatic relations develops *pari passu* with conceptual domestication of reality.

Does Vandeloise's account escape Sausserean strictures against "diachrony within synchrony"? Is the ban on mixing synchrony and diachrony justified? As for the latter question, I have mentioned two reasons for the ban. First, history does not exist for contemporary speakers, while the linguist's task is to capture their intuitions. Second, the intuitions concern the system of linguistic units, in which everything hangs together (linguistic "value" of units). There is no question that one may have wrong intuitions about past uses.[37] However, this is <u>not</u> primarily

---

[35] As investigated by the "onomasiological" approach: how a given concept (conceptual domain) is articulated lexically. It is worth pointing out that a particular historical path of development may always turn out to be relevant in use: at the general level, several words may mean "the same" thing (e.g. adj. *key*, *crucial*, *critical*, *cardinal*, *decisive*, *pivotal*), while in more specific applications their etymology may play a role.

[36] As noticed by Geeraerts in his appraisal of the definitional test of polysemy (0.4.).

[37] This is clearly a crucial problem in diachronic linguistics. Not just because available material is fragmentary and without significant context, but primarily because a modern reader applies

because the present linguistic "system" is different. As we have seen, linguistic "value" is a methodological artefact. The meaning of words is not independent of reality, but rather intertwined with it in complex ways. Consequently, our intuitive access to the past (or possible future) is difficult mainly because present reality (co-founded by language) does not provide adequate clues to capture distant intuitions. Queen Victoria, perhaps, could hardly understand the present meaning of "cool!", since an explanation would require a possibly impenetrable account of modern culture. The same goes for our attempts to understand e.g. the meaning of "nationality" in Middle Ages, or "freedom" in Ancient Greece. However, there is nothing in principle that we could not understand, if we were sufficiently open and inquisitive. As long as the human condition is common to human beings (in the Gadamerian sense: as long as we participate in the historically constituted horizon of humanity), all of its manifestations (however intricate, abstruse or revolting) are – in principle – accessible.

Saussure's ban is methodologically correct: if we want to describe the contemporary system of units, we must rely on present intuitions (there is no other access possible). However, as shown by Vandeloise, intuitions concerning the meaning of concepts (monosemic words) reflect basic pragmatic stances – impulsions. They are consistent ways of "questioning" reality, which historically "reveal" it as such-and-such, thanks to a number of oppositions (one can know what LENGTH is only in relation to WIDTH, BREADTH, HEIGTH, THICKNESS etc.). Thus, one can show that some present state reflects or encompasses a pragmatically complex set of diachronic answers. If my critique is right, Vandeloise does not offer a true historical account (nor even a chance for one), but he shows in a masterly way that the conceptual present is a "summation" of pragmatic history.[38]

4.3. The status of network models

We can see now that my original set of questions concerning the status of network models was not really adequate – it served as a first approximation, without

---

modern intuitions in interpretation. One obviously needs an extensive contact not just with the texts but also with the reality of a previous epoch to develop a feel for it (to fuse one's "horizon" with a historical one, in Gadamerian terms).

[38] This view (at one level) seems to be consonant with Łozowski's proposal to replace the opposition "synchrony" – "diachrony" (based on the idea that language is "a linear succession of discrete languages states") with the notion of cognitive "panchrony", conceived as "multi-directional progression of non-discrete categorization processes in language" (Łozowski 1999: 33–34). However, Łozowski's focus on categorization processes in language is not further elaborated and "panchrony" is a misnomer, since the notion normally refers to "relations that are everywhere and forever verifiable" (Saussure 1959: 95).

insight into the complexity of the situation.[39] Initially, one could think that different kinds of reality are linked to different temporal dimensions: a psychological present (synchrony), a social history (diachrony), the logical eternity (panchrony). I also suggested a need for a developmental account, since sense relationships must have been constituted in history. After Saussure's demonstration that the synchronic and diachronic approach have different "objects" (systematic "intuitions" of language users as opposed to speculations concerning potential links between separate systems) and after Vandeloise's analysis of a pragmatic constitution of a logical category or a set of concepts, we can try to represent the situation in a more adequate way.

When one aims to model semantic structures (whether psychological, or social, or logical), one works on the basis of contemporary intuitions. Any such model will reflect our present grasp of semantic relations: either in an active mind solving some problems, or in the intersubjective domain – the common world of a linguistic community[40] – or in an abstract conceptual system. Consequently, following Saussure's position, network models should represent contemporary intuitions concerning the relatedness of lexically available senses. To be sure, one could try to see how such a system "works" in individual minds (psychology) or whether it can be formalized (logic), but the point of network models is to show in a transparent way what is socially available – what the linguistic system offers its users.[41] From this perspective, it is imperative to distinguish "attested senses" from nonce uses or contextual construals (or social *langue* from individual *parole*).

The CL characterization of the difference between both levels in terms of "cognitive salience", "entrenchment" or "sanction" is inadequate. The terms are not interchangeable, while the last one seems more relevant. Individual "cognitive salience" or "entrenchment" do not count for much in intersubjective spaces: one must be able to rely on some senses as available to the other party. "Sanction" sounds closer to the mark; still, it is not enough that some meanings serve as schemas for elaborations or as points of departure for extensions (Langacker's account). Attested senses actually give structure to our common world and to discourse.[42] Langacker's format seems designed for an abstract conceptual space, divorced from any role in structuring reality.

---

[39] I simply enumerated the most obvious options: CL openly aims to capture "psychological reality"; commonsensical view of polysemy presupposes "diachronic" social developments; actual models of lexemes clearly represent the relatedness of concepts.

[40] Or Saussure's "social mind". Cognitivists normally find such holistic notions unacceptable as "metaphysical" (cf. Talmy 1995). Of course, "social mind" is a metaphor but it rightly suggests that a linguistic community relies on an intersubjectively available semantic system (which cognitivists try to reconstruct atomistically, on the level of individual minds).

[41] Historical uses can be integrated into such models – e.g. *kluka*, *kluczka* in Tabakowska's model of KLUCZ/KEY (1995: 51) – since one can try to "revitalize" any words (i.e. to connect them conceptually to "live" senses). To be "socially available", however, they must be felt to structure reality.

[42] These roles are described by Zlatev (2003) and McNeill (2005). I will present their views in "The hermeneutical coda" (5.).

Following Saussure's account, one must ask, however, whether language users have intuitions concerning the relatedness of senses. Since they use language, they know what words mean in a context; they will also say whether creative uses make sense to them. They cannot normally provide "definitions", except for rudimentary statements concerning the "type" or "function" of an entity ("it is a kind of...", "it is for..."). They will say that two uses are different when they bring to mind sufficiently distant or distinct situations. To recall the example quoted in 0.4., the verb *tease* has four sub-entries in a dictionary: "(1) To laugh at someone and make jokes in order to have fun by embarrassing them; (2) To deliberately annoy an animal; (3) To deliberately make someone sexually excited without intending to have sex with them; (4) (AmE) To comb your hair in the opposite direction to which it grows, so that it looks thicker". The last sense is clearly distinct and highly specific. Sense (2) could seem – in general – not distinct from (1), if one did not know that "teasing" animals takes quite specific forms (e.g. with a stick), which normally have nothing to do with (1).[43] Sense (3) seems least distinct to a Polish speaker, possibly because this "situation type" – even if equally common – is not elaborated on in the intersubjective sphere (while in English there are related expressions, e.g. *striptease*). It seems, then, that two uses are sufficiently distinct when they are felt to structure differently some domains in a socially available way. The example of "calendar month" and "four week month" – according to Croft and Cruse, possibly two closest ambiguous senses (0.4.) – seems to confirm this formulation: they provide two different "recipes" (or structurations) for social activity.

Consequently, the transfer of a sense to a different objective "domain" is not enough to get a distinct one, e.g. one can "play" with a child or with a dog; one can "tease" a child and a dog in sense (1). "Teasing" in sense (2) refers to a different kind of activity (which may be also applied to interpersonal relations) rather than to a different objective domain. Crucially, this type (*tease*2) is not just "conceived" as a possibility – it is actually "perceived" as a socially recognized situation. Once we accept this, we can easily discount putative cases of "polysemy", like *eating* "with a spoon, fork, chopsticks etc.", since they all refer to one kind of activity (performed with different tools). This case is better described as "generality" of words, when their senses do not bring to mind some referential distinctions, which can be signalled by other means. For instance, a house *window* may be contextually specified to mean the "glass" or "frame" or "opening" in the wall. This is a single general sense (with different "active zones"), not a "natural category of senses". Metaphorical uses – as long as they do not change the basic situational structure (e.g. for *eat*: an X "consumes" a Y) – do not change the sense (they are rather instantiations than extensions). But this structure – underlying an application in a new domain – may in time give way to a more direct re-description. For instance, "Rust is eating away the garden gate" has the sense

[43] The difference is lexicalized in Polish: *przekomarzać się* ("tease1") as opposed to *drażnić* ("tease2"), which suggests "courting danger".

of "erosion" (marked lexically by the particle). Such "dead metaphors" (like adj. *key*, *crucial*, *critical* etc. mentioned before) are felt to have a distinct sense, while the etymological relationship may always be brought to attention.[44] To conclude, a distinct sense brings to mind a different situation type because it has helped to structure it. Situation type is the third element or rather the basis on which the Saussurean articulation is founded.

When we return now to the relatedness of distinct senses, we can see, perhaps, why the entries for *tease* are ordered in the way proposed: sense (4) – apart from the fact that it is a regional variety – is most strongly embedded in a highly specified situation type; sense (3) – less so, and so on. One can imagine, perhaps, societies in which (2) would be more popular[45] than (1) – in such a case, it could serve as the "default" use out of context. On this basis, one can speculate that the intuitive relatedness of senses is linked to the intuitive order of situation types, or their social salience. Can one postulate anything more specific? As we have seen, Vandeloise's analysis reveals a pragmatic unity of various referential applications of a single sense. He was able to show the pragmatic logic of this referential system of uses. However, his account is clearly not diachronic – it is a pragmatic "summation" of historical vagaries.

When we turn from "monocentric" to "polycentric" categories, the "summation" in question must be of a different kind. The subject is no longer a set of related answers to a pragmatically unified enquiry, a conceptual "probing" of reality (e.g. what is the dimension providing best access to various entities?). Polycentric categories are centrifugal, they are about a conceptual domestication of reality. One is no longer concerned with how to referentially apply an already tangible concept (tangible in a range of its applications), but rather how to "capture" – make manifest to others, communicate – entities not yet articulated in a language (or articulated in inadequate ways from one's perspective). The issue in not about applying a concept but about manifesting one's perspective on (some aspect of) reality to others.

The problems posed by polycentric categories are thus more fundamental, since language is primarily about communal sharing of perspectives on various aspects of reality, or the social structuration of reality (this is also what linguistic intuition is about). Clearly, establishing a perspective on reality is chronologically prior to its application. How can one fix and communicate an individual point of view? How can one establish a communal one? These questions were not raised in Vandeloise's account but, at this fundamental level, one can only gesture at answers.

---

[44] Such "sleeping" metaphors can be "awakened", in Müller's formulation (2008).

[45] It may seem that frequency of occurrence normally correlates with social salience. One can imagine, however, that *tease*3 is statistically the most popular activity of all four, while not being salient because of some social prohibitions. *Tease*4, even if generally performed on a daily basis, would be always less socially salient that (1)–(3) because of its relatively minor social status (as long as one's hair-do is perceived as less important than one's attitude to people or animals).

In the present context one can say, in general, that this social, historical process of establishing common perspectives involves extended uses of words, which tend to cluster around referentially salient specimens. Astronomical *star* and celebrity *star* – since both are currently salient – provide good reference points for related uses. The extension from the astronomical to celebrity sense is normally classified as a metaphor and explained as an analogical use, e.g. "as a star catches one's attention in the sky, so an actor catches the attention of the public". This explanation is a *hysteron proteron* one: it is based on our present intuitions, partly shaped by the existence of the sense in question. When pressed, we could imagine a number of different scenarios underlying this extension. What is more, since a lexeme normally carries many senses, several of them can usually serve as a point of departure for a given extension. Additionally, idiosyncratic extensions (reflecting particular circumstances of use, rather than socially recognized functional and structural similarities) sometimes "make it" into general use. Historical vagaries cannot be really "explained", as they often exemplify situational serendipity or groping in the dark or confabulation. Thus, diachronic evidence rarely (if at all[46]) provides a clear-cut or unique "motivation" in single cases. What it does offer is some sense of the complexity of the process – involving an interplay of form, content and background – as well as some "patterns" of development.

More specifically, when one views a perspicuous representation of a complex category – e.g. KLUCZ/KEY (Tabakowska 1995: 51; cf. 1.2.2.) – one notices that the contemporary central sense took over this role at some point in history. There are two earlier clusters: UNPREDICTABLE MOVEMENT, as exemplified by *kluczenie* ("disguising one's tracks", "moving in circles") and CURVED OBJECT, as exemplified by *kluka* ("a curved rod"). Both are linked by the idea of "curvature", which brings to mind unpredictability or devious behaviour, as exemplified in an etymological dictionary (Brückner's Dictionary). With the passage of time, a range of items expressing "deviousness" and "curvature" fell into abeyance, and the idea of "providing access" took central stage.[47] We can see more clearly now that Langacker illegitimately fuses the diachronic and synchronic perspectives when he suggests that the category prototype "is significant because of its developmental priority and notable cognitive salience" (1987: 380; my emphasis). The latter criterion reflects the present social status of KEY; this prototypical sense is not necessarily prior in social history and need not be prior in language acquisition; e.g. in a rural area, where houses are not locked, a child could learn first the phrase *klucz gęsi* ("a wedge of geese").

Since the developmental history of a complex category is hidden from view of language users (and, as a rule, not completely transparent even to experts), the intuitive relatedness of senses apparently reflects social salience of situation types

[46] To repeat, this is true generally. Any interpretation is situated and contingent.

[47] It seems that other lexical items "took over" some senses expressed by this category, e.g. one of the senses of *kluczka* is expressed by contemporary *mieć haka na kogoś* ("to have a hook against sb", cf. Brückner's Dictionary). To be sure, "deviousness" is still present in some uses.

co-structured by a given lexeme. As the example of *tease* suggests, however, it is much easier to point out local senses – structuring narrowly defined or marginal situations – than to offer a convincing argument for one central sense among a number of candidates, or for a hierarchy of extensions. From this vantage point it is easier to understand the futility of attempts to justify on some theoretical grounds the priority of one sense of *over* or to distinguish "in a principled way" a set of distinct senses. The senses are distinguished intuitively, on the basis of our everyday orientation in situation types.

If my account is correct, then prepositions – contrary to the view expressed by some cognitive linguists – do not offer the best testing ground for polysemy. Since they express relations rather then entities, their meaning is less tangible out of co-text and context. One must place them in phrases or imagine situation types they help to structure before one can ascribe some meaning to them. Hypothetically, if one asked respondents for the central sense of *za* out of context, it is likely that "behind" would be mentioned first, since it is opposed to *przed* ("in front of"). However, if one asked about the meaning of *za* in the phrase *za pięć dwunasta* ("*za* five (to) twelve"), one could get the answer *przed* – since the point of time mentioned is <u>in front of</u> the full hour (as opposed to *po* – "past") – or perhaps *do* ("up to"), when the passage of time is placed in focus. This instability of intuitions seems linked to the dependent status of prepositions.

Can one tutor intuitions? It seems to me that the models of prepositions which aim to capture the relatedness of attested senses are precisely such attempts to extend one's intuitions by focusing one's attention on links between senses. They are acts of imagination, retracing potential steps from "more central" to "less central" senses. Thus, by analogy, if we take a sequence of adjectival phrases (adjectives are also relational words): "white wall", "white wine", "white marriage", we would probably feel that the colour <u>motivates</u> the label for "transparent" wines (centrally opposed to "non-transparent" or red ones) and the label for sexually "pure" marriages. The actual motivations are, however, contingent on historical circumstances. As for the order of extensions, the "ecological" factors mentioned by Wierzbicka (0.2.) seem to be relevant: some experiences are so widespread and elementary in human life, that they are normally taken as primary (this fact does not remove contingency: the study of colour terms reveals that some striking motives – i.e. focal colours – are not taken up by all human tribes). To conclude, prepositional network models are interpretative (or hermeneutical) attempts to relate in a transparent manner socially available senses (i.e. intuitively present in a range of linguistic expressions).

If we return, finally, to both foundational network models, they offer rather different accounts of meaning extension. Lakoff bases his model of *over* on an unspecified "imagistic" schema, which is subsequently specified in several (largely arbitrary) dimensions and transformed according to hypothetical mental rules.[48]

[48] The resultant conceptual structure is then used in "conceptual metaphors". I did not follow this story in the present account (see Pawelec 2005a, 2006a).

Langacker offers a highly flex-ible format based on schematic similarity, underlying both specifications of a schema and extensions from a prototype. Neither of the models is presented as "diachronic", while both authors invoke "psychological reality" (in a rather different meaning of the term) as their declared goal. Moreover, Langacker points to "descriptive adequacy" as his primary aim and is at places quite confusing about the synchronic status of the model.

My conclusion at this stage is perhaps entirely predictable. Since historical processes involve an interplay of formal structures, conceptual structures and the background, they cannot be properly represented by formats focused primarily on conceptual structure, even if these are offered as "dynamic", as underlying real developments (if not in history, then certainly in mental life and in discourse). Consequently, if the formats are found useful by linguists (as seems evident and as has been partly documented), they should allow them to capture a "summation" of historical processes from a particular angle.

Generally speaking, Langacker's format seems more promising in this respect, since it posits few formal requirements. As such – in skilful hands – it can be used to represent functional clusters and their intuitive conceptual unity from the present perspective. Also Lakoff's model may be found inspiring, since it invokes pragmatic factors (mostly of a perceptual kind), which are obviously operative in history. This conclusion may come as a denouement, but the fact that a new type of format has been offered (as an alternative to the feature analysis) could be in the long run more significant than the actual justifications offered for it.

To repeat, network models exemplify a search for linguistics with "a human face". CL, within which they were developed, extended research horizons after Chomsky's formalist approach, while being rooted in the mentalistic background (common to the first and second generation cognitive science). Thus, network models represent the relatedness of lexical senses on the basis of general psychological constraints and intuitively evident conceptual relations. The amount of work performed within the cognitive paradigm testifies to the intellectual potential of this approach.

5. THE HERMENEUTICAL CODA

5.0. Introductory remarks

As shown by philosophical hermeneutics, "the world", that is the world as we know it, has been revealed through constitutive activity which is normally concealed, so that the world may appear. When one starts an investigation of some aspect of the world as it manifests itself from one's vantage point (the "object" of that inquiry), one constantly runs the risk of mistaking what appears – from a certain stance, in a given theoretical paradigm, within some horizon, at a certain level of spiritual development, as established in the history of expression – for "raw reality" or "brute facts". *Hysteron proteron* fallacy, or putting the cart before the horse, is thus a constant risk in the social sciences and human studies: one tries to explain the genesis of an entity, invoking entities available only as a result of that genesis. A cognitivist example will serve as the point of departure in section 5.1., in which I would like to follow empirically a basic question concerning language genesis: should it be explained in mentalistic or in expressive terms? I will present some glimpses into the genetic relations between "language, thought, and reality" as a hermeneutical antidote to the mentalistic *hysteron proteron* approach. The antidote is to turn away from what has been constituted and focus on the process of constitution.[1]

Consequently, in our efforts to understand language, we must try to move back to the sources: to the points of genesis, which transform both the vision (i.e. one's stance towards reality) and the world. In this way we may go beyond the products of language and reveal its power of generation. This is not a new approach in language study. It can be perceived in the work of Humboldt, the greatest figure in modern linguistics before Saussure. The "genetic" approach is advocated by him in the famous "energetic" definition of language: "In itself [language] is no product (*Ergon*), but an activity (*Energeia*). Its true definition can therefore only be a genetic one. For it is the ever-repeated mental labour of making the articulated sound capable of expressing thought" (Humboldt 1999: 49).[2] More specifically in

[1] "Constitution" (Husserl's term) does not mean that we "fabricate" reality, but that we reveal it "as something" – we discover the meaning it has for us. "Bracketing" of the world – of the constituted parts relevant for a given inquiry – is for Husserl the way to provide access to the phenomenon as it is (i.e., its necessary essence). After the hermeneutical correction, one tries to reveal the phenomenon by uncovering layers of constitution in history, also in a dialogue with naturalistic accounts, as in Ricoeur's "detour" (cf. 0.1.).

[2] I will discuss some limitations of Humbold's formulation pointed out by Gadamer as well as his place in the history of linguistics in the subsequent section 5.2. The final section will contain my

our context: "the vocabulary is a continuous generation and regeneration of the word-making capacity, first in the stock to which the language owes its form, then in the learning of speech by children, and lastly in daily usage" (p. 93). Since my task is to reveal the "transformative" power of language, it seems natural to focus on the three contexts pointed out by Humboldt (in a modernized formulation): the genesis of language, language acquisition and the use of language in discourse.[3] Of course, these domains of study – linguistic phylogenesis, ontogenesis and microgenesis – cannot be explored here. Instead, I will offer some "glimpses" into these areas of investigation to show how language, thought and reality are intertwined.[4]

5.1. Language, thought, and reality

The issue of linguistic "genesis" (in all domains mentioned above) is intensely studied by the cognitive (naturalistic, scientific) approaches. If one's aim is to explain "functional wholes" – "mechanisms" in a loose sense – the description of actual causal chains (likely scenarios etc.) is of primary importance. When one can show, how an entity arises, one has a firm grasp on it. As opposed to the cognitive "just so story", discussed below, the accounts of linguistic genesis presented afterwards reveal genetic links between language, thought and reality (thus, from the hermeneutical perspective, they help to make the phenomenon of language manifest[5]).

Here is how a leading cognitive scientist, Steven Pinker, begins his popular account of language:

---

plea for "expressive" linguistics.

[3] One could also inspect other areas in which the linguistic potential abruptly changes (either increasing, or decreasing one's ability to communicate, live one's life etc.), e.g. pidginization and creolization on the one hand and various language defects and mental syndromes influencing linguistic capabilities on the other. The point is to find a perspective which may allow one to notice that one's linguistic potential and existential potential (access to reality) are intertwined. To be sure, from the scientific (naturalistic) perspective such cases are about a more extensive or more limited access to the reality independent of language. From the hermeneutical perspective, they offer glimpses how reality manifests itself more fully through language.

[4] The phrase "language, thought, and reality" – the title of Whorf's selection of papers (1956) – reappears in various versions in studies motivated by the ambition to show the inextricable links between the elements of such triads, e.g. Putnam (1975): "mind, language and reality", Tyler (1978): "mind, meaning, and culture".

[5] From the naturalistic perspective, it would be said that I simply prefer one hypothesis to another (while they all lack full confirmation and so on). One cannot answer such claims: see Merleau-Ponty's comments in note 8 below.

> As you are reading these words, you are taking part in one of the wonders of the natural world. For you and I belong to a species with a remarkable ability: we can shape events in each other's brains with exquisite precision. I am not referring to telepathy or mind control or the other obsessions of fringe science [...]. That ability is language. Simply by making noises with our mouths, we can reliably cause precise new combinations of ideas to arise in each other's minds. The ability comes so naturally that we are apt to forget what a miracle it is. (Pinker 1994: 15)

The author hastens to add that this miracle has nothing to do with "the ineffable essence of human uniqueness", but is "a biological adaptation to communicate information" (p. 19). Pinker points out the linguistic phenomenon of successful communication, while simultaneously providing two apparently equivalent accounts of it, i.e. "we can shape events in each other's brains with exquisite precision" and "we can reliably cause precise new combinations of ideas to arise in each other's minds". One can notice that the accounts are mixed up: it would be more adequate to say that we can "cause" events in brains (biological organs) and "shape" ideas in minds (spiritual entities, seats of self-consciousness etc.). By treating both accounts as interchangeable, Pinker surf-rides over the "mind-body problem" (how to get from "physical" to "semantic" explanations?).[6] He seems to accept that noises cause patterns of neuronal activation in the brain (physical phenomena), which "cause" ideas in the mind (semantic phenomena).

Pinker's account is full of confusion. First, words are not "noises", they cannot be treated as physical stimuli.[7] In his account, Pinker blurs the distinction between the semantic and "objective" levels of analysis (or "emic" and "etic", as in "phonemic" and "phonetic"). Words are made up of "phonemes" – the smallest contrastive structural units in a system of language, which can be "realised" differently on the phonetic level (the actual noises). Thus, the "shape" of words (still below the semantic level) is not equivalent to physical signals. More generally, "noises" as such cannot be reliably linked to "perceptions" (and thus, one can expect, to "neuronal patterns"). As was shown by the Gestaltists, the same signal, depending on the overall pattern of the experiential field, may be perceived differently, while different signals may be perceived as identical. Any empiricist theory

---

[6] Which is a variant of the philosophical problem of "the bridge" mentioned in 0.1. In psychology, the problem appears in the form of the "homunculus": a "little man" apparently necessary to control the machinery in the brain (a solution strange in itself, and resulting in infinite regression, for we need another homunculus to control the brain of the first one). In another book, Pinker quotes Dennett, who thinks that the problem of the homunculus is solved by the "computational theory of mind": "Homunculi are bogeymen only if they duplicate entire the talents they are rung in to explain [...]. One discharges fancy homunculi from one's scheme by organizing armies of idiots" (Pinker 1997: 79). In other words, mind-body problem is solved, if A.I. specialists can reduce semantic information to algorithms used by machines. That "solution" replaces homunculi with A.I. specialists (and their brains etc.).

[7] As in behaviourism. Chomsky, who in general opinion demolished behaviourism in his review of Skinner's *Verbal Behavior* (Chomsky 1977), apparently accepts the behaviourist perspective on linguistic "signals", as is also evident in Pinker's presentation. That perspective was shown to be inadequate (*avant la lettre*) in Saussure's discussion of linguistic units (1959: 103ff.).

linking physical stimuli to sensations requires a "constancy hypothesis", which, as shown by the Gestaltists, "conflicts with the data of consciousness".[8]

Second, as explored in the present case study, on the semantic level linguistic senses are not related in a one-to-one fashion to linguistic forms. One form normally has several conventional senses. What is more, this "underdetermination" of meaning by form is even more evident in actual use, when the meanings of a word form seem infinitely flexible. Thus, no "string of words" can be predictably (in a one-to-one fashion) linked to its "meaning" without taking into account the background of communication.[9] But Pinker describes communication as a one-way affair: an active sender shapes ideas in a passive receiver (or "sends a message through a conduit"[10]).

Pinker subsequently reveals how the "miracle" works. People are equipped by biology with "mentalese".[11] And the solution runs as follows: "Knowing a language, then, is knowing how to translate mentalese into strings of words and vice versa" (1994: 82). The process of translation is supposed to be unconscious, "automatic". However, that "hypothesis" does not solve any problems of communication, since "mentalese" – whatever its proposed content, origin etc. – is assigned the role of "code", which requires one-to-one correspondences between form and meaning.

What can one make of that story?[12] It presents "language" as a biological organ.[13] The initial credibility of that account is probably rooted in two assumptions.

[8] Merleau-Ponty (2002: 8). Cf. Merleau-Ponty's comments: "The law of constancy cannot avail itself, against the testimony of consciousness, of any crucial experiment in which it is not already implied, and wherever we believe that we are establishing it, it is already presupposed". And subsequently: "It is only fair to add that this is true of all theories, and that nowhere is there a crucial experiment. For the same reason the constancy hypothesis cannot be completely refuted on the basis of induction. It is discredited because it overlooks phenomena and does not permit any understanding of them. To discern them and to pass judgement on the hypothesis, one must 'suspend' it" (p. 9). And the final statement: "For the philosopher, as for the psychologist, there is [...] always a problem of origins, and the only method possible is to follow, in its scientific development, the causal explanation in order to make its meaning quite clear, and assign to it its proper place in the body of truth. That is why there will be found no *refutation*, but only an effort to understand the difficulties peculiar to causal thinking" (pp. 7–8).

[9] In the cognitive community the issue of the background of meaning and communication was first raised by Dreyfus (1992 [1972]: 204ff.). See also Dreyfus, Dreyfus (1986) and Searle (1999: ch. 8).

[10] See Reddy (1979) for a classic description of the "conduit model" of communication.

[11] As explained in the glossary: "The hypothetical 'language of thought', or representation of concepts and propositions in the brain in which ideas, including the meanings of words and sentences, are couched" (Pinker 1994: 478).

[12] The Reader may feel that I chose a popular exposition of mentalism to criticise a caricature, rather than the real account. However, specialist accounts normally take their assumptions for granted (as hypotheses), while Pinker feels obligated to make them explicit for the public. What is more important, my primary aim is not to criticise mentalism as a scientific perspective (which – within limits one should try to specify – is valuable), but to present it as a particular style of approaching linguistic phenomena.

[13] While the mind is supposed to be a "system of organs" (Pinker 1997: 27). The "modular" model of the mind has been the subject of a heated debate between the "first" and the "second" gen-

First, that language is produced in the mind and, consequently, in the brain, so that, in principle, a neuronal (or computational, or scientific) account of it should be possible. Second, that language works "automatically", since we can talk and understand speech effortlessly. As for the former assumption, it is obviously true that verbal activity (as perhaps any activity) runs parallel to (partly conscious) mental activity and to neuronal activity.[14] The question is whether these elements form a "functional unit", which objectifying methods can model, or whether some crucial elements of such a unit are missing. We need an evolutionary account of the biological organ in question and some account of its actual functioning, if we are to make a decision of that kind. As for the latter assumption, language must be acquired or learned – it is a skill. It seems closer to driving or playing an instrument than to biological organs, e.g. the senses.[15] At this level of discussion, one can only point out that with complex phenomena, like language, many analogies may look, *prima facie*, convincing. It is crucial to check how far the analogies may be pressed.

We can see now, perhaps, why Pinker's "positive" account of the phenomenon of communication, even though it obviously fails to deal with traditional problems, may seem initially appealing. Pinker attempts to increase that appeal by his presentation of alternatives. He suggests that if language is not a biological organ adapted for communication, then we are left with telepathy and fringe science or "the ineffable essence of human uniqueness". In other words, it is either science or obscurantism.

But if Pinker's account does not even begin to tackle the problems of communicating ideas via the physical medium of sounds (or marks on paper etc.), then we may ask in what respects it is better than telepathy. That question has a more general significance, as demonstrated by Roy Harris' charge against the model of communication (or the "language myth") adopted by linguistics of the time (the early 1980's). He says that it is based on two fallacies: "telementation" – that the function of speech is to convey thoughts from one mind to another (a version of the "conduit" metaphor); and "fixed-code fallacy" – that a language community is a group of individuals who are taught to associate words with the same mean-

---

eration of cognitive scientists (see e.g. J. Taylor 1989: 16–20). From the hermeneutical perspective, the issue is of secondary importance, since both positions assume that language is a natural ("biological") phenomenon.

[14] Still, the unconscious semantic level ("mentalese") requires special pleading, for it is hard to imagine "thinking" without an agent (even a dumb homunculus, an idiot from Dennett's army, must "get it right").

[15] I mention the senses, since this analogy is invoked by some cognitivists: "It is as though the ability to comprehend experience through metaphor were a sense, like seeing or touching or hearing, with metaphors providing the only ways to perceive and experience much of the world. Metaphor is as much a part of our functioning as our sense of touch, and as precious" (Lakoff, Johnson 1980: 239). The final statement in that seminal book has a hermeneutical ring to it, but the analogy between language and the senses is interpreted in a radically different way in both cases. Lakoff and Johnson postulate mechanisms (semantic transfers) extending what they take to be the perceptual basic level (image schemas) to the cultural world. Hermeneutical philosophers show how language is a *reprise du sens* (Ricoeur's phrase) of perceptual sense, cf. e.g. McLure (1990: 503, 513); Dillon (1988).

ings.[16] Specifically, Harris attacks the belief of generative linguists that "a language is a finite set of rules generating an infinite set of pairs, of which one member is a sound-sequence or a sequence of written characters, and the other is its meaning", and opposes to it his own understanding of language as "continuously created by the interaction of individuals" (1981: 11, 167). One may conclude, following Harris, that not only TG or CL, but linguistics as such has a fundamental problem with modelling verbal communication.

The phenomenon described in his particular manner by Pinker is obviously real. In a less theory-laden formulation, it is an ability to "share", to "make common" (lat. *communico*) some "content". At the same time, it is an ability to "reveal" to someone else what one knows, to make it "manifest".[17] From the hermeneutical perspective, one may ask if there is some affinity between the uncovering of phenomena by the senses and uncovering of "contents" by language. As was mentioned before (0.1.), perception is an activity which allows us to reach phenomena because it "hides itself". One may assume that language allows us to "share some content" also because the background of sharing is hidden from view. We do not know (all the way down) how such a sharing is possible. But we can locate the source of the problem with Pinker's position: he explains "words" in reference to ideas ("mentalese"), while ideas are not prior to words.

I will present below three accounts – glimpses into areas of massive research. The first two will concern "phylogenesis", i.e. the evolution of a type of animal: the linguistic animal or "the symbolic species", in our case.[18] The question – despite the infamous prohibition imposed on such inquiries as inherently speculative by The Paris Linguistic Society in 1866[19] – has generated enormous literature.[20] My aim here is limited to the issue at hand: should the origin of language be explained primarily in mental or in expressive terms? In other words, is the linguistic ability the result of some mental developments or of expressive activities?

In this context, it is important to remember that any inquiry of the former type faces a more acute problem of evidence. In fact, this is a more general problem of all "mentalistic" accounts: scientists have access to behaviour, not to mental states and mental "architecture". One should not go as far as the behaviourists, who refused to speculate about the mental "black box", but it seems reasonable to assume that we must point to specific behavioural changes, if we want to invoke mental evolution of one kind or another.[21]

---

[16] Harris (1981: ix). With the publication of *Relevance* by Sperber and Wilson (1986) the "code model" of communication was supplemented with the "inferential model", but the problems pointed out by Harris remain.

[17] Lat. *revelo* – "to unveil, uncover"; *manifestus* – "bound or grasped by the hand" (Smith's Dictionary). These original meanings are obviously suggestive within an account of meaning based on active involvement with reality.

[18] The title of Deacon's book (1997).

[19] As often mentioned in books on language evolution, e.g. Deacon (1997: 14).

[20] See Hurford (2007) for a recent review.

[21] I discussed some relations between the behaviourist and cognitivist view on language in Pawelec (2008).

Consequently, there is no *prima facie* warrant for mentalistic accounts of language origin which postulate some developments in brain structure or mental architecture merely on the basis that such developments are required by a corresponding theory of language ("psychologist's fallacy"). For instance, Fauconnier and Turner criticise Chomsky's idea that "language" (i.e. brain structure underlying Universal Grammar) must have evolved as a result of a genetic mutation.[22] What they propose instead, however, is of the same type. They praise Deacon, who is "the one theorist on our list who leaves ample room for relating the origin of language to the origin of other cultural behaviors". But rather than analyse some functional links between specific behaviour on the one hand and mental architecture they assume necessary for its appearance on the other, they merely state: "There is every reason to think that once the capacity [for double-scope blending] was achieved and the cultural products started to emerge, they reinforced each other. Language assisted social interaction, social interaction assisted the cultural development of language, and language assisted the elaboration of tool use, as the tree of culture put forward these exceptional new products" (Fauconnier, Turner 2003: 185–186). Fauconnier and Turner simply assume that once a new cognitive ability was in place (they never say how it got there), language development started for good. Deacon's account of experiments with chimpanzees presented below (5.1.1.) shows clearly that the genetic order assumed by Fauconnier and Turner should be reversed.

The next two accounts will provide very short glimpses into "ontogenesis" – language acquisition (the classic case of "Little Hans" described by Freud) – and "microgenesis", i.e. the use of language in discourse. They are much shorter because my aim is to illustrate the point hopefully established in reference to evolutionary research: that the expressive view of language is more convincing than the mentalistic alternative. The last section focuses on the Sapir-Whorf hypothesis.

5.1.1. Teaching chimps symbols

In Deacon (1997) we find a behaviourally motivated hierarchy of cognitive abilities underlying symbol use. Deacon weaves many elements into his explanation of language origin. I will focus here on just one: his interpretation of experiments to teach symbols to chimpanzees.[23]

Before we see what "symbols" require in terms of cognitive abilities, we need to have some grasp of operations at two lower mental levels: the "iconic" and "in-

---

[22] Chomsky pulls "a speculative, catastrophic, indeterminate, but all-powerful biological event out of a hat" (Fauconnier, Turner 2003: 184). For a more specific criticism of Chomsky in this context, see Deacon (1997: 35, 103ff).

[23] Two not exceptionally bright chimps called Sherman and Austin trained in the 1970's to use simple symbols by Sue Savage-Rumbaugh and Duane Rumbaugh. Subsequent work with the pygmy chimp (or bonobo) Kanzi showed a much greater potential of the apes for acquiring symbols.

dexical". Deacon invokes Peirce's terms[24] to describe various types of interpretative processes in the animal world. The iconic level should be viewed as the "default" option of interpretation, i.e. in negative terms as the lack of need or ability to make a distinction. For instance, a bird which does not recognise a moth sitting on the bark of a tree (a case of successful mimicry), does not find enough clues which would indicate the behaviourally important difference. Hence, the iconic level is limited to what an animal can already recognise, and requires the least interpretative effort. As for its origin, it is based on an inferential process based on the recognition of "similarity" (regular association), says Deacon (pp. 71–76).[25]

Indices are well exemplified by Pavlov's dog salivating at the sound of a buzzer. We talk here about associating one type of experiential context (or "icon") with another (rather than two "entities", defined by their physical features). In a standard behaviourist account, this type of situation is represented in terms of "stimulus" and "response": some distinct element ("buzz") close in space and time to an icon ("food served") "triggers" an animal's corresponding reaction on its own, when the sequence has occurred often enough (conditioned response learning). Behaviourists assume that, with sufficient exposition, the association is "automatic" (one "thing" replaces another as the "cause" of some action). Deacon shows how much mental work is necessary in this case and what kind of change in mental architecture is involved.

We need not go into details. It is enough to realise that what looks, from the behaviourist perspective, like a replacement of "triggers", requires an interpretative blending of two icons ("buzz", "food served"). Only the third icon – comprising both on a higher level of mental organisation[26] – may be used for indexical purposes. In experiential terms, indexical interpretation allows to shape (adapt to the "standard" conditions) the "vortices" of experience.[27] Naturally, that interpretative process is constrained by the mental potential of a species.[28]

---

[24] Deacon uses Peirce's terms in a rather idiosyncratic fashion. For the original meaning of "index", "icon" and "symbol", see e.g. Nöth (1995). It is important to underline here that "symbol use" in the experiments analysed by Deacon has little to do with human "language use".

[25] It is crucial to realize that "similarity" invoked in the explanation of the iconic level is not based on some prior, physical resemblance (as we would see it in our terms). "Similarity" here is a break-off point in the process of interpretation: the animal does not find clues (whether of boredom, or lack of attention or the limitations of its mental system) for making an experiential distinction (i.e. for a differential response). Thus, "anything" can be iconic of "anything" else (Deacon 1997: 76).

[26] More complex mental representation of reality (from icons to indices) is explained here in terms of "internal communication" between levels of mental architecture (Deacon 1997: 78). This idea was developed in neurological terms by Edelman (1992).

[27] Deacon's explanation shows in some detail what Cassirer meant (in his interpretation of perception pathologies) when he described normal perception (quoted in 0.2.) in the following way: "What was previously an unremitting flow of events now coalesces, as it were, about ['favored points' which interrupt the stream of experience in various ways]: in the very midst of the stream there form separate vortices, whose parts seem to be linked in a common movement" (Cassirer 1957: 221).

[28] Deacon says that the same "physical" signal – "laughter" – will be interpreted differently, depending on the mental potential of a creature. A fish would recognise it merely as "vibration" (an "icon" meaning "danger" or "nothing of importance"). A dog would take it as evidence that humans

We can now move to the experiments with chimps, which may be treated as a case of "enculturation" – an attempt to find out how much of the human symbolic culture can be appropriated by animals. Two chimps, Austin and Sherman, were trained to use sequences of "lexigrams" (simple abstract shapes without any iconic resemblance to their referents) on large illuminated keys on a keyboard. There were two "verb" and four "noun" lexigrams to choose from ("give"/"pour" going with solid or liquid food, e.g. a "banana" or "orange juice"). The animals were first taught successfully the "right" pairs, one by one (4 in all). However, when required to choose from all available options, they failed to do so (they repeated the last sequence taught or tried at random). This shows that they learnt to link the lexigrams with their referents indexically, with no grasp of the meaning relation.

The problem they faced is easier to appreciate when we notice that 6 lexigrams may be arranged in 720 ordered sequences and 64 ordered pairs. The four "correct" pairs taught during initial training were not enough for them to guess the "logic" of the system (i.e. "classes" of allowed combinations). To make this task easier, the researchers decided to train the animals which sequences are not allowed (i.e. what not to do – a very complex training task). After thousands of trials, the chimps produced correct pairs every time.

To check, if the animals had learnt the liquid / solid distinction (and that a new lexigram is for a new item), the experimenters introduced some new food items with corresponding lexigrams. This time, Austin and Sherman made almost no mistakes – they got the "logic" right. The animals learnt that the meaning of a lexigram (its reference to something experientially significant) depends on its relations to other lexigrams. "This is the essence of a symbolic relationship", concludes Deacon (pp. 84–86).

Let us have another look at the training process to see how the transformation took place. The animals learnt the initial four pairs separately (let us say: A1, A2, B3, B4) as indices. But when faced with the whole repertoire, in which only 4 out of 64 pairs "worked", they were helpless – their errors immediately obscured the right choices. Only after the "wrong" pairs were indexically excluded, Austin and Sherman could be successful again. Deacon assumes that the symbolic reconfiguration happened at this stage, to reduce the memory load:

> Try to imagine yourself in their situation for a moment. You have just come to the point where you are not making errors. What is your strategy? Probably, you are struggling to remember what specific things worked and did not work, still at the level of one-by-one associations. The problem is, it is hard to remember all the details. What you need are aids to help organize what you know, because there are a lot of possibilities. But in the internal search for supports you discover that there is another source of redundancy and regularity that begins to appear, besides just the individual stimulus-response-reward regularities: the relationships between lexigrams! And these redundant patterns are far fewer than the messy

are around (an "index"). For chimps (which can produce it), laughter is indicative of a "relaxed atmosphere". For us, it is symbolic (an experiential response to a situation, e.g. a recognition of the point of a joke) (Deacon 1997: 73).

> set of dozens of individual associations that you are trying to keep track of [...] Forced to repeat errorless trials over and over, Sherman and Austin didn't just learn the details well, they also became aware of something they couldn't have noticed otherwise, that there was a system behind it all [...]. They could now afford to forget about individual correlations so long as they could keep track of them via the lexigram-lexigram rules". (Deacon 1997: 88–89)

Thus, according to Deacon, the transformation may be described as a change in "mnemonic strategy". The indexical relation: "index tokens – referents" was replaced by an indexical relation of a higher order between index tokens "to offload redundant details". Deacon's interpretation makes it clear that the symbolic relation is built on top of numerous indexical relations, whose "structure" (interrelatedness from some perspective) may become tangible thanks to at least three factors: numerous repetitions of indexical activity, in a relative separation from other actions, and (crucially in the experiment) a set of stable "structural hints" (lexigrams). Deacon notes that "nature seldom offers such nice neat logical systems that can help organize our associations. There are not many chances to use such strategies, so not much selection for this sort of process" (p. 89). Deacon's comment makes it very clear that while his interpretation reveals some important structural features of "symbolic interpretation", it cannot tell us much about the evolutionary context – the origin of language. The structural hints or lexigrams provided by the experimenters, and procedurally "deciphered" by Austin and Sherman, are not to be found in nature; symbols had to be invented by *homo sapiens* as repeatable, clearly differentiated behavioural units. We will have a closer look at the evolutionary context in the next section.

Nevertheless, Deacon's account of "symbolic interpretation" is much more illuminating than the mentalist stories of language origin proposed by Chomsky or Fauconnier and Turner. He shows, first, that a new mental stance is rooted in exploratory action. On the indexical level, animals search for clues or develop new behavioural patterns when they are frustrated by lack of success. When they fail at a task, they do not know the way to proceed (there is no mental plan, conscious or unconscious) – they must try again. Only subsequently, as a result of consistent behaviour (successful "tries" are repeated[29]), is a mental reconfiguration of experience possible.

Second, the symbolic "recoding" requires that a creature unlearns (or suspends) the search for "immediate satisfaction". This general change of "stance" must be rooted in behaviour which is not a direct response to environmental pressure. The most obvious candidate is "play" – adaptive behaviour allowing the young to learn adult behavioural patterns by imitation.

---

[29] The driving force of a successful try was demonstrated in a cruel experiment recorded in a Polish documentary "The Rat-catcher" (Andrzej Czarnecki, *Szczurołap*, 1986): a rat could swim for about 10 minutes in a large aquarium, before it drowned; another one, after less than 10 minutes in another tank, was given a chance to rest on a prop for a few seconds; subsequently, it had swum for almost 15 hours, mostly around the spot where it expected to be rescued, before it drowned.

Third, indices may stand on their own, while symbols can appear and function only in a system. A "symbol – referent" pair is an abstraction, viewed outside of a network of symbolic relations.[30]

Fourth, the discovery of symbolic meaning is an insight into an experiential whole: what one already "knows" implicitly, in a situation, is revealed as a structure; abstract links are forged, which allow an overall vision (Ricoeur's *reprise du sens*). In this context, Deacon invokes the opposition between "insight learning" and "learning by rote". An insight is possible only after one already "knows" how to handle a given task (with some obstacles and lack of transparency). One cannot be expected to understand structural hints without a prior practical acquaintance with a domain.[31]

Fifth, structural clarity in a domain is gained because the relations between tokens (allowed combinations) are consistently built on experiential relations. The social use of tokens imposes a cognitive map on the reality, previously available to an animal only in a behavioural way. As we have noticed, reality can be represented, because it has already been differentially structured in action. The symbolic restructuring is also differential: what we call "orange juice" – and interpret as a physical entity with some properties – would be revealed in the experiment as [not solid] [not apple liquid]. As long as further symbolic distinctions are not introduced into the system, an animal will call <u>any new drink</u> either "orange juice" or "apple juice". This habit – a series of attempts to make consistent choices – would probably reveal some criterion of differentiation (e.g. [sweet] vs. [sour]). We can see now that the initial characterization of the referents was made from the human perspective.

Sixth, once a system of symbols is installed, it allows to restructure <u>all</u> experience. Primarily, experience no longer takes the form of indexical relations, triggering reactions, but is shaped by abstract categories, revealed in linguistic expression. A symbolic species is no longer on the leash of its environment.[32]

To be sure, this effect was not achieved in the experiment reported (nor in any other). Austin and Sherman did not learn symbols, as we normally understand them: conventional signs used for "conveying ideas". They learnt to use lexigrams, they acquired "procedural" knowledge of symbols as "structural hints".

---

[30] This is the standard way of describing symbols: "token-meaning" pairs linked by convention (as opposed to the original Saussurean system of differences). We can see, by now, that such a description is a result of focusing on end-states, without proper attention to the process of "constitution".

[31] In everyday life, this is perhaps best seen when one deals with "instructions" of various kind (e.g. how to get to some location, cook a dish, operate a device etc.). As long as one is not in touch with the reality in question, an instruction may seem to be clear but means little; when used in a situation, it proves to be ambiguous at various crucial junctures, until one acquires an overall grasp of the whole semantic field to which it applies.

[32] As a result, the symbolic species can learn not only by exploration and imitation but also through linguistic "hearsay", which increases its chances exponentially (learning by "hearsay" is invoked by Harnad 2005: 16).

But that achievement did not constitute a step on the path to symbolic communicative behaviour.

5.1.2. The mimetic origins of language

Deacon's interpretation of experiments with chimps shows with greater clarity several problems of mentalistic accounts of language origin. In general, they disregard the basic rule of cognitive development (and, as a result, they reverse the order of explanation): mental reconfiguration of experience is rooted in active engagements with environment. One must "know" something procedurally ("knowing how"), before one may develop a conceptual (abstract, structural) grasp of it ("knowing that"). More specifically, the development of a "structural grasp" cannot be automatic, as is vividly shown by the acquisition of lexigrams. It requires "structural hints", which may be used to form (in a long and painstaking process) abstract categories. The appearance of such symbolic "tokens" in nature is an important gap in Deacon's interpretation.[33]

This gap is narrowed in Donald's account of "mimesis" (1991, 1993, 1999, 2000, 2001) – the crucial "exaptation" for language.[34] Donald frames the problem of language origin in terms of "voluntary access" of animals to their "memory banks". Animals rely on their environment to provide "hints" for recalling proper behavioural patterns. Humans, however, have the ability for "autocueing": they can retrieve their memories voluntarily (Donald 1993: 146). How did this ability evolve?

Donald postulates a "mimetic skill" – imitation with one's body. Mimesis requires a memory system that can "rehearse and refine movement voluntarily and systematically, in terms of a coherent perceptual model of the body" (p. 150). In other words, one can produce a sequence of movements matching some previous sequence, because one develops a perception of one's body (*proprioception*), resulting in a conscious "body image". When one has a model of one's body (or voluntary "control", in everyday terms[35]), one can stop, replay and edit any action of the body. This is a "supramodal" skill – it can be exercised with any means: eyes, hands, feet, posture, locomotion, facial expression, voice (p. 151). Thus, a rhythm

---

[33] Assuming that the author believes that his interpretation helps explain the origin of language (as seems probable, considering the title and the suggestion that nature rarely offers structural hints).

[34] The term "exaptation" is used for a function which changed its role in the evolutionary process – which was co-opted for some other task. This notion is a naturalistic way out of the *hysteron proteron* trap (i.e. an attempt not to invoke present functionality in genetic explanations).

[35] To give an example of missing "voluntary" control: a patient suffering from a rare syndrome can slap a mosquito on his cheek but cannot point to the cheek, when asked by the doctor. For more examples of that kind see Cassirer (1957), Merleau-Ponty (2002). This point illustrates the more general difference between what is available behaviourally, in a situation, and what is available semantically, out of context. The difference between relative and absolute discrimination described by Harnad (0.2.) is of the same kind.

initiated by foot tapping can be taken over by finger tapping, tongue clicks, hand or head movements, jumping, singing etc.

Mimesis is clearly adaptive. It may have evolved from animal play or ritual displays, when similar sequences of movements are repeated by a pair or a group of individuals (without voluntary control, by "contagion"). Whatever its source, it is obviously advantageous, once acquired: the intentional reproduction of movements can be used e.g. for tool making, practising hunting skills or communicating by mime.

For Donald, mimesis is the first step in the human co-evolution of mind and culture. Donald postulates three stages of development: mimetic culture, mythic culture (based on language and story telling), theoretic culture (based on external memory systems: writing and other cultural artefacts, like abacus or computer). Donald's grand vision need not be inspected in detail here. It is important, however, to notice two elements missing in Deacon's account: the development of mental abilities is intensely social (anchored in interactions of a collective, rather than in interactions with environment); and it requires the control of one's body, which turns into "an organ of mimicry" (cf. Merleau-Ponty 2002: 479).

Donald's proposal has been developed by Zlatev. He offers a definition of bodily mimesis which shows clearly how it differs from simpler acts of imitation on the one hand, and from symbolic representation on the other:

> Def: A particular bodily act of cognition or communication is an act of bodily mimesis if and only if:
> a) it involves a cross-modal[36] mapping between *exteroception* (i.e. perception of the environment, normally dominated by vision) and *proprioception* (perception of one's own body, normally through kinesthetic sense);
> b) it is under conscious control and corresponds to – either iconically or indexically – to some action, object or event, while at the same time being *differentiated* from it by the subject;
> c) the subject *intends* the act *to stand for* some action, object or event for an addressee (and for the addressee to recognize this intention);
> d) without the act being conventional-normative, and
> e) without the act dividing (semi)compositionally into meaningful sub-acts that systematically relate to each other and other similar acts". (Zlatev 2007c: 9; emphasis in the original)

Condition (a) states that all acts of imitation involve mapping between external and internal perception. In other words, one becomes aware of one's body (develops "body image") through acts of imitation. Zlatev mentions "contagion" as an example of the simplest, "proto-mimetic" level of imitation. Contagion – as with "contagious" laughter or yawning – does not involve voluntary control and is not representational for the subject. Representation on the level (b) is "dyadic",

---

[36] The term "cross-modal" is applied to perception, as coming through any (number of) sensory channels. It seems related to "supramodal" as used by Donald (i.e. activity through any channels of expression).

i.e. it involves a differentiation between "signifier" (a bodily act) and "signified" from the subject's point of view. An example of iconic mimesis, described by Piaget, is "an infant opening and closing her mouth to model the opening and closing of a matchbox". Children pointing at objects to help guide their attention is a case of indexical mimesis. Only when condition (c) is fulfilled, mimesis becomes "triadic" – it is used for communication and involves an addressee (thus, gestures turn into mimetic signs). Miming an action to communicate something about it would be an iconic mimetic sign, while "declarative pointing" is a paradigmatic indexical mimetic sign. Only when signs become "conventional" – that is "normative" – and they are systematically linked, we cross the border of "symbolic" acts, i.e. language (conditions d-e).

On the basis of bodily mimesis, Zlatev proposes the notion of "mimetic schemas", i.e. pre-linguistic concepts, which categorise activities (EATING, CRYING, RUNNIG) and actions (goal-directed acts: GRASP-X, PUSH-X). He mentions five properties of "mimetic schemas"[37]: they are "(a) representational, (b) accessible to consciousness, (c) relatively concrete, (d) proprioceptively based and (e) pre-reflectively shared" (p. 11).

We may stop here to recapitulate. Donald and Zlatev's account paints a picture of language genesis which is directly opposed to mentalistic explanations. The latter are based on the A.I. assumption that mental capacities require a "program" to be functional.[38] That assumption takes radically different forms, e.g. that "language" requires an algorithmic "syntactic module" (Chomsky's "Platonic" nativism), possibly operated by "an army of idiots" (Dennett), or that it is based on "image schemas" developed in direct interactions with environment (Lakoff and Johnson's empiricism). But these differences merely point to an essential arbitrariness of mentalism, which cannot propose functional explanations, except for "freak" mutations or automatic semantic processes and transfers in the "cognitive unconscious". Mentalism is "agenetic", as clearly demonstrated by the evolutionary accounts presented in this section.

The mimetic account of complex mental abilities may seem at first counterintuitive. It proposes, for instance, that acts of imagination – when we voluntarily picture things "in the mind" – are dependent on prior symbolic imitation (i.e. social gesturing). Thus, it opposes the commonsensical view that the objective world is "external", while our "internal" mental world is somehow based on it (a view shared by mentalistic accounts of language). However, our mental world is primarily "external": it is born and develops in contact with things and co-specifics; it is dependent on control of one's body and on acts of expressive communication (consequently, the "individual" mind is genetically "social"). The "objec-

[37] On all five counts "mimetic schemas" are opposed to "image schemas" proposed by Johnson and Lakoff.

[38] As stated by a Polish psychologist and a critic of cognitivism, this is an "old assumption" that "all complex behaviour must be based on a prior plan of action" (Bobryk 1996: 107). We can see now that it is a result of focusing on end-states, or *hysteron proteron* fallacy.

tive" world, on the other hand, could be viewed in some sense as "internal": its appearance is shaped by our stance, by the ways we approach it, by our frames of reference and horizons (to repeat: there is no intention here to deny independent reality and non-arbitrariness in our vision of things). It is perhaps best to say that the opposition "external"/"internal" is not originary.

5.1.3. First words of a child

Freud in *Jenseits des Lustprinzips* recounts playful behaviour of a 1,5 year old boy (1988: 13–18).[39] The child was not precocious, spoke only a few words understood by his family, never cried when left alone, and was generally not a nuisance – with one exception . He used to throw away all small objects he could grab, producing at the same time a long "oooo" sound, interpreted by his carers as *fort* ("away"). In time, Freud realised that the boy played only this one game with his toys: "away with it" game. One day, the boy was playing with a spool. Rather than throw it away, he made it disappear behind the edge of the bed and then recovered it, pulling the thread attached. This game was accompanied by loud "ooo" in the first stage and *da* ("here", "back") in the second one. The child never tired of this game and was visibly enjoying himself, more so when the spool appeared again.

We need not go into specific interpretations of this behaviour provided by Freud and Lacan (cf. Lang 1973) to see its probable psychological meaning and its relevance in our context. The boy was deprived of his mother's presence. His reaction was not crying (the standard expression of rage and helplessness at this stage) but an attempt at a symbolic control of the situation. The act of imitation gave him some power to channel his emotions: "I can throw you away" or "I do not need you" (if mind-reading could yield any specific results at this psychologically "undifferentiated" stage). The discovery that there is a happy ending to his plight – that disappearance and return are linked – allowed him to "represent" his situation, gave him some insight.

The case of Little Hans exemplifies the actual mental work in "symbol acquisition": the boy repeats with the means available to him the act ("disappearance") that disturbs him the most – taking symbolic "revenge" – and discovers in the process that this act is linked with another one, which brings more satisfaction ("return"). This work cannot be properly described as "unconscious", or even "cognitive". The boy seeks relief in his existential plight. He does not burst into tears as most of his peers would, but takes an active role. By re-enacting the situation, he hits upon scenarios which bring relief – the second one more effectively than the first one. The schema provided by the more successful scenario ("away" – "back") allows satisfactory orientation in the situation at hand. Its verbal representation (*fort*, *da*) may be easily invoked when the child finds himself in (for

[39] I used this example in Pawelec (2007a: 213–215).

him) analogous situations. Thus, symbolic representations expressing emotional attitudes towards existentially important phenomena lead to cognitive representations as a by-product.

5.1.4. Words as "stopping orders"

So far, I have focused on the genetic relations between "language, thought, and reality" (in phylogenesis and ontogenesis). I have tried to demonstrate, following evolutionary and developmental research, that the genetic order assumed in mentalistic accounts should be reversed: exploratory, expressive and at some stage linguistic behaviour necessarily precedes (pre)conceptual structures. This must be so if mental structures re-code or provide insight into experiential structures developed via rote-learning. Equally necessary is the eclipse of the constitutive process by its outcome: the revelatory procedures must fade into the background, if we are to be able to "see" the world the way it has been "revealed". This does not mean, however, that the constituted world may be replaced by its mental representation – that language may be identified with conceptual structures. As stated by Merleau-Ponty: "The link between the word and its living meaning is not an external link of association, the meaning inhabits the word [...]. Language certainly has an inner content, but this is not self-subsistent and self-conscious thought. What then does language express, if it does not express thoughts? It presents or rather it *is* the subject's taking up of a position in the world of his meanings" (2002: 224–225; emphasis in the original).

David McNeill provides an interpretation of Merleau-Ponty's idea that "meaning inhabits the word" (McNeill 2005: 91–92). His interpretation is part of a detailed theory explaining the role of gestures which accompany speech. McNeill captures Merleau-Ponty's idea in terms of a dialectic (or an opposition leading to a resolution through change) between gestures and words in an utterance: "imagery-language dialectic". The opposition results from a combination of different modes of expression: gestural imagery is holistic, it signals the position taken up by the speaker against some common background, while verbal articulation is linear – it successively "unpacks" the holistic stance, translates it into categorial content. From a complementary point of view, it is an opposition between an individual stance and the social means of expression. The change in question is a mutual propulsion and clarification through an interplay of these channels of expression: gestures differentiate significant contrasts in a way which is not transparent to the listener and which requires unpacking in words, while words make sense in the field of oppositions signalled by gestures. What is of special interest in our context, verbal articulations serve as "stopping points", signalling a temporary resolution of the dialectic. Our linguistic intuition tells us that a given formulation is "good enough" as an articulation of our actual stance in a discourse situation. In other words, an individual vision is judged to be sufficiently available thanks to the social means of expression, which do not code or trigger conceptual structures, but serve to satisfy our intuition that we have made ourselves understood (McNeill 2005: 92–95). This approach allows us to understand why people effectively use words even if they are often unable to provide their definitions (to say nothing about rules of grammar). Meanings "inhabit" words, because words allow us to take stances towards situation types. When we talk about something, we do not express ready-made thoughts with verbal labels attached to them but we enact our stance to a situation.

5.1.5. The Sapir-Whorf hypothesis

In CL, the relations between "language, thought, and reality" are discussed in reference to the Sapir-Whorf hypothesis.[40] It is usually presented in two versions: the stronger interpretation called "linguistic determinism", and the weaker one called "linguistic relativity". The former states (in Pinker's formulation) that "people's thoughts are determined by the categories made available by their language", while according to the latter "differences among languages cause differences in the thoughts of their speakers" (1994: 57). The strong position is clearly untenable (e.g. in view of bilingualism). The weak position – linguistic relativity[41] – is quite unspecific. It merely states that the language we speak "influences" the way we think. Its most tangible interpretation, known as "thinking for speaking", was developed by Slobin. He makes the assumption that in the process of speaking (or any other process of verbal coding, decoding or re-coding), "experiences are filtered through language into *verbalized events*" (Slobin 2000: 107; emphasis in the original). In other words, in order to be expressed in a particular language, experience must be accessed from a particular point of view (a conventional one, if imposed by grammar). Thus, linguistic structures make available conventional ways of viewing reality, while language in use is a "window" on online conceptual activity.

Slobin has carried out several experiments to confirm the influence of "available" coding structures on the way experience is expressed.[42] As an example, he

---

[40] E.g. Lakoff (1987: ch. 18); Bickel (1998); Hopper (1998); Lee (1998); Slobin (1998, 2000, 2003); Niemeier, Dirven (2000). For other points of view, see e.g. Black (1962: 244–257); Tyler (1978: 68–70).

[41] Whorf expressly calls his position "a new principle of relativity, which holds that all observers are not led by the same physical evidence to the same picture of the universe, unless their linguistic backgrounds are similar, or can in some way be calibrated" (1956: 214). However, his position, rather confusingly (see Leavitt 2006: 66–68), does not amount to "linguistic relativism". It is only the deterministic interpretation which states that we are imprisoned in our "linguistic-cultural" vision of the world – that all our "truth-claims" are relative to that system of reference. Since Whorf does not reject the view that linguistic backgrounds "can in some way be calibrated", he is not a relativist. However, a deterministic (i.e. relativist) interpretation of Whorf's position was prevalent in the early reception of his work. No wonder that Berlin and Kay, in their classic work on the semantic universals in colour terminology, explicitly reject "the Whorfian tradition" (1969: 2, 160) (cf. 0.2).

[42] This is not a new type of research. One can see affinities with e.g. Chafe's study of narrative structuring of events in different cultures (Chafe 1980). The view that language in use is a window

hypothesised that there should be systematic differences in the way experience is coded when one compares two types of languages called (after Talmy) "verb-framed" and "satellite-framed". The latter (e.g. English or Polish) indicate "path" by a satellite to the verb:

(1)	a. *He ran*	*into*	*the house.*
	b. *Wbiegł*	*do*	*domu.*[43]
	He in-run	to	the house

The former (e.g. French, Spanish) indicate "path" by the main verb:

(2)	a. *Il est entré dans*	*la maison*	*en courant.*
	b. He is entered in	the house	by running[44]

As a result, verb-framed languages tend to code the manner of movement in an optional adjunct phrase (*en courant*), while satellite-framed languages tend to code "manner" in the main verb.

In the experiment, Slobin's team asked respondents[45] to describe events from a picture storybook *Frog, where are you?* – a fairy-tale in 24 pictures without words. In one episode, a little boy climbs a tree to look into a hole, and an owl flies out and knocks him down. While in satellite-framed languages the owl's movement was described (in various proportions) both by manner verbs and path verbs, in verb-framed languages only path verbs were used (with a single exception – one description of a Hebrew speaker). Slobin concludes that "speakers of the two language types differ in their *habitual attention* to manner of motion – as evidenced [...] in relative differences in frequency of mention". Specifically, speakers of verb-framed languages tend to focus on "path" (rather than "manner" of action) and tend not to choose manner verbs. On the structural level, Slobin notices that verb-framed languages have far fewer expressive manner verbs. He explains this fact by a smaller "cost" of filling one combined "slot" for "motion" and "manner" in satellite-framed languages (which has encouraged language users to be inventive) than of filling the additional optional slot for "manner" in verb-framed languages (2000: 113; emphasis in the original).

Slobin provides more evidence, but his overall conclusion is cautious and still rather vague: "it seems that users of [verb-framed] languages build mental images

---

on on-line conceptual activity is best exemplified by the research conducted by Chafe (1976, 1990, 1994, 1998) and McNeill (1992, 2005), also Drey, McNeill (1990).

[43] The division into both types is somewhat fuzzy: in Polish, "path" is coded both by the preposition (*do* - "to") and the verbal prefix (*w-*) - ("into"); the English translation of example (2a) shows that there are English verbs ("entered") which code "path" more completely than French verbs (*est entré dans*). Cf. Slobin (2000: 133–134, note 3).

[44] Slobin (2000: 108). Except for the Polish sentence, the examples are Slobin's.

[45] Both children (aged 3–11), and adults. The languages tested: English, German, Dutch, Russian (satellite-framed); French, Spanish, Turkish, Hebrew (verb-framed).

of physical scenes with minimal focus on manner of movement, and with rather different conceptualizations of manner when it *is* in focus. [...] These differences are exceptionally difficult to pin down, but the considerable range of evidence examined here is at least suggestive of rather divergent mental worlds of speakers of the two language types" (2000: 133; emphasis in the original).

Slobin's interpretation of "linguistic relativity" is so "weak" that the final suggestion concerning "rather divergent mental worlds of speakers of the two language types" comes as a surprise. After all, he talks only about "habitual attention" to certain features of the physical environment linked to the use of linguistic categories. To put it in more general terms, if one uses a tool, then some features of the environment "stand out" as relevant for the task at hand. For instance, since one uses articles in English, the feature of referents "presumably known/unknown to the addressee" is constantly monitored in speech and writing.[46] In Polish, that feature is not coded in grammar, but it can be expressed by other means, when relevant. The existence of a tool – e.g. a grammatical construction or a lexical item – may perhaps say something important about the social world, in which it developed and is still found useful, but – in itself – it is not enough to reveal the "mental world" of its users. Some crucial elements must be missing from Slobin's argument.

Slobin's attempt to find "Whorfian effects" in the use of grammatical categories shares an important feature with Berlin and Kay's famous attempt to disprove such effects in "colour naming" (mentioned in section 0.2). Both approaches treat the principle of linguistic relativity as a testable "hypothesis" and, accordingly, try to confront linguistic data with the perception of physical evidence (colours, actions). Since we have access to everyday perceptual things independently of linguistic expression,[47] it seems natural for scientists to look for effects of linguistic categories on that level.

But the effect of language on the perception of "middle-size dry goods" seems to be primarily general. Language lets "things" appear. It reduces the pressure of environment and allows its users to see a stable "world". Consequently, they may freely focus on any part of it. If some elements of their world play a significant part in daily commerce, they will be lexicalized. Thus, there is nothing essentially "relative" (incommensurable) in the fact that Eskimos have many words for different kinds of snow (if they do), to mention just one example from a large collection of "odd cases" presented in the literature. Eskimos must focus on snow collectively – with the help of linguistic distinctions – to survive. But, in principle, anyone can "see" snow the way they do. If not always directly, then certainly in the context of relevant activities (e.g. "a snow" good for making an igloo). This

---

[46] I presented this example in Pawelec (2006c).

[47] An access which can be standardised by the use of "pictures", presenting "entities" in question (drawings, films, colour samples etc.). As mentioned in 0.2., Lucy comments on the problem of using only linguistic data for investigating Whorfian effects (2000: xi–xii).

is true for any kind of "expert" knowledge, i.e. the knowledge of distinctions relevant for some activity (e.g. wine-tasting, driving a car or chicken-sexing).[48]

Taylor points out that the situation is different as concerns entities constituted in a language: "The reason why this is bound to be so is evident. Human beings in different societies constitute different ways of life. They recognize different emotions, different virtues, build different institutions, practices, and footings. [...] A given emotion, a given virtue, a certain prized act, a certain kind of footing, may only make sense within the institutions and practices of that society, and in relation to its favoured ends" (Taylor 2006: 36–37). Apparently the same point is made by Lucy: "There are many domains of experience that are primarily or exclusively verbal and we might expect linguistic relativity to have its most dramatic effects in such domains" (2000: xii).[49]

We are now in a better position to assess the principle of linguistic relativity. A language – as Taylor shows – expresses and partly constitutes a "way of life": a collective way of dealing with reality. A social group develops various practices as an answer to life's exigencies and in an attempt to make its existence worthwhile. In the process, distinctions relevant for practices are verbalized. If we return now to Berlin and Kay's study on colours (0.2.),[50] we may repeat what we know from work on "language genesis": linguistic categories express existentially important distinctions. If they happen to be universal (as in the case in question), this is not a direct result of physiology, but of some commonalities of human experience. Light and dark, the sun, fire, vegetation, the sky, the soil – these features of environment (as pointed out by Wierzbicka) are common enough and sufficiently important to prompt expression of the system of colour categories found in human communication. One may wonder, of course, why some communities did not feel the need to develop a richer system of distinctions and were satisfied with a

---

[48] It is true in principle that one can learn to see relevant distinctions; in practice, there are natural limitations of taste, skill, persistence etc. In this context, it is perhaps important to add that in many, if not most cases expertise does not in itself require (or even allow) verbalizing of the finest distinctions: one can perceive or perform something proficiently without naming; nevertheless, naming helps steer attention and seems indispensable when passing one's expertise to novices. On the issues involved in developing expertise, see Dreyfus, Dreyfus (1986); on chicken-sexers and supervised learning, see Harnad (2005).

[49] Lucy's remark is, of course, cogent in the context of attempts to test the principle of linguistic relativity. It does not help, however, to understand it. It would be more adequate to say that many domains of experience are primarily or exclusively constituted by expressive social practices and that, consequently, an access to experience of that kind is mostly linguistic.

[50] This is their conclusion: " Our essentially linguistic investigations have led, seemingly inescapably, to the conclusion that the eleven basic color categories are pan-human perceptual universals. But we can offer no physical or physiological explanation for the apparently greater perceptual salience of these particular eleven color stimuli, nor can we explain in any satisfying way the relative ordering among them. Existing theories of color perception, both classical and recent, offer several plausible suggestions for parts of the observed pattern, but none will serve as the basis of an adequate explanation" (Berlin, Kay 1969: 109).

single opposition.[51] Still, we see in this case that the experiential spectrum is to some extent shaped prior to language, that particular languages "divide" it in an experientially motivated fashion, and that – in principle – there is no limit to making and verbalizing ever finer distinctions (our "dialogue" with colour reality can go on for ever, if we perceive further differentiations significant in some spheres of activity).

What about Whorfian effects? Once we accept that linguistic categories express experientially relevant distinctions, we will not be surprised that language influences "habitual" responses to reality. If nothing special is expected, it is natural that people will use standard "slots" prompted by linguistic categories. Since "verb-framed" constructions, mentioned above require only a specification of "path" (and not necessarily of "manner"), there is little point in providing "extra" detail, unless one is asked to. Since Polish has not grammaticalised the feature "presumably known/unknown to the addressee", it is verbalized only when the speaker finds it relevant (as opposed to English). Whorfian effects of that kind are not significant (they say nothing about the "mental world" of language users), because we normally have or may have experiential access to relevant physical distinctions and, in most cases, some verbal means to draw them.[52]

However, if the required experience is rooted in a social reality – if it is developed in the context of specific collective practices and institutions – then language marks distinctions which may not be accessible to members of other communities (like "cool!" to Queen Victoria). To give an example from Poland under the communist rule, the English word "customer" could be easily translated into Polish at that time, since shops existed, but the underlying idea of the relevant social practice (as expressed by the phrase "Thank you for your custom!") made little sense. In Poland, one "hunted" for better commodities – usually sold "under the counter" – and "customers" were treated by shop "assistants" as pests. This example is relatively superficial, as "doing shopping" is perhaps not a deeply "formative" experience.[53] Still, it shows well enough that the source of strongest Whorfian effects lies not simply in the linguistic character of a domain, but in social practices, which shape the experience in a given sphere of activity. Accordingly (to return to Slobin's statement), when one wants to investigate "mental worlds", one should focus primarily on social practices underlying linguistic distinctions. However, since this task necessitates highly interpretative, culture- and language-

[51] The opposition which is difficult to verbalize (and imagine) when one operates on the basis of a more complex system of distinctions: perhaps "light vs. dark" or "cold vs. warm colours"? Cf. Wierzbicka's comments (1990a: 128 ff.) and 0.2.

[52] In the classic work on the "descriptive function" of language, Bühler notices that in each language family there are at least rudiments of structures fully developed in other families (1965: 152). At this point, a philosopher may raise a more general issue: what structures are necessary for a language to allow a description of the world, cf. Patočka (1987: 123ff).

[53] For a linguistic analysis of a formative social practice – "the cult of Mary, Mother of God" in Poland – see Tabakowska (2000).

bound explorations, cognitive scientists tend to focus on perceptual domains and cross-linguistic structural patterns.

5.2. The formalism of linguistics: a Gadamerian view

I have already quoted Humboldt's "energetic" definition of language (5.0). Let me quote now another passage, made famous by Chomsky, which presents in some detail the relationship between thought and language: "For language is quite peculiarly confronted by an unending and truly boundless domain, the essence of all that can be thought. It must therefore make infinite employment of finite means, and is able to do so through the power which produces identity of language and thought. But this also necessarily implies that language should exert its effect in two directions at once, in that it first proceeds outwards to the utterance, but then also back again to the powers that engender it" (1999: 91).

The energetic definition emphasizes the processual nature of language as mental labour necessary for the expression of thought.[54] The second passage, as pointed out by Gadamer, captures its essence as "a faculty that is aware of itself", i.e. which is "able to make infinite use of finite means" (Gadamer 1993: 441). This involves a two-way traffic, which underlies the fundamental identity of thought and language: thinking arises in linguistic expression, which is subsequently appropriated through reflection and thus increases the ability to express thought (or one's awareness), which in turn calls for subtler means of linguistic expression. As Humboldt puts it: "if the mental powers be lively enough, there issues from this constant striving and counter-striving of the soul an ever-greater *refinement* of language, a growing *enrichment* thereof in spiritual content, which enhances the demands made of language in precisely the same measure as they are better satisfied" (1999: 92; emphasis in the original).

In his appreciation of Humboldt's position, Gadamer notes that Humboldt limits "the universality of the connection between language and thought to the formalism of a faculty" (1993: 440). As we have seen, Humboldt captures the development of mental powers (or ideality) in terms of a positive reinforcement between linguistic and conceptual articulation. In his account, however, there is no source of propulsion, giving impetus to the process of expression, apart from arbitrarily distributed "will" ("if the mental powers be lively enough"). To be sure, the originary "will to speak" remains the central problem for all theories of the genesis of language. Even if we can sketch plausible scenarios of this kind (as we have seen in 5.1.1.–2.), it is still an unfathomable mystery why an ape species

[54] The material in this section and partly in the next one has been presented in Pawelec (to appear: b).

discovered language (a mystery of the same order, perhaps, as other enigmas of reality: why is there life?; why is there consciousness?; why is there something rather than nothing?).[55] One thing is clear by now. Contrary to Humboldt's intuition, what speech serves to articulate is primarily not thought, but a common situation. The will to speak is the will to connect with some aspects of reality[56] and to make others see something in the world. This point is clearly made by Gadamer: "there is no reflection when the word is formed, for the word is not expressing the mind but the thing intended" (1993: 426). The word is an attempt to articulate something about the world. Reflection may come later as an effort to see whether (or how well) a given take fits in with one's general grasp of the situation.

Let us ask now about the fate of the Humboldtian heritage in modern linguistics. As we have seen (4.1.), Saussure is fully aware of the inextricable connection between thought and language. To quote again: "Without language, thought is a vague, unchartered nebula. There are no pre-existing ideas, and nothing is distinct before the appearance of language [...] Neither are thoughts given material form nor are sounds transformed into mental entities; the somewhat mysterious fact is rather that 'thought-sound' implies division, and that language works out its units while taking shape between two shapeless masses" (1959: 112). Saussure's notion of "linguistic value" appears to be close to Humboldt's insight: language is "the domain of articulations", or "reciprocal delimitations" of sounds and concepts (p. 112). However, Saussure argues at length (1959: 79–100) for a systematic approach to linguistic phenomena, which he finds possible only in synchronic linguistics. As a result, Humboldt's focus on dynamic *energeia* – the linguistic energy which leads to an enrichment of mental powers and a parallel refinement of linguistic structures – is replaced by the focus on static value: "the pairing of a certain number of acoustical signs with as many cuts made from the mass of thought engenders a system of values" (1959: 120). For Humboldt, a linguistic change may be a sign of spiritual development (assuming the change embodies mental labour). For Saussure, it results from the influence of external social forces, which rather limit freedom and rationality. Since the linguistic sign is arbitrary, in principle the linguistic system could be organized at will in a perfectly rational manner. However, due to the influence of time, which produces deformations and even "teratological cases", it cannot be improved by individual actions (1959: 32, 78). In general, the arbitrariness of the linguistic sign makes the idea of spiritual development in language incomprehensible.

When we move on to Chomsky's interpretation of Humboldt – which, ironically perhaps, led to the present-day revival of his thought – we lose sight of the genetic link between language and thought ever more completely. Although Chomsky presents Humboldt's views under the rubric "creative aspects of lan-

---

[55] To be sure, such questions are raised by philosophers, rather than scientists. Cf. a statement by a psychologist: "Brains that pulse with certain patterns of electrical activity are conscious. Why? They just are" (Donald 2001: 178).

[56] In performative uses and most explicitly in verbal magic, cf. e.g. Leeuw (1997).

guage use", he does not relate the "patterned organization" of linguistic elements to mental labour necessary for articulation, but to "the finite system of generative principles" (Chomsky 1966: 22). In other words, Chomsky replaces "creativity" in language use as commonly understood (as acts generating new means of expression) with his own reinterpretation of it as the capacity to produce infinitely many new sentences thanks to the application of recursive rules (cf. McLure 1990: 500). As noted by a critic: "The idea that we create and understand novel sentences because we know a set of rules is a travesty of the meaning of creativity, for it construes creativity as the mechanical action of rules in reproducing and comprehending what is already known" (Tyler 1978: 140). In Chomsky's formalist account of language there is no place for spiritual development. Additionally, since generative principles are supposed to operate in individual minds, the social nature of language is lost from view.

CL apparently overcomes the formalist limitations of TG, as it places meaning at the centre of linguistic analysis and even promises to explain "what people find *meaningful* in their lives" (Lakoff, Johnson 1980: ix). However, in the mainstream it takes for granted the mentalistic perspective on language developed by Chomsky: conceptual processes are prior to and independent of linguistic "surface structures"; language should be explained on the conceptual ("deep") level. Since Chomsky's focus is limited to the "combinatorial potential" of syntactic forms, his hypothetical "mentalese" may be purely formal: algorithmic and unmotivated. Cognitive linguists, on the other hand, are interested in the semantic potential of verbal units at all levels of generality and complexity. Consequently, the "mentalese" they postulate must be much richer and motivated psychologically: by apparently universal rules of perception and by more specific rules imposed by one's cultural environment. However, in both cases the process of conceptualization is divorced from the mental labour inherent in verbal articulation, as described by Humboldt. At the same time, there is no recognition of the essentially social nature of the linguistic sign, as dependent on its place in the system of differences (linguistic value). Thus, language is reduced "to a simple naming-process" (Saussure 1959: 65, 114).

In spite of important differences, all modern accounts of language mentioned above treat it merely as a "tool". This perspective was most clearly articulated by Bühler with the Aristotelian notion of *organon* (1965: 24–28) and subsequently developed by Jakobson (1960). Bühler pointed out three basic functions of language: representational, expressive[57] and appellative, while Jakobson mentioned several additional ones, which may play a more or less important role in various acts of communication, e.g. poetic, magical, phatic. It should be clear at this point that a functionalist description of language, valid in its own limits and important

[57] Bühler's "expressive" function is limited to acts of communication involving one's inner states (emotions etc.). It should not be confused with hermeneutical "expression", which involves a linguistic articulation of opaque reality.

as an antidote to formalist tendencies, takes for granted common horizons opened up by linguistic expression.

When we look at language from the hermeneutical perspective – as a new way of collective being which opens up horizons in which reality may progressively appear for us – theories put forward by linguists are bound to seem limited. Gadamer accuses Humboldt of "formalism", because language conceived as *energeia* allows to differentiate thought and refine the means of its expression, rather than provides an altogether more transparent access to reality.[58] Subsequent conceptions may seem even more constrained: Saussure views language as a socially constituted system of values, Chomsky – as a generative system biologically implanted in individual heads, cognitive linguists – as networks of conceptualizations functioning according to psychological rules, while all of them view language as a tool of communication rather than a transforming way of being.

But we may also treat these theories in the standard way: as steps along the path of scientific progress. Even if linguistics divorces language from the originary context of "opening up" for us a range of mute experience, this is properly so. Linguistics as a science must "objectify", i.e. focus on language as separate from the world it helps to reveal. It is a set of "methods" – constrained ways of dealing with phenomena. As such, the theories mentioned above are necessarily "perspectival", throwing light only on a particular aspect of language. And it may be argued that each of them is an improvement on its predecessor (even if gains are bought at a price). Consequently, the hermeneutical approach to language need not imply a criticism of linguistics (certainly, that was not Gadamer's intention). Nevertheless, it may serve as a reminder to linguists of the scale and, ultimately, mysteriousness of the phenomenon they subject to analysis.[59]

Finally, we may see better now that the interpretation of CL as "a return of [prestructuralist] hermeneutics to lexical semantics" put forward by Geeraerts and Tabakowska is only partly right. It is true that a wealth of interpretative observations concerning "psychological" motivations of linguistic forms made by linguists in the 19th and early 20th century has been integrated into a mentalistic paradigm. One may ask, however, whether in the process the very hermeneutical character of those observations has not been obscured. Any statements concerning the history of linguistic ideas would obviously require a separate study. If one assumes, however, that the prestructuralist linguistics was (at least partly) Humboldtian in spirit – i.e. exploring a situated and social mental labour of linguistic articulation within particular communities – then CL's *reprise* of that heritage in mostly individualistic and universalist terms (a generic human being coping with its environment) brings with it both gains and losses which I have tried to capture.

[58] This "accessive" role of language is described by C. Taylor (2006). Cf. Pawelec (2009a, b).

[59] I do not suggest that linguists require such reminders. As already mentioned, Saussure (1959: 112) and Croft, Cruse (2004: 115) – for instance – freely admit the mysteriousness of linguistic phenomena they aim to capture. My point is to underline the tension between the hermeneutical vision of language as transformative of reality and human life on the one hand and the vision of language as a tool of communication analysed in various ways by linguists on the other hand.

In short, while CL can represent in a transparent way the results of processes of linguistic expression, it misrepresents their nature due to its cognitivist assumptions.

5.3. A plea for "expressive" linguistics

As I have already pointed out, a phenomenal success of CL is indicative of a disillusionment with (what is felt to be by many) arid formalisms of TG and of a widespread longing for linguistics "with a human face". Despite its limitations – which I have tried to delineate in this book – CL has generated a vast body of work which reveals the "human factor" in language. Can one go further in the direction laid down by CL, while at the same time modifying its fundamental assumptions? Let us inspect one such proposal.

Zlatev offers the notion of "a minimal, differentiated language game" (MDLG) as a correction of the idea of "embodiment" which was developed in cognitive semantics (e.g. Johnson 1987). Basically, he wants to replace the view that linguistic meaning is "grounded" in physical interactions with environment (preconceptual "image schemas") with the Wittgensteinian "view of language as constituting 'forms of life', embedded or *situated* within sociocultural practices". As he says, if cognitive semantics does not complement "physical" with "social" embodiment, it "is bound to remain individualistic, trapped in solipsism or neural reductionism" (Zlatev 2003: 454; emphasis in the original).

We already know the force of this objection. The notion of "image schemas" refers back to Kantian "transcendental schemas" and, more generally, to the problem of knowledge: how can we know anything, assuming that reality is in constant flux? Plato famously proposed the realm of immutable ideas but subsequently demolished his own theory in *Parmenides*. The problems with all such *a priori* systems of categories are similar: any framework devised for the organization of experience is bound to seem arbitrary, while the application of a fixed form to changing content involves endless regression (one needs a more general schema to apply a given schema, and so on). If one rejects idealism, and chooses to derive categories *a posteriori* from experience, the problems are even greater: experience is in flux, anything can be compared with anything else along an infinite number of dimensions, and – crucially – comparison requires a standard (thus one returns to idealism). Johnson does not show a way out of such problems; he merely postulates a limited set of categories (e.g. CONTAINER, PATH, BALANCE, CENTRE/PERIPHERY) which supposedly emerge in universal physical experience and "ground" linguistic meanings. Despite empirical rhetoric (including the neuronal level), this is an idealistic solution, which is open to all typical objections. Specifically, it does not face the problem of other minds, or (in its more relevant version for us) the problem of communication: how can one know what someone else has in mind? An "ostensive definition" is never enough: it can be interpreted in an infinite number of ways. Hence Zlatev's charge of solipsism.

The solution proposed by hermeneutics, and followed by Zlatev, is to reject that "meanings are in the head" (brain, mind). Meanings arise as ways to structure situations. Biological meanings arise in a habitat (or the field of activity of a species) as a set of differentiations (of the type: "food/non-food", "home/foreign territory", "friend/foe" etc.) imposed by a generic search to satisfy the needs of a given type of creature. Such meanings are not conceptual (or ideal): they are available only as responses to a situation. Linguistic or conceptual meanings arise in the communal field of expression and "sediment" – become freely available, can be used to actively structure any situation (real or imagined). As a result, a linguistic creature is at a distance from its environment (rather than at its beck and call) and can freely zoom in on things, not just in pressing circumstances, when it is on the look out for food or a predator. This means that even our "mute" experience – when we do not feel the need to use words or when we are confused and grope for words – is qualitatively different from the wordless world of animals. Such experience appears against the already structured background of cultural meanings – infinitely richer than the biological meanings of an animal.

This account shows that when we talk about something in the world, we do not refer to an objective, language-independent state of affairs (with the concomitant problem of ostensive definition), or to a conceptualization, a node in an internalised network of definitions (with the concomitant problem of other minds), but to "a humanly significant, in part linguistically construed aspect of reality". Consequently, Zlatev proposes that the "semantic pole" of linguistic symbols should be conceived not as a "conceptualization", but as a "situation (type)" (2003: 455; cf. Zielińska 2007a, b for a related proposal). His notion of MDLG emphasizes our social (i.e. partly linguistically constituted) situatedness. He talks of a "language game" to underline the fact that symbols are a matter of social convention; thus, it is social norms – rather than "truth conditions" or "conceptualizations" in individual minds – which constitute criteria of their appropriate use. The "minimal" unit of language is an utterance – the smallest move in discourse. Crucially, the minimal unit is one which still possesses essential attributes of the entity in question (as opposed to "atomistic" accounts). It is "differentiated", since it consists of smaller entities: words or phrases, but it retains its holistic character (words have meanings only in situated use; one cannot properly base a linguistic theory on a lower level of structure than the minimal unit).

Zlatev's notion of MDLG captures the social nature of linguistic meaning. It points to the fact that we inhabit a socially structured reality, which our language has helped to articulate (thus, in a sense, we inhabit language). Let us notice that this idea is different from the Sapir-Whorf hypothesis (in its strong version), which presents language almost as a set of animal habits one cannot but follow. It is more adequate to say, after Gadamer, that language opens up a horizon within which things appear for the first time and may be articulated *ad infinitum* (as opposed to the animal realm, in which things have no independent status – they appear only fleetingly in a situation as correlates of drives). Consequently, we are not forced to follow current articulations, while they are necessary as stepping-stones for all attempts at reformulating reality (and, of course, may be used unreflectively).

We can perhaps appreciate better now the significance of the sequence invoked in the Introduction: "the issue of the representation of lexical senses (available out of context) presupposes the issue of distinct meanings of words in use, which in turn presupposes the question of the transformative power of words". To be sure, the last question is bound to remain hardly transparent, since it concerns the contours of our life-world: the background of our understanding, underlying both unreflective, habitual practices and attempts at extending the boundaries of "domesticated" reality, which may transform its shape. This is necessarily so, if the hermeneutical diagnosis is right: something may appear only against an opaque background as a result of active engagements. In semantic terms, there are no single, "atomic" meanings. A meaning may appear only in a semantic field, as a result of differentiations. In the animal world, meanings are available in a generic behavioural field (or a habitat), constituted by basic polarizations reflecting "biological" needs. In the human world, meanings reflect existentially significant entities and features (perhaps best exemplified by such fundamental oppositions as "male/female", "human/animal", "night/day" or "earth/sky") and they "sediment" in communicative fields, or become articulated and freely available. This communal, intersubjective process forms the necessary, intuitively accessible background of all acts of communication, thus providing a way out of the problems with ostensive definitions and other minds.

When we accept this semantic, linguistically articulated and intuitively accessible background of communication, we may try to see more clearly the problem of "distinct" senses. Apparently, they are distinct when relevant referential situations are not only intersubjectively differentiated, but also felt to be opposed. The four senses of *tease*, mentioned in 0.4. and 4.3., are felt to be distinct because they refer to situations which are taken to be mutually exclusive (full "antagonism" pointed out by Croft and Cruse, cf. 0.4). This intuitive background of communication is far from transparent. Referentially distinct activities, e.g. "to paint" pictures vs. walls, need not be opposed, or felt to be distinct senses (cf. Tuggy 1993). Why can one say: "John paints, and so does Jane" (when John paints walls in a gallery, and Jane paints pictures hanging in the gallery)? Such a statement may cause mild amusement, while "John teases Rex, and so does Jane" (when John teases the dog with a stick, while Jane – with a sausage) is openly aberrant (or zeugmatic). This intuitive difference calls for some explanation. One can speculate, for instance, that the former sentence is acceptable because painting as an art is felt to be a specialist variant of a more general activity (a "microsense" of sorts, to use the terminology provided by Croft and Cruse). Apparently, microsenses are felt to become "distinct" senses when the situations they co-articulate drift apart in social perception (one can imagine that "teasing" a dog with a stick or a sausage would be perceived as a single sense in some "macho" cultures). To conclude, whatever explanations one puts forward, they should clarify our intuitions about what senses are felt to be socially antagonistic.

When we turn to the issue of the representation of distinct "senses", we can see now that some of the accounts presented above "change the subject" (cf. 0.1.). Most blatantly, both Lakoff and Dewell – who invoke "imagistic" explanations – abstract from the intuitive background of communication in the name of some theoretical constructs (the "linguist's fallacy"). When one begins with attested senses – as done by Queller and Taylor in a small segment of a lexeme's application, and more extensively by Tabakowska – the problem of the relatedness of senses looms large. It is perhaps intuitively tangible when one focuses on "recursive" extensions of a single sense in phrases – their sequence seems transparent, since they are all covered by contemporary intuitions. When one tries, however, to relate the whole range of dictionary senses, one is at a loss because such senses were established in a history of expression, which is not intuitively accessible (as demonstrated by Saussure). The cognitivist solution is to represent the results of that history around the central senses, as revealed by contemporary intuitions. Can one do better? Can one actually uncover the layers of constitution? Is "expressive" linguistics possible?

We have seen one such attempt by Vandeloise (4.2.). Even though it does not represent the actual development of a single sense (a monosemic category), it clearly shows the pragmatic character of that process and the crucial role of oppositions in it (LENGTH as opposed to WIDTH, BREADTH, HEIGHT, THICKNESS etc.). Another example known to me concerns a grammatical category – the French verbal adjective (McLure, Reed 1990). In both cases, it is the unity of a linguistic category which is at stake. Such examples suggest that one can imaginatively recreate the logical or notional (as opposed to the actual, diachronic) unity of a lexical category, when one focuses on "some vestiges [...] of [a category's] evolution", i.e. "seemingly arbitrary aspects of the distribution of [a given term or category] and most notably their selection restrictions" (Vandeloise 1990: 418). Such attempts are openly interpretative and merely suggestive of the processes of meaning extension that must have taken place (while particulars and contingencies are obviously hidden from view).

Consequently, my plea for "expressive linguistics" is tentative and limited. I do not propose a new "paradigm", which could rival CL or other linguistic schools. Expressive linguistics would be necessarily based on individual insight, helping one to transcend contemporary intuitions. One thing is clear, though: such attempts would have to take as their point of departure exceptions and irregularities, which are "regularized" or swept aside by mainstream linguistics.

REFERENCES

Achard, M. and S. Niemeier (eds.) (2004). *Cognitive Linguistics, Second Language Acquisition, Foreign Language Teaching*. Berlin: Mouton de Gruyter.

Allwood, J. and P. Gardenfors (eds.) (1998). *Cognitive Semantics. Meaning and Cognition*. Amsterdam / Philadelphia: John Benjamins.

Alm-Arvius, C. (2007). Lexical polysemy. In: Magnusson, H. et al. (eds.), 43–56.

Antas, J. (2000). *O kłamstwie i kłamaniu*. Kraków: Universitas.

Bacz, B. (2004). On the meaning of *za* in the Polish title of *Kidnapped* by Louis Stevenson. In: Branny, G. and A. Branny (eds.), 439–448.

Baumgartner, P. and S. Payr (eds.) (1995). *Speaking Minds. Interviews with Twenty Cognitive Scientists*. Princeton: Princeton University Press.

Bechtel, W. and G. Graham (eds.) (1998). *A Companion to Cognitive Science*. Oxford: Oxford University Press.

Becker, L.C. (1986). *Reciprocity*. London/New York: Routledge & Kegan Paul.

Behrens, L. (ed.) (2002). *Lexicon in Focus. Competition and Convergence in Current Lexicology*. Frankfurt/New York: Peter Lang.

Berlin, B. and P. Kay (1969). *Basic Color Terms: Their Universality and Evolution*. Berkeley: University of California Press.

Bickel, B. (1998). *Grammar and social practice: On the role of culture in linguistic relativity*. Essen: LAUD 425.

Bird, A. and E. Tobin (2008). Natural kinds. *Stanford Encyclopedia of Philosophy* (online).

Black, M. (1962). *Models and metaphors*. Ithaca: Cornell University Press.

Blank, A. and P. Koch (eds.) (1999). *Historical Semantics and Cognition*. Berlin/New York: Mouton de Gruyter.

Bobryk, J. (1996). *Akty świadomości i procesy poznawcze*. Wrocław: Fundacja Na Rzecz Nauki Polskiej.

Bolinger, D. (1992). About furniture and birds. *Cognitive Linguistics* 1, 111–117.

Branny, G. and A. Branny (2004). *Ways of looking at a blackbird. Essays in British and American Literature and Studies in Honor of Prof. Irena Przemecka*. Kraków: IFA UJ.

Britton, B.K. and A.D. Pellegrini (eds.) (1990). *Narrative thought and narrative language*. Mahwah: LEA.

Bühler, K. (1965). *Sprachtheorie. Die Darstellungsfunktion der Sprache*. Stuttgart: Gustav Fischer Verlag.

Buttler, D. (1988). *Słownik polskich homonimów całkowitych*. Wrocław: PAN.

Cassirer, E. (1957). *The Phenomenology of Knowledge*. New Haven/London: Yale University Press.

Chafe, W. (1976). Givenness, contrastiveness, definiteness, subjects, topics, and point of view. In: Li, C.N. (ed.), 25–55.

Chafe, W. (1980). *The Pear Stories*. Norwood, N.J.: Ablex.

Chafe, W. (1990). Some things that narrativess tell us about the mind. In: Britton, B.K. and A.D. Pellegrini (eds.), 79–98.

Chafe, W. (1994). *Discourse, consciousness, and time*. Chicago: University of Chicago Press.

Chafe, W. (1998). Language and the flow of thought. In: Tomasello M. (ed.), 93–112.

Chłopicki, W. et al. (eds.) (2007). *Cognition in Language. Volume in Honour of Professor Elżbieta Tabakowska*. Kraków: Tertium.

Chomsky, N. (1966). *Cartesian Linguistics*. New York: Harper & Row.

Chomsky, N. (1977). A Polish translation of the review of B.F. Skinner's *Verbal Behavior*. In: Stanosz, B. (ed.), 23–81.

Chrzanowska-Kluczewska, E. and G. Szpila (eds.) (2009). *In search of (non)sense*. Newcastle upon Tyne: Cambridge Scholars Publishing.

Corballis, M.C. and I. Lea (eds.) (1999). *The descent of mind*. Oxford: Oxford University Press.

Coulmas, F. (ed.) (1981). *A Festschrift for native speaker*. The Hague: Mouton.

Croft, W. (2000). *Explaining language change. An evolutionary approach*. Harlow: Longman/Pearson Education.

Croft, W. (2009). Toward a social cognitive linguistics. In: Evans, V. and S. Pourcel (eds.), 395–420.

Croft, W. and D.A. Cruse (2004). *Cognitive Linguistics*. Cambridge: Cambridge University Press.

Cuyckens, H. (1999). Grammaticalization in the English Prepositions "to" and "for". In: Lewandowska-Tomaszczyk, B. (ed.), 53–76.

Cuyckens, H. et al. (eds.) (2003a). *Motivation in Language*. Amsterdam/Philadelphia: John Benjamins.

Cuyckens, H. et al. (eds.) (2003b). *Cognitive approaches to lexical semantics*. Berlin/New York: Mouton de Gruyter.

Dąbrowska, E. (1996). The spatial structuring of events: A study of Polish perfectivizing prefixes. In: Puetz, M. and R. Dirven (eds.), 467–490.

Dąbrowska, E. and W. Kubiński (2003). *Akwizycja języka w świetle językoznawstwa kognitywnego*. Kraków: Universitas.

Deacon, T. (1997). *The symbolic species*. London: Penguin.

Dewell, R.B. (1994). *Over* again: Image-schema transformations in semantic analysis. *Cognitive Linguistics* 4, 351–380.

Dirven, R. and J. Vanparys (eds.) (1995). *Current approaches to the lexicon*. Frankfurt am Mein: Peter Lang.

Dillon, M.C. (1988). *Merleau-Ponty's Ontology*. Evanston, Ill.: Northwestern University Press.

Donald, M. (1991). *Origins of the modern mind*. Cambridge, Mass.: Harvard University Press.

Donald, M. (1993). Human cognitive evolution. *Social Research* 60/1, 143–170.

Donald, M. (1999). Preconditions for the evolution of protolanguages. In: Corballis, M.C. and I. Lea (eds.), 355–365. [author's web page]

Donald, M. (2000). The central role of culture in cognitive evolution: A reflection on the myth of the "isolated mind". In: Nucci, L. (ed.), 19–38.

Donald, M. (2001). *A mind so rare. The evolution of human consciousness*. New York: Norton.

Donald, M. (2004). The virtues of rigorous interdisciplinarity. In: Lucariello, J.M. et al. (eds.), 245–256. [author's web page]

Donaldson, M. (1986). *Myślenie dzieci*. Warszawa: WP [M. Donaldson (1986). *Children's minds*. HarperCollins] .

Drey, N.L. and D. McNeill (1990). Gestures during discourse. In: Tsohatzidis, S.L. (ed.), 465–487.

Dreyfus, H.L. (1991). *Being-in-the-World. A commentary to Heidegger's* Being and Time. Cambridge, Mass./London: MIT Press.

Dreyfus, H.L. (1992 [1972]). *What computers still can't do*. Cambridge, Mass.: MIT Press.

Dreyfus, H.L. and S. Dreyfus (1986). *Mind over machine*. The Free Press.

Dunbar, G. (1991). *The Cognitive Lexicon*. Tübingen: G. Narr.

Edelman, G. (1992). *Bright air, brilliant fire: On the matter of the mind*. New York: Basic Books.

Eiser, R. (1994). *Attitudes, chaos, and the connectionist mind*. Oxford: Blackwell.

Ereshefsky, M. (2007). Species. *Stanford Encyclopedia of Philosophy* (on-line).

Evans, V. (2007). Towards a cognitive compositional semantics: An overview of LCCM theory. In: Magnusson, U. et al. (eds.), 11–42.

Evans, V. and M. Green (2006). *Cognitive Linguistics*. Edinburgh: Edinburgh University Press.

Evans, V. and S. Pourcel (eds.) (2009). *New Directions in Cognitive Linguistics*. Amsterdam / Philadelphia: John Benjamins.

Evens, M.W. (ed.) (1988). *Relational models of the lexicon. Representing knowledge in semantic networks*. Cambridge: Cambridge University Press.

Fauconnier, G. (1994). *Mental Spaces*. Cambridge: Cambridge University Press.

Fauconnier, G. (1997). *Mappings in Thought and Language*. Cambridge: Cambridge University Press.

Fauconnier, G. (2003). Cognitive Linguistics. In: L. Nadel (ed.), [internet version: 1–14].

Fauconnier, G. and M. Turner (2003). *The way we think*. New York: Basic Books.

Fleck, L. (1986 [1935]). *Powstanie i rozwój faktu naukowego*. Lublin: Wydawnictwo Lubelskie [L. Fleck (1981). *Genesis and development of scientific fact*. Chicago: The University of Chicago Press].

Foucault, M. (1994). *The Order of Things. An Archeology of Human Sciences*. New York: Vintage.

Frank, R.M. et al. (eds.) (2008). *Body, Language and Mind*. Vol. 2. Berlin/New York: Mouton de Gruyter.

Frege, G. (1993). On Sense and Reference. In: Moore, A.W. (ed.), 23–42 [internet].

Freud, S. (1988). *Essays III. Auswahl 1920–1937*. Berlin: Verlag Volk und Welt.

Gadamer, H.-G. (1993). *Truth and method*. London: Sheed & Ward.

Garbowski, C. et al. (eds.) (2009). *Charles Taylor's Vision of Modernity. Reconstructions and Interpretations*. Newcastle upon Tyne: Cambridge Scholars Publishing.

Gardner, H. (1987). *The mind's new science. A history of the cognitive revolution*. New York: Basic Books.

Geeraerts, D. (1988a). Where does prototypicality comes from? In: Rudzka-Ostyn, B. (ed.), 207–230.

Geeraerts, D. (1988b). Cognitive Grammar and the History of Lexical Semantics. In: Rudzka-Ostyn, B. (ed.), 647–677.

Geeraerts, D. (1990). The lexicographical treatment of prototypical polysemy. In: Tsohatzidis, S.L. (ed.), 195–210.

Geeraerts, D. (1992a). Polysemy and prototypicality [a review of Kleiber 1990]. *Cognitive Linguistics* 2, 219–231.

Geeraerts, D. (1992b). The return of hermeneutics to lexical semantics. In: Pütz, M. (ed.), 257–282.

Geeraerts, D. (1993). Vagueness's puzzles, polysemy's vagaries. *Cognitive Linguistics* 3, 223–272.

Geeraerts, D. (2002). The theoretical and descriptive development of lexical semantics. In: Behrens, L. (ed.), 23–42 [internet version: 1–13].

Geeraerts, D. (2007). Lexicography. In: Geeraerts, D. and H. Cuyckens (eds.), 1160–1175.

Geeraerts, D. and H. Cuyckens (eds.) (2007). *The Oxford Handbook of Cognitive Linguistics*. Oxford/New York: Oxford University Press.

Geiger, R.A. and B. Rudzka-Ostyn (eds.) (1993). *Conceptualizations and Mental Processing in Language*. Berlin/New York: Mouton de Gruyter.

Glynn, D. (2009). Polysemy, syntax, and variation. A usage-based method for Cognitive Semantics. In: Evans, V. and S. Pourcel (eds.), 77–104 [internet].

Górska, E. (ed.) (1993). *Images from the cognitive scene*. Kraków: Universitas.

Gould, S.J. (1983). *Hen's Teeth and Horse's Toes*. New York: Norton.

Halliday, M.A.K. and R. Hasan (1976). *Cohesion in English*. London/New York: Longman.

Harder, P. (1999). Partial Autonomy. Ontology and Methodology in Cognitive Linguistics. In: Janssen, T. and G. Redeker (eds.), 195–222.

Harder, P. (2006). Recursion in a functional-semantic grammar. In: Haukioja, T. (ed.), 67–105 [author's web page].

Harder, P. (2007). Cognitive Linguistics and Philosophy. In: Geeraerts, D. and H. Cuyckens (eds.), 1241–1265.

Harder, P. (2009). Meaning as input: the instructional perspective. In: Evans, V. and S. Pourcel (eds.), 27–55.

Harnad, S. (2005). To Cognize is to Categorize: Cognition is Categorization. In: Lefebvre, C. and H. Cohen (eds.), [internet version: 1–30].

Harris, R. (1981). *The Language Myth*. London: Duckworth.

Harris, R. (1988). *Language, Saussure and Wittgenstein*. London: Routledge.

Harris, R. and T.J. Taylor (1989). *Landmarks in Linguistic Thought. The Western Tradition from Socrates to Saussure*. London/New York: Routledge.

Haukioja, T. (ed.) (2006). *Publications in General Linguistics 10. Papers on Language Theory*. Turku.

Hayek, F. (1978). *New Studies in Philosophy, Politics, Economics and the History of Ideas*. London/Henley: Routledge & Kegan Paul.

Heidegger, M. (1994). *Bycie i czas*. Warszawa: PWN [M. Heidegger (1996). *Being and Time*. New York: Suny Press].

Hopper, P. (1998). *Verbs and their Whorfian ways: The view from discourse*. Essen: LAUD 439.

Humboldt, W. von (1999). *On Language*. Cambridge: Cambridge University Press.

Hurford, J.R. (2007). *The origins of meaning. Language in the light of evolution*. Oxford: Oxford University Press.

Itkonen, E. (1977). The relation between grammar and sociolinguistics. *Forum Linguisticum* 1/3, 238–254 [internet].

Itkonen, E. (1981). The concept of linguistic intuition. In: Coulmas, F. (ed.), 127–140 [internet].

Itkonen, E. (1997). The social ontology of linguistic meaning. *SKY: The Yearbook of the Linguistic Association of Finland*, 49–80 [internet].

Itkonen, E. (2002). Grammaticalization as an analogue of hypothetico-deductive thinking. In: Wischer, I. and G. Diewald (eds.), 413–422 [internet].

Itkonen, E. (2008). The central role of normativity in language and linguistics. In: Zlatev, J. et al. (eds.), [internet version: 1–25].

Jakobson, R. (1960). Linguistics and Poetics. In: Sebeok, T.A. (ed.), 350–377.

Jameson, F. (1972). *The prison-house of language*. Princeton: Princeton University Press.

Jankowsky, K. (1972). *The Neogrammarians*. The Hague/Paris: Mouton.

Janowska, A. (2007a). *Polisemia staropolskich czasowników. Źródła, swoistość, konsekwencje.* Katowice: Wydawnictwo UŚ.

Janowska, A. (2007b). O roli analogii w słowotwórstwie (na przykładzie czasowników staropolskich). *LingVaria* 2/4, 115–129.

Janowska, A. and M. Pastuchowa (2005). *Słowotwórstwo czasowników staropolskich: stan i tendencje rozwojowe*. Kraków: Universitas.

Janssen, T. and G. Redeker (eds.) (1999). *Cognitive Linguistics: foundations, scope, and methodology*. Berlin/New York: Mouton de Gruyter.

Jespersen, O. (1922). *Language. Its Nature, Development and Origin*. London: Allen & Unwin.

Johnson, M. (1987). *The body in the mind*. Chicago: University of Chicago Press.

Johnson, M. (1992). Philosophical implications of cognitive semantics. *Cognitive Linguistics* 4, 345–366.

Johnson, M. (1993a). *Moral imagination*. Chicago: University of Chicago Press.

Johnson, M. (1993b). Why cognitive semantics matters to philosophy. *Cognitive Linguistics* 1, 62–74.

Johnson, M. and G. Lakoff (2002). Why cognitive linguistics requires embodied realism? *Cognitive Linguistics* 3, 245–263.

Jonas, H. (1974). "Sight and Thought: A review of 'Visual Thinking'". *Philosophical Essays*. Chicago: University of Chicago Press, 224–236.

Joseph, J.E. (2004). The linguistic sign. In: Sanders, C. (ed.), 59–75.

Jourdan, C. and K. Tuite (eds.) (2006). *Language, culture, and society*. Cambridge: Cambridge University Press.

Kalisz, R. and W. Kubiński (1998). Przyimki, przypadki i domeny. In: Kubiński, W. et al. (eds.), 189–198.

Kardela, H. (1993). Of *false pearls*, *angry storms* and *artificial tears*. Toward a cognitive analysis of collocations. In: Górska, E. (ed.), 43–58.

Kardela, H. et al. (eds.) (2005). *Kognitywistyka. Problemy i Perspektywy*. Lublin: Wydawnictwo UMCS.

Katz, J. (1971). *The underlying reality of language*. New York: Harper & Row.

Keller, R. (1994). *On language change: The invisible hand in language*. London: Routledge.

Kellermann, G. and M.D. Morrissey (eds.) (1992). *Diachrony within synchrony: Language history and cognition*. Frankfurt am Mein: Peter Lang.

Kleiber, G. (2003). *Semantyka prototypu. Kategorie i znaczenie leksykalne*. Tr. by B. Ligara. Kraków: Universitas [*La sémantique du prototype. Catégories et sens lexical*. PUF 1990].

Kochańska, A. (1996). Temporal meanings of spatial prepositions in Polish: The case of *przez* and *w*. In: Pütz, M. and R. Dirven (eds.), 491–508.

Kołakowski, L. (1975). *Husserl and the search for certitude*. Chicago/London: University of Chicago Press.

Kövecses, Z. (1986). *Metaphors of Anger, Pride, and Love*. Amsterdam: Benjamins.

Kövecses, Z. (1988). *The Language of Love*. Lewisburg: Bucknell University Press.

Kövecses, Z. (1990). *Emotion Concepts*. New York: Springer.

Kreitzer, A. (1997). Multiple levels of schematization: A study in the conceptualization of space. *Cognitive Linguistics* 4, 291–325.

Kristiansen, G. et al. (eds.) (2006). *Cognitive Linguistics: Current Applications and Future Perspectives*. Berlin/New York: Mouton de Gruyter.

Krzeszowski, T.P. (1993). The axiological parameter in preconceptual image schemata. In: Geiger, R.A. and B. Rudzka-Ostyn (eds.), 307–330.

Krzeszowski, T.P. (1997). *Angels and Devils in Hell*. Warszawa: Energeia.

Krzeszowski, T.P. (2002). Problems that are not supposed to arise? *Cognitive Linguistics* 3, 265–269.

Kubiński, W. et al. (eds.) (1998). *Językoznawstwo kognitywne: Wybór tekstów*. Gdańsk: Wydawnictwo Uniwersytetu Gdańskiego.

Kuhn, T. (1996). *The structure of scientific revolutions*. Chicago: University of Chicago Press.

Kula, W. (2004). *Miary i ludzie*. Warszawa: Książka i Wiedza.

Kurek, H. and M. Brzezina (eds.) (1999). *Collectanea Linguistica in honorem Casimiri Polański*. Kraków: Księgarnia Akademicka.

Kurtyka, A. (2001). Teaching English phrasal verbs: a cognitive approach. In: Pütz, M. et al. (eds.), 29–54.

Lakoff, G. (1987). *Women, Fire, and Dangerous Things. What Categories Reveal about the Mind*. Chicago: University of Chicago Press.

Lakoff, G. (1990). The Invariance Hypothesis: is abstract reason based on image-schemas? *Cognitive Linguistics* 1, 39–74.

Lakoff, G. (1996). *Moral Politics*. Chicago: University of Chicago Press.

Lakoff, G. and M. Johnson (1980). *Metaphors we live by*. Chicago: University of Chicago Press.

Lakoff, G. and M. Johnson (1999). *Philosophy in the Flesh*. New York: Basic Books.

Lakoff, G. and R. Núñez (2001). *Where Mathematics Comes From*. New York: Basic Books.

Lakoff, G. and M. Turner (1989). *More Than Cool Reason*. Chicago: University of Chicago Press.

Lang, H. (1973). *Die Sprache und das Unbewusste*. Frankfurt am Main: Suhrkamp Verlag.

Langacker, R. (1987). *Foundations of Cognitive Grammar*. Vol. 1: *Theoretical prerequisites*. Stanford: Stanford University Press.

Langacker, R. (1988a). A View of Linguistic Semantics. In: Rudzka-Ostyn, B. (ed.), 49–90.

Langacker, R. (1988b). A Usage-Based Model. In: Rudzka-Ostyn, B. (ed.), 127–161.

Langacker, R. (1991). *Concept, Image, and Symbol*. Berlin/New York: Mouton de Gruyter.

Leavitt, J. (2006). Linguistic relativities. In: Jourdan, C. and K. Tuite (eds.), 47–81.

Lee, P. (1998). *The operation of linguistic relativity in the cognitive domain*. Essen: LAUD 433.

Leeuw, G. van der (1997). *Fenomenologia religii*. Warszawa: Książka i Wiedza [G. van der Leeuw (1963). *Religion in essence and manifestation: A Study in Phenomenology*. New York: Harper & Row].

Lefebvre, C. and H. Cohen (eds.) (2005). *Handbook on Categorization*. Elsevier.

Lehrer, A. (1990). Prototype theory and its implications for lexical analysis. In: Tsohatzidis, S.L. (ed.), 368–381.

Lewandowska-Tomaszczyk, B. (ed.) (1999). *Cognitive perspectives on language*. Frankfurt am Mein: Peter Lang.

Lewandowska-Tomaszczyk, B. (2007). Polysemy, prototypes, and radial categories. In: Geeraerts, D. and H. Cuyckens (eds.), 139–169.

Li, C.N. (ed.) (1976). *Subject and Topic*. Academic Press.

Lorenz, K. (1963). *On Agression*. New York/Toronto: Bantam Books.

Lucariello, J.M. et al. (eds.) (2004). *The development of the mediated mind*. Mahwah: LEA.

Lucy, J.A. (2000). Introductory comments. In: Niemeier, S. and R. Dirven (eds.), ix–xxi.

Łozowski, P. (1999). Panchrony, or linguistics without synchrony. In: Lewandowska-Tomaszczyk, B. (ed.), 23–35.

Magnusson, U. et al. (eds.) (2007). *Further Insights into Semantics and Lexicography*. Lublin: Wydawnictwo UMCS.

Mannheim, K. (1955). *Ideology and Utopia: An Introduction to the Sociology of Knowledge*. Harvest Books.

McLure, R. (1990). Why words have to be vague? In: Tsohatzidis, S. (ed.), 488–520.

McLure, R. (1993). On "Philosophical implications of cognitive semantics". *Cognitive Linguistics* 1, 39–47.

McLure, R. and P. Reed (1990). A notional approach to the French verbal adjective. In: Tsohatzidis, S.L. (ed.), 247–266.

McNeill, D. (1992). *Hand and Mind*. Chicago: University of Chicago Press.

McNeill, D. (2005). *Gesture and Thought*. Chicago/London: University of Chicago Press.

Mehler, J. and S. Franck (eds.) (1995). *"Cognition" on Cognition*. Cambridge, Mass.: MIT Press.

Merleau-Ponty M. (2002). *Phenomenology of Perception*. London/New York: Routledge [M. Merleau-Ponty (2001). *Fenomenologia percepcji*. Warszawa: Aletheia].

Michalski, K. (1998). *Heidegger i filozofia współczesna*. Warszawa: PIW.

Moore, A.W. (ed.) (1993). *Meaning and Reference*. Oxford: Oxford University Press.

Morris, D. (2004). *The sense of space*. Albany: SUNY Press.

Müller, C. (2008). *Metaphors dead and alive, sleeping and waking*. Chicago: University of Chicago Press.

Nadel, L. (ed.) (2003). *Encyclopedia of Cognitive Science*. London: Macmillan.

Nerlich, B. et al. (eds.) (2003). *Flexible Patterns of Meaning in Mind and Language*. Berlin/New York: Mouton de Gruyter.

Nerlich, B. and D.D. Clarke (2007). Cognitive Linguistics and the History of Linguistics. In: Geeraerts, D. and H. Cuyckens (eds.), 589–610.

Niemeier, S. and R. Dirven (eds.) (2000). *Evidence for linguistic relativity*. Amsterdam/ Philadelphia: John Benjamins.

Normand, C. (2004). System, arbitrariness, value. In: Sanders, C. (ed.), 88–104.

Nöth, W. (1995). *Handbook of Semiotics*. Bloomington: Indiana University Press.

Nucci, L. (ed.) (2000). *Culture, thought and development*. Mahwah, NJ: L. Erlbaum.

Nuyts, J. (2007). Cognitive Linguistics and Functional Linguistics. In: Geeraerts, D. and H. Cuyckens (eds.), 543–565.

Oakley, T. (2007). Image schemas. In: Geeraerts, D. and H. Cuyckens (eds.), 214–235.

Ortony, A. (1979). *Metaphor and Thought*. Cambridge: Cambridge University Press.

Ortony, A. (1988). Are emotion metaphors conceptual or lexical? *Cognition and Emotion* 2/2, 95–103.

Pasich-Piasecka, A. (1993). Polysemy of the Polish verbal prefix *prze-*. In: Górska, E. (ed.), 11–26.

Pateman, T. (1987). *Language in mind and language in society. Studies in Linguistic Reproduction*. Oxford: Clarendon Press.

Patočka, J. (1986). *Świat naturalny i fenomenologia*. Kraków: Wydział Filozoficzny.

Patočka, J. (1998). *Body, community, language, world*. Chicago/La Salle, Ill.: Open Court.

Pawelec, A. (2005a). *Znaczenie ucieleśnione. Propozycje kręgu Lakoffa*. Kraków: Universitas.

Pawelec, A. (2005b). Druga rewolucja kognitywistyczna. In: Kardela, H. et al. (eds.), 279–284.

Pawelec, A. (2005c). Znaczenie ucieleśnione. *Przestrzenie Teorii* 5/6, 253–263.

Pawelec, A. (2005d). "Grounding of meaning in the history of expression". Paper presented at NDCL Conference in Brighton.

Pawelec, A. (2006a). *Metafora pojęciowa a tradycja*. Universitas: Kraków.

Pawelec, A. (2006b). The death of metaphor. *Studia Linguistica UJ*, 117–121.

Pawelec, A. (2006c). Relatywizm językowy. Czy można „przyswoić sobie" inny język? *Kwartalnik Pedagogiczny UW* 4, 155–162.

Pawelec, A. (2007a). *Metaphor and the unconscious*. In: Chłopicki, W. et al. (eds.), 210–223.

Pawelec, A. (2007b). A note on the "formalism" of Cognitive Linguistics. *Studia Linguistica UJ*, 99–102.

Pawelec, A. (2007c). A note on iconicity and motivation of expression. *Research in Language* 5, 205–212.

Pawelec, A. (2008). Mentalizm w badaniach nad językiem. In: Stalmaszczyk, P. (ed.), 105–119.

Pawelec, A. (2009a). The Romantic theory of language and metaphor. In: Garbowski, C. et al. (eds.), 194–204.

Pawelec, B. (2009b). Metaphor in philosophical discourse. In: Chrzanowska-Kluczewska, E. and G. Szpila (eds.), 59–65.

Pawelec, A. (to appear: a). *Językoznawstwo kognitywne a hermeneutyka*. In: Stalmaszczyk, P. (ed.) *Metodologie językoznawstwa III*.

Pawelec, A. (to appear: b). The formalism of linguistics? A Gadamerian view. In: Stalmaszczyk, P. (ed.) *Philosophy of Language and Linguistics*. Vol. II: *The Philosophical Turn*.

Piaget, J. (1966a). *Studia z psychologii dziecka*. Warszawa: PWN [J. Piaget (2000). *The psychology of the child*. New York: Basic Books].

Piaget, J. (1966b). *Narodziny inteligencji dziecka*. Warszawa: PWN [J. Piaget (1992). *Origins of intelligence in children*. International Universities Press].

Piaget, J. (1972). *Strukturalizm*. Warszawa: Wiedza Powszechna [J. Piaget (1970). *Structuralism*. New York: Basic Books].

Piatelli-Palmarini, M. (1995). Ever since language and learning: After-thoughts on the Piaget-Chomsky debate. In: Mehler, J. and S. Franck (eds.), 361–392.

Pinker, S. (1994). *The language instinct. The new science of language and mind*. London: Penguin Books.

Pinker, S. (1997). *How the mind works*. London: Allen Lane/The Penguin Press.

Pinker, S. (2007). *The stuff of thought. Language as a window into human nature*. London: Allen Lane / Penguin Books.

Plamenatz, J. (1950). Rights. *Proceedings of Aristotelian Society* 24, 75–82.

Plamenatz, J. (1973). *Democracy and Illusion*. Macmillan.

Plato, *Complete Works*, tr. by B. Jowett [internet].

Przybylska, R. (2002). *Polisemia przyimków polskich w świetle semantyki kognitywnej*. Kraków: Universitas.

Przybylska, R. (2006). *Schematy wyobrażeniowe a semantyka polskich prefiksów czasownikowych do-, od-, prze-, roz-, u-*. Kraków: Universitas.

Pütz, M. (ed.) (1992). *Thirty Years of Linguistic Evolution*. Philadelphia/Amsterdam: John Benjamins.

Pütz, M. and R. Dirven (eds.) (1996). *The Construal of Space in Language and Thought*. Berlin/New York: Mouton de Gruyter.

Pütz, M. et al. (eds.) (2001). *Applied Cognitive Linguistics II: Language Pedagogy*. Berlin/New York: Mouton de Gruyter.

Putnam, H. (1975). The meaning of "meaning". In: *Mind, Language and Reality. Philosophical Papers vol.2*. Cambridge: Cambridge University Press, 215–271.

Queller, K. (2001). A usage-based approach to modeling and teaching the phrasal lexicon. In: Puetz, M. et al. (eds.), 55–83.

Queller, K. (2008). Toward a socially situated, functionally embodied lexical semantics: the case of *(all) over*. In: Frank, R.M. et al. (eds.), 265–300 [internet: 1–38].

Radden, G. and K. Panther (eds.) (2004). *Studies in Linguistic Motivation*. Berlin/New York: Mouton de Gruyter.

Rakova, M. (2002). The philosophy of embodied realism: A high price to pay? *Cognitive Linguistics* 3, 215–244.

Ravin, Y. and C. Leacock (2000). Polysemy: An overview, In: Ravin, Y. and C. Leacock (eds.), 1–21. [internet]

Ravin, Y. and C. Leacock (eds.) (2000). *Polysemy. Theoretical and Computational Approaches*. Oxford: Oxford University Press.

Reddy, M. (1979). The conduit metaphor. In: Ortony, A. (ed.), 284–324.

Rice, S. (1996). Prepositional Prototypes. In: Pütz, M. and R. Dirven (eds.), 135–165.

Richards, I.A. (1965). *The Philosophy of Rhetoric*. Oxford: Oxford University Press.

Ricoeur, P. (1977). *The rule of metaphor*. London/New York: Routledge.

Ricoeur, P. (1985). *Egzystencja i hermeneutyka*. Warszawa: PAX.

Ricoeur, P. (1986). *Symbolika zła*. Warszawa: PAX [P. Ricoeur (1986). *The symbolism of evil*. Beacon Press].

Ricoeur, P. (1989). *Język, tekst, interpretacja*. Warszawa: PIW.

Ricoeur, P. (2003). *O sobie samym jako innym*. Warszawa: PWN [P. Ricoeur (1995). *Oneself as another*. Chicago: University of Chicago Press].

Ricoeur, P. (2004). *Drogi rozpoznania*. Kraków: Znak [P. Ricoeur (2005). *The course of recognition*. Harvard University Press].

Rosner, K. (1995). *Noama Chomsky'ego próba rewolucji naukowej*. Vol. 1. Warszawa: IFiS PAN.

Rosner, K. (1996). *Noama Chomsky'ego próba rewolucji naukowej*. Vol. 2. Warszawa: IFiS PAN.

Rúa, P. L. (2003). *Birds, Colours and Prepositions. The Theory of Categorization and its Applications in Linguistics*. München: Lincom.

Rudzka-Ostyn, B. (ed.) (1988). *Topics in Cognitive Linguistics*. Amsterdam/Philadelphia: John Benjamins.

Rudzka-Ostyn, B. (2003). *Word Power: Phrasal Verbs and Compounds. A Cognitive Approach*. Berlin/New York: Mouton de Gruyter.

Sanders, C. (ed.) (2004). *The Cambridge Companion to Saussure*. Cambridge: Cambridge University Press.

Sandra, D. and S. Rice (1995). Network analyses of prepositional meaning: Mirroring whose mind – the linguist's or the language user's? *Cognitive Linguistics* 1, 89–130.

Saussure, F. de (1959). *Course in General Linguistics*. New York: Philosophical Library.

Searle, J. (1999). *Umysł na nowo odkryty*. Warszawa: PIW [J. Searle (1992). *The rediscovery of the mind*. MIT Press].

Sebeok, T.A. (ed.) (1960). *Style in Language*. Cambridge, Mass: MIT Press.

Seuren, P.A.M. (1998). *Western Linguistics. An historical introduction*. Oxford/Malden, Mass.: Blackwell Publishers.

Sinha, C. (1993). On Representing and Referring. In: Geiger, R.A. and B. Rudzka-Ostyn (eds.), 227–246.

Sinha, C. (1999). Grounding, mapping, and acts of meaning. In: Janssen, T. and G. Redeker (eds.), 223–256.

Sinha, C. (2009). Language as a biocultural niche and a social institution. In: Evans, V. and S. Pourcel (eds.), 289–309.

Slobin, D. (1998). *Verbalized events*. Essen: LAUD 449.

Slobin, D. (2000) Verbalized events: a dynamic approach to linguistic relativity and determinism. In: Niemeier, S. and R. Dirven (eds.), 107–138.

Slobin, D. (2003). Od „myśli i języka" do „myślenia dla mówienia". In: Dąbrowska, E. and W. Kubiński (eds.), 361–402.

Sperber, D. and D. Wilson (1986). *Relevance*. Oxford: Blackwell.

Stalmaszczyk, P. (ed.) (2008). *Metodologie językoznawstwa. Współczesne tendencje i kontrowersje*. Kraków: Lexis.

Stanosz, B. (ed.) (1977). *Lingwistyka a filozofia*. Warszawa: PWN.

Sweetser, E. (1990). *From Etymology to Pragmatics. Metaphorical and Cultural Aspects of Semantic Structure*. Cambridge: Cambridge University Press.

Szwedek, A. (2007). Polysemy and metaphorization. In: Chłopicki, W. et al. (eds.), 255––272.

Szymanek, B. (1993). *Introduction to Morphological Analysis*. Warszawa: PWN.

Tabakowska, E. (1995). *Gramatyka i obrazowanie*. Kraków: PAN.

Tabakowska, E. (1999). Pobłądzić po malowniczych zaułkach Starego Miasta: semantyka polskiego przyimka *po* i przedrostka *po-*. In: Kurek, H. and M. Brzezina (eds.), 269–278 ["Prepositions and Verbal prefixes in Polish: *Po(-)*". Paper presented at the International Workshop 'Motivation in Grammar', Hamburg University, July 1999].

Tabakowska, E. (2000). Grammar and the cult of the virgin: A case study of Polish religious discourse. In: Niemeier, S. and R. Dirven (eds.), 223–233.

Tabakowska, E. (2003). Space and Time in Polish. The Preposition *za* and the Verbal Prefix *za-*. In: Cuyckens, H. et al. (eds.) (2003a), 153–177.

Tabakowska, E. (2004). *Kognitywizm po polsku – wczoraj i dziś*. Kraków: Universitas.

Tabakowska, E. (to appear). The story of ZA: a defence of the radial category [1–10].

Tabakowska, E. and C. Ljungberg (eds.) (2007). *Insistent images. Iconicity in Language and Literature*. Amsterdam: John Benjamins.

Talmy, L. (1995). *The Cognitive Culture System*. Duisburg: LAUD 357.

Talmy, L. (2000). *Toward a Cognitive Semantics: Concept Structuring Systems*. Cambridge, Mass.: MIT Press.

Taylor, C. (1985). *Philosophical Papers*, 2 vols. Cambridge: Cambridge University Press.

Taylor, C. (1989). *Sources of the self*. Cambridge: Cambridge University Press.

Taylor, C. (1991). *The Ethics of Authenticity*. Cambridge, Mass.: Harvard University Press.

Taylor, C. (1995). *Philosophical Arguments*. Cambridge, Mass.: Harvard University Press.

Taylor, C. (2004). *Modern Social Imaginaries*. Durham: Duke University.

Taylor, C. (2006). An issue about language. In: Jourdan, C. and K. Tuite (eds.), 16–46.

Taylor, C. (2007). *A secular age*. Cambridge, Mass./London: Belknap Press.

Taylor, J. (1988). Contrasting Prepositional Categories: English and Italian. In: Rudzka-Ostyn, B. (ed.), 299–326.

Taylor, J. (1989). *Linguistic Categorization. Prototypes in Linguistic Theory*. Oxford: Clarendon Press.

Taylor, J. (1990). Schemas, prototypes, and models. In: Tsohatzidis, S.L. (ed.), 521–534.

Taylor, J. (1995). Models of word meaning in comparison: The two-level model (Manfred Bierwisch) and the network model (Ronald Langacker). In: Dirven, R. and J. Vanparys (eds.), 3–26.

Taylor, J. (1996). On running and jogging. *Cognitive Linguistics* 1, 21–34.

Taylor, J. (1999). Cognitive semantics and structural semantics. In: Blank, A. and P. Koch (eds.), 17–48.

Taylor, J. (2006). Polysemy and the lexicon. In: Kristiansen, G. et al. (eds.), 51–80.

Taylor, J. (2007). Cognitive Linguistics and Autonomous Linguistics. In: Geeraerts, D. and H. Cuyckens (eds.), 566–588.

Tomasello, M. (ed.) (1998). *The New Psychology of Language*. Mahwah: LEA.

Tsohatzidis, S.L. (ed.) (1990). *Meaning and Prototypes. Studies in Linguistic Categorization*. London/New York: Routledge.

Tuggy, D. (1993). Ambiguity, polysemy, and vagueness. *Cognitive Linguistics* 3, 273–290.

Tuggy, D. (2007). Schematicity. In: Geeraerts, D. and H. Cuyckens (eds.), 82–116.

Turner, M. (1991). *Reading Minds*. Princeton: Princeton University Press.
Turner, M. (2001). *Cognitive Dimensions of Social Science*. Oxford: Oxford University Press.
Tyler, A. and V. Evans (2003a). *The Semantics of English Prepositions*. Cambridge: Cambridge University Press.
Tyler, A. and V. Evans (2003b). Reconsidering prepositional polysemy networks: The case of *over*. In: Nerlich, B. et al. (eds.), 95–159. [Evans' page]
Tyler, A. and V. Evans (2004a). Spatial experience, lexical structure and motivation: The case of *In*. In: Radden, G. and K. Panther (eds.), 157–192. [Evans' page]
Tyler, A. and V. Evans (2004b). Rethinking "English prepositions of movement": The case of *To* and *Through*. *Belgian Journal of Linguistics* 18, 247–270 [Evans' page]
Tyler, A. and V. Evans (2004c). Applying Cognitive Linguistics to Pedagogical Grammar: The case of *Over*. In: Achard, M. and S. Niemeier (eds.), 257–280. [Evans' page]
Tyler, S. (1978). *The said and the unsaid: mind, meaning, and culture*. New York: Academic Press.
Ungerer, F. and H.-J. Schmid (1996). *An Introduction to Cognitive Linguistics*. London/New York: Longman.
Vandeloise, C. (1988). Length, width, and potential passing. In: Rudzka-Ostyn, B. (ed.), 403–427.
Vandeloise, C. (1990). Representation, prototypes, and centrality. In: Tsohatzidis, S.L. (ed.), 403-437.
Varela, F.J., E. Thompson and E. Rosch (1993). *The Embodied Mind*. Cambridge, Mass.: MIT Press.
Vygotsky, L.S. (1962). *Thought and Language*. Cambridge, Mass.: MIT Press.
Weiner, J. (1994). *The beak of the finch. A story of evolution in our time*. New York: Alfred Knopf.
Weinsberg, A. (1973). *Przyimki przestrzenne w języku polskim, niemieckim i rumuńskim*. Wrocław: Ossolineum.
Werner, H. and B. Kaplan (1963). *Symbol formation. An organismic-developmental approach to language and the expression of thought*. New York: John Wiley & Sons.
Whorf, B.L. (1956). *Language, thought, and reality*. Cambridge, Mass.: Harvard University Press.
Wierzbicka, A. (1990a). The meaning of color terms: semantics, culture, and cognition. *Cognitive Linguistics* 1, 99–150.
Wierzbicka, A. (1990b). Prototypes save: on the uses and abuses of the notion "prototype" in linguistics and related fields. In: Tsohatzidis, S.L. (ed.), 347–367.
Wierzbicka, A. (1992). Furniture and birds: A reply to Dwight Bolinger. *Cognitive Linguistics* 1, 119–123.
Wischer, I. and G. Diewald (eds.) (2002). *New reflections on grammaticalization*. Amsterdam: Benjamins.
Wittgenstein, L. (2000). *Dociekania filozoficzne*. Warszawa: PWN [L. Wittgenstein (1978). *Philosophical Investigations*. Oxford: Blackwell].
Zielińska, D. (2007a). *Proceduralny model języka*. Kraków: WUJ.
Zielińska, D. (2007b). The selective mode of language use and the quantized communicative field. *Journal of Pragmatics* 39/5, 813–830.
Ziemke, T. et al. (eds.) (2007). *Body, Language, and Mind*. Vol. 1. Berlin/New York: Mouton de Gruyter.

Zlatev, J. (1998). Situated embodied semantics and connectionist modelling. In: Allwood, J. and P. Gardenfors (eds.), 173–194.

Zlatev, J. (2003). Polysemy or generality? Mu. In: Cuyckens, H. et al. (eds.) (2003b), 447–494 [internet].

Zlatev, J. (2007a). Spatial Semantics. In: Geeraerts D. and H. Cuyckens (eds.). *Handbook in Cognitive Linguistics*, chapter 13 [internet version: 1–27].

Zlatev, J. (2007b). Embodiment, language, and mimesis. In: Ziemke, T. et al. (eds.), 297–338 [internet].

Zlatev, J. (2007c). Intersubjectivity, mimetic schemas and the emergence of language. *Intellectica* 46/7, 123–152 [internet: 1–29].

Zlatev, J. et al. (eds.) (2008), *The shared mind: Perspectives on intersubjectivity*. Amsterdam: Benjamins.

Dictionaries

Brückner, A. (1927). *Słownik etymologiczny języka polskiego*. Kraków: Krakowska Spółka Wydawnicza.

Chamber's Twentieth Century Dictionary (1952). Edinburgh/London: Chambers.

Longman Dictionary of Contemporary English (2003). Harlow: Pearson Education Limited.

Smith, W. (1926 [1851]). *A Latin-English Dictionary*. London.

INDEX

TECHNICAL EDITORS *Jadwiga Makowiec*
Marta Lupa

TYPE SETTER *Wojciech Wojewoda*

Wydawnictwo Uniwersytetu Jagiellońskiego
Redakcja: ul. Michałowskiego 9/2, 31-126 Kraków
tel. 012-631-18-81, 012-631-18-82, fax 012-631-18-83

Errata

Andrzej Pawelec, *Prepositional network models. A hermeneutical case study,* Jagiellonian University Press, Kraków 2009.

At the final stage of the production process the following errors, misprints and omissions were noticed. The corrected version:

Page 25, line 13 from bottom:	COUCH
Page 35, footnote 39, line 2:	Geeraerts'
Page 45, line 21 from top:	book
Page 51, footnote 65, line 1:	Weinreich
Page 51, footnote 66, line 4:	The reference is to: Langacker, R. (1991). *Foundations of Cognitive Grammar.* Vol. 2: *Descriptive application*. Stanford: Stanford University Press.
Page 70, line 9 from top:	Geeraerts'
Page 70, line 19 from top:	(1.4.)
Page 72, line 18 from top:	gives
Page 82, figure 3:	The caption should be only below the schema.
Page 137, line 14 from top:	vision"
Page 142, line 7 from bottom:	Saussurean
Page 151, footnote 2, line 1:	Humboldt's
Page 163, line 8 from bottom:	acts.
Page 165, line 10 from top:	exception.
Page 170, footnote 50, line 1:	"Our
Page 171, line 11 from top:	above,

Index

Page 195:	Brugman C.
Page 195:	Coseriu, E. 10
Page 196:	Hopper – to be placed after Heidegger.

Despite efforts to achieve stylistic unity, several inconsistencies were noticed:

The division of words was a painstaking process. In some cases the dashes were not removed after text conversion: p. 103, l. 12 from bottom; p. 113, l. 5 from top; p. 149, l. 1 from top. In other cases, inconsistencies remained: p. 167, l. 4 from bottom: "online" vs. p. 168, ft. 42, l. 1 "on-line". Some divisions are still wrong, e.g. p.160, l. 9 from top: "off-load" (such cases are likely to be the most numerous).

In the text:

– in the possessive form of names ending with "s", an "s" was not normally added after the apostrophe, but see p. 25, ft. 22, l. 1.

– the authors of publications are mentioned in the alphabetical order, but see p. 104, l. 4 from top.

– the adjective form of "Saussure" is normally "Saussurean", but "Saussurian" also appears: 105, l. 6 from bottom; p. 106, ft. 5, l. 1.

– there are normally no spaces around a slash, but see pp. 28, 35, 44, 66, 67, 76, 115, 159.